CANTICLES II
(LOST SCROLLS)

ESSENTIAL POETS SERIES 263

Canada Council for the Arts
Conseil des Arts du Canada

ONTARIO ARTS COUNCIL
CONSEIL DES ARTS DE L'ONTARIO
an Ontario government agency
un organisme du gouvernement de l'Ontario

Canada

Guernica Editions Inc. acknowledges the support of the Canada Council for the Arts and the Ontario Arts Council. The Ontario Arts Council is an agency of the Government of Ontario.

We acknowledge the financial support of the Government of Canada.

GEORGE ELLIOTT CLARKE

CANTICLES

II

(LOST SCROLLS)

GUERNICA EDITIONS
TORONTO • BUFFALO • LANCASTER (U.K.)
2019

Michael Mirolla, editor
David Moratto, cover and interior design
Cover font, interior drop caps: Bill Clarke Caps
Guernica Editions Inc.
287 Templemead Drive, Hasmilton (ON), Canada L8W 2W4
2250 Military Road, Tonawanda, N.Y. 14150-6000 U.S.A.
www.guernicaeditions.com

Distributors:
University of Toronto Press Distribution
5201 Dufferin Street, Toronto (ON), Canada M3H 5T8
Gazelle Book Services, White Cross Mills
High Town, Lancaster LA1 4XS U.K.

First edition.
Printed in Canada.

Legal Deposit – Third Quarter
Library of Congress Catalog Card Number: 2019936902
Library and Archives Canada Cataloguing in Publication
Title: Canticles II : (MMXIX) : (lost scrolls) / George Elliott Clarke.
Names: Clarke, George Elliott, author.
Series: Essential poets ; 263.
Description: Series statement: Essential poets series ; 263 | Poems.
Identifiers: Canadiana 20190084596 | ISBN 9781771834094 (softcover)
Classification: LCC PS8555.L3748 C36 2019 | DDC C811/.54—dc23

I must Create a System or
be enslav'd by another Man's.

—William Blake, *Milton: A Poem in Two Books.*

I'm wondering: to edit the Holy Book and it be read
what could be said or unsaid.

—Boyd Warren Chubbs, "Sonnet #2"

For Geraldine Elizabeth Clarke (1939–2000)
& William Lloyd Clarke (1935–2005):
Adepts, Believers, African Baptists.

& For St. James Hampton (1909–1964):
Creator of *The Throne of the Third Heaven of the Nations' Millennium General Assembly*
& Author of *The Book of the 7 Dispensation.*

& For Thích Quảng Đức (1897–1963)
& Norman Morrison (1933–1965):
Honorary Africadian Martyrs.

THE BOOK OF BEING

Compassings

INTRODUCTORY

We romance between pages, enter through epic.
— Giovanna Riccio

Canticles is a lyric-styled epic. The subject of Testament I (issued in two parts—*Canticles I [MMXVI]* and *Canticles I [MMXVII]*) is *History*, principally, of slavery and the resistance to enslavement; of imperialism and the struggle to overthrow European (and American) racial hierarchies; and also of the image or symbolism of the 'Negro' or 'black' in the Euro-Caucasian and pseudo-Christian Occident. Testament II—these *Canticles II (MMXIX)* and *Canticles II (MMXX)*—enacts re-readings—revisions, rewrites—of Hebraic and other scriptures annexed by the emergent (Anglophone) African Diaspora in the Americas. Testament III (to appear last) will chronicle the creation of the African Baptist Association churches of Nova Scotia in 1853.

My method? Oulipo, elliptical, and serendipitous. Upon my meditating on a particular set of canonical or apocryphal, sacred texts, I would review phrases and words composed randomly in my notebooks to select potential replacements for the received, established strictures and narratives of *Faith*. Yet, I dismiss categorically any allegations of *Blasphemy*. My transcriptions are merely new translations. (Aye, some chapters and/or verses are utterly invented; others deviate substantively from the once-upon-a-time originals.) However, *Irreverence* is relevant to all revisions, all adaptations. I say so—reverently.

My constraints? Again, 1) to write no poem in Toronto, Ontario, and 2) always to write in black ink (usually *via* a fountain pen). Hence, *Canticles* is a species of travel writing in black-and-white. I pray that the reader will find some extra pleasure in connecting a chapter of, say, Ecclesiastes writ in New Scotland with another writ in Nouvelle-Orléans. That is to say, the spirit generative of these inklings is both boundless and/or always out-of-bounds.

In short, the Reader encounters in *Canticles II* an imaginary 'Africadian' Bible. One will be careful *not* to read it as if it were *The* Bible …

George Elliott Clarke
Toronto (Ontario)
19/1/19*

* 19 *janvier* mmxix.

Furthermore.

Gentile scripture so jesuit of knowledge and canticle in subdued contemplation ...
—Joel Calvin Simmons, *Mistral*, viii

In his article on "Religion and Theology" in *The Oxford Companion to Canadian Literature* (1997), John Webster Grant posits the indebtedness of Canadian writers like Leonard Cohen and Margaret Laurence to religious interests and themes, and he finds that colonial Canadian literature includes religious writings by poet Henry Alline and comic-sketch scribe Thomas McCullough. Grant also posits that the critical discourses of literary theorist Northrop Frye and philosopher George Grant also rely upon or address—specifically—Christian belief. However, John Webster Grant does not examine the possibility of a religious literature that is, in fact, the *formative* literature of a subculture or minority. However, there are potentially many such literatures in Canada, from Jewish to Mennonite, or from Cape Breton Catholic to British Columbian Doukhobor. The one that I know enough about to say, authoritatively, that its origins lay in ecclesiastical commentary, is, African-Canadian literature, and, even more precisely, Africadian (i.e. Afro-Maritime) literature.

Certainly, Africadian literature commences with the publication of slave memoirs by David George (Baptist) and Boston King (Methodist), transcribed and published by Caucasian Christians in 1793 and 1798 respectively. There is also a captivity narrative by John Marrant (Methodist), that saw at least twenty-one printings pursuant to its initial publication in 1785. In 1854, John William Robertson published in Halifax a slave narrative that is, in part, a theological argument, titled *The Book of the Bible Against Slavery*. 1854 also witnessed the inception of the publication of the annual Minutes of the African Baptist Association of Nova Scotia. In 1882, African Baptist pastor Reverend F.R. Langford published, likely at his own expense, a collection of spirituals titled, *A Call from Zion: Jubilee Songs and Old Revival Hymns*. By 1895, Antigua-native Peter Evander McKerrow published in Halifax the very first text by a Caribbean-Canadian writer, namely, *History of the Coloured Baptists of Nova Scotia*. Some secularists may disparage these 'churchy' publications. I—being worldly—do not.

Indeed, I believe that the original Homers of African-Canadian literature must be, then, the church-and-community chroniclers: Closer to bards than they are drabs (prosaic historians), they are, as scribers of congregational *Memory*, latter-day versions of the anonymous crafters—makers, *poets*—of the spirituals. It is sensible that I honour their creativity (and scholarship) with the poetry of *Canticles II*, this continuation of my lyric epic (see *Canticles I: MMXVI* & *MMXVII*, 2 vols.), wherein documents and personages are set in narrative contestation (disputation) with each other.*

Note: The poetry is faithful to *Psychology*, not canonical *Theology*, which is itself, as far as I know, in constant *Crisis* and *Doubt*. *Selah*!

---

* *The quarrel is doubtless the explanation.*
—Massimo Bacigalupo, xix, *Ezra Pound: Posthumous Cantos*

*Beloved Reader**

As you unfurl these leaves,
Parting lushly before your eyes,
They shiver before your sweet breath.

In your passage, your pilgrimage,
From beginning to beginning,
Remember you will also be leaves,

Frail blossoms upon the wind—
Then other leaves in another hand.

* Cf. "The Table of Verses."

THE BOOK OF BEAUTY

Some Apocryphal Texts of Africadian Baptism

The poet is the sayer, the namer, and represents Beauty.

—Ralph Waldo Emerson, "The Poet"

Beauty is not a matter of perception but an arena for creating hegemony....

—Russ Castronovo, "Beauty Along the Color Line"

No Beauty without struggle.

—Rev. Dr. Anthony Bailey,
"Honouring Howard D. McCurdy (1932–2018)"
@ St. Andrew's Presbyterian Church
[Ottawa (Ontario), 19 *mai* mmxviii]

THE LOST SCROLLS SEQUENCED

From: ***The King James Version, et cetera***

Genesis (Selected)
Fragments I
Samson (Repressed)
The Saga of Jezebel
The Book of Ruth
The Book of Ezra
Job (Conclusions)
Fragments II
Ecclesiastes
The Lectures of Solomon
The Song of Solomon
The Canticle of Sheba
The Book of Amos
Fragments III
The Book of Nahum
The Book of Enoch

From: ***The Apocryphal / Deuterocanonical Books***

Wisdom of Solomon
Addendum to Solomon
Ecclesiasticus, or the Wisdom of Jesus, Son of Sirach
Singular Circulars

LOST SCROLLS

GENESIS (SELECTED)

בראשית א'

מאת ג'ורג' אליוט קלארק

1 מן האפס המוחלט, מעלטת הכלום
מאפלה געשית סמיכה
צר לו אלוהים מין דבר
מתוך השום-דבר.

2 ולעצם העגול הזה קרא "ארץ".
לא היה אפשר להבחין
בין הגוש הנוזלי, הכהה כדיו,
לבין הרִיק השחור שמתוכו נוצר.

3 אבל אלוהים שרטט את גבולותיו של הכדור החשוך—
חצץ בינו לבין האַיִן—
תחם אותו באור.

4 עם האור נולדו יום ולילה
ואיתם, בה בעת, הטבלה המחזורית
והאסטרונומיה.

5 כך התיר האור לרקיע
לרחף מעל מים סוערים.

6 נפרשו השמים מעל ימים עכורים:
אור גלש על גב גלים נגללים לרווחה.

7 ויהי יום שני לבריאה.

8 כִּיֵּיל אלוהים את הצבע הירוק
למען יצבע מרקמים מנוגדים לרוב:
מִשְׁיִי, קוצני, עֵצִי, גבשושי,
קטיפתי, גַרְמִי וכו'.
חורשות, בוסתנים, יערות, ג'ונגלים,
קקטוסים, פירות, פרחים, ירקות,
כולם ארוכים, מֻנֻצים, סבוכים,
ירוקי גבעול לרוב
(או חומי גזע),
וחמניות חצופות, רברבניות,
ותַפּוּחים תְפוּחים, עסיסיים, מתוקים,
וכו'.

9 "מהמם! לא ככה?"
ראה אלוהים בעיני רוחו את הירוק
כמעודן ורקבובי ופריך,
כחרדל בגוון כתום-שרוף, ספוג סיגליות,
כצאצאם העשבוני הישיר
של אור זהוב וגשם סַפִּירִי.

10 ויהי לילה, ויהי יום. יום שלישי.

11 הגדיר אלוהים את שני חצאי היממה,
העניק את הבכורה לשמש —
ואת הסיומת לירח —
כדי ששני שעוני הטבע האלה
יוכלו לקצוב שבועות מתוך חודשים
ולחצוב חודשים מתוך שנים
ולחלוש על מחזורי הגאות והשפל והאישה...

12 המעדנים האסטרונומיים הללו
(גסטרונומיה לעין)
התעצמו והלכו
הודות להתעבות הכוכבים
במפולת סמיכה וזורמת —
רוטב רותח, לוהב,
נופל בשצף...

13 אחרת, איך היינו מבדילים בין חושך לאור
ומשלחים את הזמן לדרכו הדועכת אל הנצח?

14 אחרת, איך היינו מבחינים בין ימי עבודה
לימי חופש?
איך היינו יודעים מהן שעות נוספות (מאה חמישים אחוז),
מהם מחזורי חיים, מהן עונות?

15 אחרת, איך היינו יודעים מתי לשתול
ומתי לקטוף?
מתי לזרוע, מתי לקצור?

16 כך ביום הרביעי.

17 בינתיים, הימים והאוקיינוסים נצבעים ירוק
מקום שם שטים עשבי ים
או עוגנות אצות.
לכן אלוהים מציף את המים
בשפע של סנפירים וזימים
ופִּיוֹת שנושמים נוזלים
מלוחים או מתוקים.

18 טייסות של כנפיים,
יעפים של נוֹצות משחירים כל כך
את שמי הטורקיז שעמדו פעם בשיממונם,
שאור השמש מגיע אל האדמה
פסים-פסים.

19 אלוהים מצווה על הכנפיים והסנפירים להתרבות,
לסלסל בקולם במרומים
ולפזז במחולם בזרמים,
להגזים עד בלי די במחוות של יְפִי הטבע.

20 כך ביום החמישי.

21 כעת מעלה אלוהים אל הבמה את חיות הבר —
ואת חיות המשק —
כל אחת בהתאם למטען הגנטי שלה.
ולמראן הוא מהנהן בתבונה: "יפה!"

22 ואז מחליט אלוהים ליצור את האנושות —
בצלמו ובדמותו —
ולהעניק לנו את הריבונות על הארץ.

23 כך חישל אותנו אלוהים בדמותו;
זכר ונקבה ברא —
וציווה עלינו
להתיך איברים בחדווה
ולייצר אהבה.

24 גבר ואישה ברא אותם
למען יחסירו פעימה זה מול זה
ולעולם לא יחסרו אהבה.

25 והמליך אותם אלוהים למלך ולמלכה
על כל יתר היצורים החיים.

26 ועל הזוג ציווה לאכול
רק עלים, פירות, זרעים, שורשים, אגוזים —
שכן התזונה המוסרית (אז) היתה צמחונית.

27 ובדיעבד התבונן אלוהים — בכל אשר עשה —
באהבה רבה: "שיחקתי אותה!" חשב.

28 (הבריאה מוכיחה כי אין הוא אדריכל מוכה ירח
וכי יש לו תוכניות בשבילנו,
גם אם נדמה שהן מעורפלות-משהו.)

29 ויהי ערב ויהי בוקר יום שישי.

[מונטריאול (קוובק) 31 בינואר 2019
ומקסיקו סיטי (מקסיקו) 17–15 בפברואר 2019]

תרגמה מאנגלית: גליה וורגן
Hebrew translation by Galia Vurgan.

I.

1. Out of sable *Zero*, the pitch of *Zilch*,
stable, obsidian *Opacity*,
God rounded off some *Thing*
outta the surrounding *Nothing*.

2. He dubbed this dark sphere, "Earth."
Undiscernible was it from the black *Void*
outta which it got scooped and shaped,
this glob of inky liquid.

3. But God delineated the benighted globe—
separated it from the basic *Emptiness*—
by scheming up *Light*.

4. Thus was born Day and Night,
simultaneous with the *Periodic Table*
and *Astronomy*.

5. Thus, light licensed the sky
to hover over seething waters.

6. The sky stretched over the roiled oceans:
Light surfed over unscrolling waters.

7. Cometh the Second Day of *Creation*.

8. Now, God calibrated the colour *Green*
to tint contradictory textures:
Silken, prickly, wooden, gnarly,
plush, bony, *et cetera.*
Groves, orchards, forests, jungles,
cacti, fruits, flowers, vegetables,
all gangled up, sprang up, tangled,
often green-stemmed
(or brown-trunked),
and then flaunting raunchy sunflowers,
luscious fat, juicy, burgeoning apples,
et cetera.

9. "What's not to like?"
God could envision *Green*
as suave and musty and crunchy,
as burnt-orange mustard infused with violets,
as constituting the leafy, unmediated breeding
of gold light and sapphire rain.

10. Night came; then Day. The Third.

11. Indeed, God now demarcated the two halves
of 24 hours,
granting the debut portion to the sun—
the terminal portion to the moon—
so that these natural timepieces
could divvy weeks outta months
and devise months outta years,
govern tides (and *Menses*)....

12. These astronomical delights
(ocular *Gastronomy*)
got intensified,
thanks to the condensation of stars
in a streaming, creamy avalanche—
a blazing, blanching sauce,
cascading....

13. How else to split light from dark
and set *Time* ebbin toward *Eternity*?

14. How else to figure out work weeks
and holidays,
what's overtime (time and a half),
cycles, seasons?

15. How else to know when to plant
and when to harvest?
When to sow, when to reap?

16. The Fourth Day ensues.

17. Currently, the seas and oceans tinge green
where seaweed streams
or where algae anchors.
So, God saturates waterways
with fins and gills
and mouths that inhale liquids,
briny or fresh.

18. Now, squadrons of wings,
squalls of feathers, blacken so massively
the once-void turquoise vault above,
that sunlight reaches earth
only as stripes and strips.

19. God commands wing and fin to multiply,
to warble and to riot in the air
and to splash and frolic through tides,
dramatizing episodes of elemental *Beauty.*

20. Ensues now the Fifth Day.

21. Now God brought forth beasts—
and livestock—
each after its DNA.
And He nods sagely: "Good!"

22. Then God decided to fashion *Humanity*—
in His own image—
and grant us *Dominion* o'er the Earth.

23. So, God wrought us in His image;
created Male and Female—
and commanded us
to fuse loins profusely
and produce *Love.*

24. Thus, God made Man and Woman
to want each other
and never want for *Love.*

25. And God set each up to be King and Queen
o'er all other critters.

26. And God commanded the pair to eat
only leaves, fruits, seeds, roots, nuts—
for the righteous diet (then) is vegetarian.

27. God beheld belatedly—all that He'd made—
so lovingly: *Pretty damn fine!*, thought God.

28. (The *Creation* proves He's no lunatic architect,
but got plans for us,
even if conclusions seem elusive.)

29. Here is the Sixth Day.

[Montréal (Québec) 31 *janvier* mmxix
& Cuidad de México (México) 15–17 *février* mmxix]

II.

1. *Presto*! The world and the cosmos,
completed, debuted perfect. *Consummate.*

2. Come the Seventh Day, God decreed *Rest*,
to savour the *Creation*,
its wholly Holy *Poetry*.

3. God plumped up Adam outta clay,
clumps of wet dust,
then puffed air into his lungs.

4. And bade him to govern the Garden,
Oriental, in torrid Eden;
to nurture perpetually florid and fruitful orchards;
to pluck, non-stop, the apples,
peaches, pears, plums, figs, *etc.*

5. But God forbade Adam to try
the mortally wounding
Tree of Knowledge of Good and Evil:
"It be deadly, 'mon,' deadly!"

6. God watched Adam wrestle soft-pawed lions
and tutor songbirds in scales and melodies.
But, each night, the man sighed himself a-snooze.

7. Now, God hypothesized,
Perhaps Adam requires a mate—
to know Happiness *galore.*

8. (*Life* lives to love;
Love loves to live.)

9. But God hesitated to conjure a woman.
Instead, he paraded before the man
an unfenced zoo of interminable critters,
so Adam could terminate their blank *Anonymity.*

10. Pleasant it was to have Adam all to Himself,
but God did fret that this man—
this one creature disallowed coupling—
might crave such *Parity*—
to the point of *Despondency.*

11. So, as the last day's animal-canonizing ended,
and dawned the moon's *Somnolence*-inducing *Luminescence,*
and Adam yawned and laid his head to dream
against a tiger's purring tummy,
God excised a section of rib,
to configure Adam a *conjoint*—
less physically imposing than the male—
except for her intimidating blessing
of being able to usher new persons—
reasoning Innocents—
into being.

12. When Adam stirred, woke, he felt an absence
in and about his heart.
He knew *Pain*—suddenly—*Yearning.*

13. Then, ecstatic in His sculpting,
God unveiled the woman to Adam,
who quit at once all his pruning and planting
and pronouncements,
to explore this being, his *Perfection.*

14. Backed by songbirds, Adam enthused,
"She be the supreme, most excellent *Creation,*
this *Woman*—
for she be '*Wombed Man,*'
and is myself equalled."

15. Eve whispered, "Poesy *me fecit.*"

16. Ever since, a man or woman quits mom and dad
to cleave to his/her love—
and savour *Love* that's prodigious, imperative;*
Love that's never invalidated,
for *Loving* is never invalid.

17. Adam and his *sposa*—Eve—both *au naturel*,
revelled in each other's bodies,
guiltless of *Prudery* or *Shame*.

[Cuidad de México (México) 17/2/19
& Valle de Bravo (México) 18 *février* mmxix]

---

* Coitus instantiates *Sankofa*: All of *History* surges forth in every orgasm, that exquisite *Lucidity*. *Passion* / *Love* underwrites all *Action*, all efforts to attain Nirvana.

III.

1. The wiliest intellectual that God conceived?
Easy! That slick, insinuating Serpent!
His hissing—or lisping—rhetoric
schmoozes lawyerly, sounds slyly papal,
politico-slippery, plus by-the-book snide.

2. Discovering Eve alone—
and envious of her disorienting *Beauty*
(this mindful, soulful seraph,
this craft of no paltry Deity—
all ochre complexion, onyx eyes,
indigo-tint introitus,
with lips of Madeira sherry,
breasts like graspable stars,
plus bumper-brushing molasses tresses),
but praying her prone to *Vanity*—
prone to being supine and/or prone—
the serpent lisped saccharine *Intrigue*:
"Why spurn that most intoxicating fruit:
That of *The Tree of Knowledge of Good and Evil*?

3. Eve swung her head from side to side: "*Nyet*!
To gulp that pulp is to taste *Death*."

4. The serpent stuck out his tongue, chortled,
to debunk God:
"What a ninny thou art!
Why would God root that tree in Paradise,
and then scare you off?
It don't compute!
Lookit, once you eat,
you'll acquire instant, godly *Wisdom*; not die!"

5. Eve snuck a glance at the tempting tree.
Then, she strode toward it,
only to be staggered by the fragrance of its fruit.
She snatched down a piece,
bit into the juicy, perfumed flesh—
and found it awfully tasty and satisfying.

6. Except for feeling extra blissful
due to her adventurist act,
Eve observed that all was just as it'd been:
Apparently, the Serpent had aired errantless *Truth*.

7. So, Eve tracked down Adam and let him sniff
the entrancing and arousing aroma,
and then chew and nosh the wet, gushing innards.

8. But once Adam swallowed, *Light* itself darkened,
and *Heat* slumped chill.

9. Instantly, the duo recognized they were bare-assed,
and flinched, flushed.

10. Frantically, they rampaged among,
ripped apart, greenery,
to strip vines into belts
and fasten fig leaves as girdles—
to shroud their now tawdry genitals.

11. As was His wont at dusk, God boomed His voice
through the lanes and alleys of the Garden,
calling for His beloved Adam and Eve
to join Him and share the looming spectacle
of 1 billion, blooming, glittering stars.

12. But the pair were skulking behind bushes,
and craved now to chomp lamb meat, rare,
and felt crazed and manic for furs.
Now they puzzled out, animals could be produce.

13. Aggravated, God hollered: "Enough!
You two, show yo'selves! Now!"

14. They arose from the depression
where they cowered, craven,
and lurched into the open.

15. Adam expounded their predicament:
"Big Sir, we're secreting ourselves
cos we see our bodies are indecent."

16. God bellowed,"If you now detest your flesh,
it's cos you've plundered
The Tree of the Knowledge of Good and Evil!"

17. Adam blamed this "blunder" on Eve.
Eve claimed the Serpent had beguiled her....

18. Adam knelt and cried, "I repent,"
but then asserted, piously, that God's drafting of Eve—
this "crafty and artful lady"—
was how *Wrong* commenced.

19. God spat, sucked-teeth, at Adam: "Hush!
From this moment on, the viper's gonna slither
through slime and crap and dust.
And all women will haste to hack off its head,
lest the snake anchor fangs through their ankles."

20. To Eve, God vowed,
"You'll burst out babes in yelping, yowling *Agony*.
Moreover, thy *Equality*'s revoked.
Be serf, and kowtow to thy husband!"

21. To Adam, God tut-tutted,
"Thy *Easy Livin*'s done.
You's gonna be your own ox,
shoulderin hitches,
and sloggin or stumpin through barrens,
either swampy or stony.

22. "Sometimes, you's gonna be hungry enough
to tumble onto your belly—
humble down like a creepy-crawly—
and grub in grass.

23. "You wanted *Wisdom*?
Here's your *Primary Lesson*:
'You's gonna die and become tread upon dust.'

24. 'Eve, every person you mother's gonna die.
You's gonna communicate *Mortality* forever.'"

25. Next, God swivelled His head east and west:
"Those fig-leaf aprons are a joke!
I now license *Hunting* and *Killing*."
(Thus was founded *Fashion* and *Style*.)

26. God then pivoted to his Host:
"We can't let these humans
utilize *Know-How* and *Can-Do*
to become—like us—deathless."

27. So, God dispatched angels to sword-point prod—
Adam and Eve way, way, way, far outta Paradise:
The debut refugees, the original exiles.

[Valle de Bravo (México) 21/2/19]

Eve's Version of the Subversion

My debut memory, post-*Creation* (my own),
was of coming to—in a *louche*, dingy library
(much bad—poor—lighting),
in a dark barrack of books—
picturing (and vaunting) *Naval Design*,
Architecture, Aerodynamics—
and I knew instantly that the Old Man
had plagriarized and perfected
illuminated blueprints—
to conceive my Georgian curves and cupolas
to accord with Adam's Gothic spire
and his relative sparseness, paucity, of flesh.

A spunky stench arose
from the mainly mouldering books
(so many mothballed precepts)....

Also present when I discovered *Consciousness*
was a saturnalian congress of grey pates,
all sniffing about my fragrant *Nudity*.
One member of this parliament—
this murky intelligentsia—
was the Serpent,
who argued vehemently for my *Nudity*
(while he pulled smoke from a hookah),
although God pooh-poohed the issue as "irrelevant":
For, I wasn't to need clothes—
or lingerie—
to urge *Comfort* or imp *Lust*.

(Twisty and twisted, the viper surely was,
but he was also a kind of pack-rat,
convenient to archives.
That bookish devil was
as white-bellied as an imperialist.)

I did sense—*ex nihilo*—that the Serpent
represented a defunct bard,
a *roué*,
who was permitted his midnight rambles
and rambling meditations
(the panoply of insinuations)—
to be a sparring partner for God.*

Clearly, the Serpent defined a demonic poet,
for he wondered aloud (in the library)
whether my "portals" were "excessive"....

Well, not for me, and not for Adam!
But I get ahead of myself already....

Refreshing it was to be delivered unto Eden—
to launch glorious *Concubinage*:
I could hardly trust how mesmerizing—
magnificent—was Adam—
mahogany in face and limb
(ebony in member).
My untrammeled sex felt
fervent urge to vex and annex the man
in vigorous, amorous ventures!

Our reciprocal gyrations—
among the incoherent miscellany
of the lodgings the Old Codger allotted—
as days met their weird darkening—
allowed no fringe passions
gingerly vented.

(Adam loved the blushing of his own *Joy*.
Went totally gaga over and gung-ho for me!
We fucked and fucked and fucked....
We were personages of *Rectitude* then.)

---

* Cf. Job 1.

The star-cinema gala each night
flared pure fluorescence bleaching
the flowers of any colourful difference.

It was a monochrome monotony—
if also tony—
a tonic and an aphrodisiac—
to ready Adam for our panting—
our loins hunting—haunting—each other,
pell mell.

Adam was punctilious in backbone—
unto the interregnum of temporary *Exhaustion.*

And I was unctuous, kneeling,
at crotch, uncringing.

I loved to ogle the manly zealot,
as I acted the salty debauchee
with my tongue, shifting about his body,
so he crooned like a loud-mouthed lecher.

Our angular pivots about each other were doctrinal,
imitating the sleek fluidity of swans, necking.

I wish the Old Man had warned us firmly
re: the poets to seek out, the poets to memorize,
but also the poets to flee, to avoid.

Instead, the crowning *Infiltration*
of the Garden was perpetrated
by that dissembling semanticist—
The Serpent,
who was hellishly jealous of our ensexment,
because he had no ennabling organs
to purpose his would-be slimy sexiveness.

The Serpent's vengeance for being a eunuch
was to substitute, for Paradise,
a fiasco.

I explain plainly:
As solemn as autumn came he unto me....

I recognize that that Fruit (forbidden)
was palatable poison—
toxic sugar.

But I was no feeble *femme*,
and felt strong enough to want to know everything.
(*Damnation* be damned!)

Besides, to turn a doorknob—
to enter or to leave—
one's hand must make a fist.

Now, Adam and I are *Theology*'s homeless:
Persona non grata in Paradise,
and *Religion* mandates the shackling of women.

[YUL—Dorval (Québec) 7 *avril* mmxix]

IX. *(20–27): The Curse Against Ham.*

1. Plush with gangrene'd flesh
plus green plants gone dun,
soils, post-Flood, thus supersaturated,
exuded dews and oils:
So, Noah staked vineyards all about.
All grapes that sprang forth
were as potent as Christ's blood
(or *Sangre de Cristo, hecho en México*).

2. (The unconscionably stagnant flood waters
had looked a stew
the colour of Champagne—
dirtied with olive juice.)

3. Soon, Noah was commonly,
uncommonly wasted,
so polluted that, nightly,
benighted,
he sprawled out,
lewdly nude,
from woolly head to down past nappy crotch.

4. Ham shrugged to behold his pop's manhood,
dark as mahogany
and as long and no-nonsense
as a horse's or a bull's.*

5. Ham joked to his brothers
about their "Negroid Elder,
this specimen of *Black Power*,"
exhibiting such a ludicrous *Spectacle*.

*** Leviticus 20:11 suggests that "nakedness" is a euphemism for a junior's cuckolding of his own daddy. Had Ham and Noah's wifey paired off, all hush-hush, yet pseudo-incestuous?**

6. Scandalized, Sham and Caché cornered a blanket
and, mincing backward into the tent,
while eyeing a mirror,
recoiled at the drool and burp-breath at Noah's lips,
but cast over him the bed-clothing,
so as to black out his loins and groin.

7. When Big Daddy awoke, groggy—
angry blood thudding his brains—
he speculated that Ham would've let him
lie there, as exposed as a dog turd.

8. Noah blared, "Accursed is Canaan!
Let he and descendants be chattel
for even Europe's Neanderthals!

9. "Blessed then be Sham, who shall whip
Ham's backside forever and forever
to compel *Free Labour*—
and rape his daughters and wives
to whelp extra *Free Labour*—
and merchandise the Ham host
(really hostages),
kit and caboodle,
for as little coin as anyone cares to pay."

10. (Thus were born the serfdom of Slavic states—
and Europe's beat-down peasants.)

11. "And let Caché reside in Sham's lodgings,
and let Caché also claim Ham's services,
utterly *gratuit*, or at dirt-cheap rates, always."

12. This tirade, these imprecations,
configured no chitchat!

13. Canaan's brats were gonna be galley-slaves,
with their cleft palates and hare lips—
glub-glubbing the Latin of pigs,
and their crotches pumping out rat-finks.

14. Their children would be grunts
and chamber maids,
slaves to *Pawn Shops*,
and/or enslaved by *Student Loans*.

15. These folks prove as obstinate as mud,
and all shy from em.

16. They puke, unequivocally,
old ale and stale bread.

17. Each Cannanite's studious
in *Depravity*,
while also being childishly stupid.

18. Pitiless *Luxury*'s the purview of Caché,
totalitarian as acid.

19. But Caché's clan is diligently royal,
while Ham's folks toil bitterly in grime,
see their daughters pimped out—
fucked like mules and worked like horses;
watch their sons become septic in trade
cos sluggish in morals,
and so extravagantly thuggish.

20. Sham's descendants mount paranoid,
Yellow Peril poeting,
attacking Caché's *Success*
at copycatting their luxuries and inventions,
and improvin upon em;
and thanks to their heavy dollars,
crowdin out the lightweights,
they hike *Real-Estate* prices
(while demonizing old-growth trees
for their "seed-garbage,"
and so choppin em down *sans* consultation,
thus agonizin the white-bread neighbours).

21. Each Sham son is a minor Homer,
weepin Gothic and oneiric lyrics.

22. They are elegiac dandies, specializing in
the onrush of ink—
outta the deficit of wine bottles—
into unlovely volumes,
a rubbish heap of worn-out poems—
and, lastly,
burnt—charred—leaves of poems.

[YVR—Richmond (British Columbia)
22 *décembre* mmxviii]

XI.

1. Despite endless feuds, uncancellable massacres,
Humanity had one tongue, shared one voice:
No translators necessary.

2. However, a mishmash, *hoi polloi* assembly,
schemed to attain Heaven
by craning up a tower at Pisa.
An indescribable tower!

3. Thanks to *beaucoup* shekels, *beaucoup* cash,
thousands of *sang-mélee*
(the Métis and multi-melanin'd indigent)
got commissioned to set up backyard blast furnaces
(foreshadowing the Great Proletarian Cultural Revolution),
and fire em up to forge bricks.

4. Barefoot theologians and sandalled engineers
figured that a sky-high tower—
could let all call on God directly—
voiding bureaucratic delay.

5. But God heard this godawful din of *Industry*:
Metal clanging, bosses shouting,
minions grunting and/or singing,
the boom and bam of bricks
being slammed in place as trowels slathered slime.

6. Instantly, God knew that *Mortality*
could not alone stop humans
from striving to ape *Divinity*.

7. To prevent their acquiring demi-god savvy,
God imposed on the diverse lot
an insane hodgepodge of lingoes.

8. Such a babble—bedlam—erupted at Pisa,
the tower was abandoned—left listing,
as everyone vamoosed *ex* the construction site,
each to seek speakers projecting his/her select tongue.

[Windsor (Ontario) 31 *mars* mmxix]

XIX. *(Unexpurgated Version).*

1. Each as 6-pack-ribbed as Icarus—
the chiselled, tag-team, he-man types—
touched down at Sodom at dusk.

2. True: The angels Osama and Obama
mirrored husky, beefy, Mormon evangelists
(right down to their underwear).*

3. They reconnoitered with Lot,
slumped at the fringe
of the Porte-de-Pantine dump.

4. Due to those Chippendale-buff physiques,
Osama and Obama defined the angelic.
So, Lot, divining their celestial anatomies,
up and bellyflopped,
nosing dirt in meet *Homage.*

5. "Heaven's Emissaries, please honour my home:
Steamy water and bergamot soap will cleanse your bods.
And my beds are well-built."

6. "No," the star-born aristocrats intoned:
"We'll lodge in the Square—at the Y."

7. Daring now to lift his once-dug-in chin,
Lot pooh-poohed this "preposterous" notion.
So, the dusk-descended duo condescended
to bunk at Lot's mundane abode.

---

* Cf. R. Nixon.

8. Soon, Obama and Osama perched at Lot's table.
Spiced lemon scents scaling from their scoured frames
didn't contradict the aromas of butter-bathed sourdough,
plus vinegar-soaked sardines, pimento'd olives,
and *vino locale bianco.*

9. But as the diners tucked into the fare,
a rabble's din built in brawling *Volume.*

10. The sound imitated a Million Man March—
as once-murmurs differentiated into shouts,
pitched loudly bout Lot's detached crib.

11. Quitting his now-reticent table,
Lot scouted, out a curtain'd window, the outside:
He surveilled an Adamic multitude milling,
commandeering street, gutter, sidewalk.

12. Yahoos who didn't grip stones, ready to fling—
to splatter—painstakingly—
every pane of glass in Lot's dwelling—
gripped bottles instead, downing swigs.

13. Rednecks, rude boys, a pack of no-goodniks!
And, strangely, dangerously, homogeneously male....

14. Lot scoffed at (but wheezingly)
those raucous mugs without.
He mused: *Why this ruckus?*

15. Soon as Lot set foot on his front-stoop,
caterwauls and cat-calls walloped his ears.

16. The chief of this presumptive Klan—
Onan—in a muscle-shirt,
aimed his phallic bullhorn
at the now-queasy-nauseated, quivering Lot.

17. "Lot, ya got two very finessed rascals—
not rough-trade, but finically cut twinks,
abiding with ya, and we intend
to raffle off and rumpus at their rears.
So, hand over their butts, lickety-split!

18. "Elsewise, all us worthies is gonna ransack
thy shack, slay the whole lot of Lots (*lots*)—
and then rough-house with dem fine-ass fellas...."

19. *Fear* negates *Reason*:
Lot blurted out that two Zara swains
(namely, Butch and Biff)—
fiancés to his daughters—
were also his houseguests.

20. "Including me, that makes five fighters,
and we've arms—
and some of you will die
before you break through my bricks."

21. That was the gist of Lot's aposematic ruse—
or bluff.

22. The rioters' publicist,
Onan, megaphoned anew:
"Stab us with your fingernails, eh?!!
We ain't gonna be—um—'pussywhipped'
by any So-and-So's say-so!

23. "Naw, we's gonna bum-rush ya, Lot:
We'll ravage the young quartet;
make these Fab Four our bed-buddy quadrupeds,
kneeling before our thousands!"

24. *Fear* nixes *Reason*:
Lot thought now to sacrifice his girls—
Melania and Sarah-Palaska—
to the brazen horde.

25. (The congregation's *furor sexualis* rendered em
a bunch of simian imitations—
but more reptilian, actually, than mammalian.)

26. Lot shouted back—desperate
to halt a rock barrage from pelting down;
to forestall battering rams tattering his doors:

27. "I'll share my virgins with y'all.
Their bodies are pure.
These are nubile debs—
spring-fresh—undoubtedly—at every vent.
But spare my honourable visitors!"

28. The literate dung-spitter loud-speakered back:
"Our *Lust*'s first for lads, only latterly ladies!"
Braying, the mob lobbed boos.

29. Lot's wife, Mimi, and his daughters,
Melania and Sarah-Palaska, clutched each other
and whimpered and wailed and wept:
How could Lot—husband and father—
plot to trade their only credit—
their coral-pink, coral-white, carnation Chastity?

30. Cowering in the basement,
quavering in their beds,
were dough-faced Biff and whey-faced Butch:
They feared becoming
no-nonsense, Spartan Sodomites'
Byzantine-bent-over bitches.
They cared nada bout preservin their fiancées.

31. The bullhorn yapped:
"Get the fuck out the way, Lot!
We mean to drill dem blokes!"

32. The aroused rowdies swamped forward,
Raunch in their haunches.

33. But Osama and Obama
oped the front door and hauled their host within,
and overturned the dining-room table,
to turn up a barricade.

34. Wine scattered and dishes nattered
o'er the food-splattered floor.

35. Alarmed by Lot's sycophantic parley,
the women snatched up dirtied forks and knives,
improvising weapons.

36. The orangutang-vipers outside
brabbled up crescendo upon crescendo:
Having glimpsed the angels,
Vice now ramped up, vicious.

37. Each angel knelt, prayed, crossed imself,
arrowed glances toward the table-stopped door.

38. Instantly, a neutron-bomb of blindness
(so to speak) detonated,
thus irradiating the louts' eyeballs outside,
so that the crowd disintegrated into screeching,
moaning, stumbling, doleful, individualized sad-sacks.

39. Once the yelling fellers' eyes went blank,
their buggery-hungry rods drooped,
deflated.

40. The Sodomites outraged Obama and Osama—
"up the yin-yang."
Their fates were the angels' *fiat*:
"Lot, Mimi, daughters, suitors, scram!
We're gonna immolate this cesspool!"

41. Biff and Butch, swishing silk dressing gowns,
now chimed in with their perspective:

42. "Lookit! We don't know how you two
gents broke up that lynch-mob.
But you boys gotta be joking
about obliterating this burgh!"

43. Melania and Sarah-Palaska whined:
"Butch, Biff, doncha still wanna marry us?"

44. Their now-ex-fiancés guffawed:
"Your own papa just offered yas
to be gang-raped and DAPed!
If he don't value your—alleged—*Virginity*,
why should we?

45. "So, well, we're gonna skedaddle, too,
but we'll linger long nuf
to shut down your house.
We'll drop your keys wherever you like,
and then say *'adios'* to this version of Hell."

46. Melania and Sarah-Palaska wept and tore
their evening gowns.
Their mama tried to shush their kerfuffle,
but Lot's *Emergency* tactics had cost em
plausible husbands and nice-nice dowries.

47. The angels intoned, "Pray, you two poofs!
This sewer is *History*!

48. "We's gonna blast Sodom with sulphur fumes,
chased by napalm:
Fire's gonna blizzard—sizzling—
blitzing every morsel of flesh.

49. "Furthermore, don't look back!
Or else!"

50. Prodding Lot on ahead,
the angels Obama and Osama seized the hands
of Mimi, Melania, and Sarah-Palaska,
and hauled em out the city.

51. Lot whined to settle at the Zara foothills,
for he said they'd scant "odds"
to survive long the mountains.

52. Now, God permitted O & O
to settle a stinking, suffocating, sulphur cloud
over Sodom and its satellite in *Fornication*—
Gomorrah,
that iniquitous suburb.

53. Sulphur, heavy as gravel,
chunked down upon blinded buggers.
A putrid, stifling miasma hunkered.

54. Next, the golden sulphur caught fire,
burning with a lovely sapphire flame mass—
so the smoke resembled a fallen sky.

55. The denizens of the "Twin Cities" died blind,
choking, and ablaze.

56. In their basement hideout, Biff and Butch
evaporated in each other's arms.
(Who saw the other vapourize first
is a question for Einsteinian *Physics*.)

57. But Mimi turned her head
to ogle the lurid sapphire glow
saturating the horizon.
Instantly, she shriveled horizontally
and sprouted vertically,
becoming a pillar of pink salt
(a *plein-air*, Himalayan stalagmite).

58. Suspicious of the chronology
between Lot's lot's arrival
and th'extinction of Sodom and Gomorrah,
the Zara burghers voted to expel,
at gunpoint, Lot & Dotters.

59. The truncated family relocated
to a mountain cave.

60. Exiled from all *Civilization*,
how could the two beautiful,
but self-wounding daughters
(given to slashing their arms with brambles),
their bellies big up with babes?

61. The eldest, Sarah-Palaska,
spelled out—to Melania—this stratagem:
"Get the old man sloshed to the gills,
then bounce up and down on his loins
til he studs."

62. Hot to trump her sis, Melania agreed.
In fact, Melania was the first to hump
her alcohol-addled widower-*pater*.
To sluice his spunk into her squirting depths.

63. Jealous, Sarah-Palaska repeated
the operation the next night:
To feel paternal jism spurt and spatter her innards.

64. Lot never guessed which was pleasuring
him at her leisure.
No matter:
Sarah-Palaska's son got named Mob;
Melania named her son, Moroni.

[Tropea (Italia) 14 *juin* mmxviii]

XXXIV.*

1. The damsel of Jacob and Leah,
Dinah piggybacked on a horseback ride
to go kibbutzing with Canaanite kinswomen.

2. The son of Hammer
(The Thane of Canaan),
Sessions—that skin-dog and booze-hound—
binocular'd Dinah, then, accosted her,
once she was afoot;
to slake his eyes upon her nakedness.
Quick, before his unbuttoned pantaloons,
he scissored wide her legs.

3. Time and again was Sessions sassy and scrappy
at Dinah's precincts,
hammering deep, deep, deep.

4. His prong got stuck in her—
like a sugar-cane stalk clamped in a rat's jaws.

5. But, as he stroked, Sessions felt stricken;
he now hankered to re-classify *Rape* as *Romance*:
To woo Dinah so he could twice daily, justly,
spade and churn her lil grotto.

6. Sessions bugged daddy-o:
"Yeah, I spunked in her 'functioning wound'—
but I'll take the chit now as my wife."

7. Jacob heard that Dinah'd been distressed.
But his sons were herding sheep:
No hands were free to brandish arms.

*** In discussing Genesis XIX with Rick Salutin, he suggested I scope out Genesis XXXIV.**

8. Hammer saddled up, camel'd diplomatically
to Jake, to set right his boy's wrongs.

9. Finally, Jacob's sons stalled their pacific herds,
but they were not pacifists:
They deemed Sessions's tupping of Dinah
an insult against Israel.

10. Dinah was, they judged,
a diamond tumbled in dirt.

11. Hammer havered, nevertheless, for *Peace*:
"Let Sessions marry Dinah!
Thus, we couple Canaan and Israel."
(He prayed a truce weren't *Verboten*.)

12. Also, in tandem with the nuptials,
they'd finagle a Free Trade Agreement,
allowing cross-border, untaxed exchanges
of goods, services, and workers.

13. Sessions also galloped to beseech Jake & Sons,
the permit to wed Dinah:
"No price for her is too high."

14. But Jacob's boys believed
Sessions's violent ejaculations'd
besmirched their sis
and bespattered Israel.

15. Their *de facto Foreign Policy*
reflected uncompromising *Reason*.

16. So, they treated the Canaanites to this treaty:
"No Jewess may marry a Canaanite
unless *all* of yas be circumcised."

17. "All Caananite gents must go 'under the knife.'
Agree, and *Marriage* and customs unions
become possible.

18. "Disagree, and we'll keep Dinah;
Sessions will keep a criminal record."

19. Canaan's Thane and *Dauphin* trumpeted this deal.

20. "Israel's an honest broker.
We shall be as one as fingers are to a hand.

21. "Only one condition:
Circumcision for us all.

22. "Just dock our dicks a nick;
then we nick Israeli brides, coins, herds, lands."

23. The Canaanite gentry voted, *"Oui!"*
Guys lined up to have their foreskins lopped,
but the operation was sloppy:
Linoleum knives got used.
Manly blood and unmanly tears jointly glopped.

24. 72 hours after, with Canaan's cock-o-the-walks
still flailing in immedicable *Pain*,
their groins and bowels expectorating blood
impossible to bandage,
two of Jacob's sons—
Simon and Levi,
took their blades
(sheathed to insulate moonlight
from illuminating their intentions),
snuck into Canaan,
and belly-stuck and throat-ruptured
each Canaanite male,
thus turning grunts into wheezes,
groans into sighs.

25. The two brothers moved velvetly,
i.e., as soundlessly as clouds.

26. Ensued now a lump-sum sacking;
each smack-down ranked top-notch.

27. Cold-bloodedly wormed the Hebrew steel:
Sumptuous chrome, thrusting,
disgusted each tummy, busted each wind-pipe.

28. Blood burped up and slurped out.
Dead dudes laid out as blatant as defecate.
The campaign was as dirty as *True Crime* always is.

29. Simon and Levi (in *Levi's Red Tab*, blue-denim)
sliced up Hammer and Sessions.
Was no insignificant gore.
And nothin finicky, nothin sporadic.

30. While Dinah watched, her bros whacked off
Sessions's pallid weenie
and rammed the ruddied bit
down Hammer's throat:
The prince bled pallid,
while the king choked, suffocated.

31. Then, the Hebrew bros looted Canaan,
while widows and sonless mamas wailed—
unleashed cacophonies of howling.

32. All was pillaged—
Art (paintings, scultptures), pantries,
liquor cabinets, all the flocks.

33. Canaanite women and *filles* had to help
cart the plunder and/or shepherdess
now unshephered herds.

34. Daylight surveyed *Subtraction*;
Jewish poets soon inked accounts
of arrogant life-spans blunted.

35. The post-*Rapine* caravan,
rolling thunderously to Israel,
was prophetic of Iraqis evacuatin out Kuwait—
if not of the hovering, Christian, *War* machinery
that repurposed pirates as burnt-up cadavers.

36. When Simon, Levi, and Dinah returned home,
toting booty and booting along captives,
Jacob griped, "Well, now you've started a war
with the Canaanites and all parasitic foreigners,
that outnumber us handily."

37. Simon and Levi shrugged:
"Look at it this way, pops:
We've warned all heathens
our women can't be treated
like gutter whores."

38. But the Canaanite widows would soon prove
polyrhythmic "hussies," perennial honey,
a bunch of nightly encumbered "bitches."

39. The orgies copied 1 million Monarch butterflies—
simultaneously mating—
orange-and-black shimmering,
smouldering.

[YVR—Richmond (British Columbia)
21 & 22 *décembre* mmxviii]

FRAGMENTS I

Joseph; or, Madama Potiphar (on the Verge).

1. Shit! I don't want a "drink."
I want Champagne!

2. I urge Joey—Adonis—
"Play along, stay with me.
You're not my husband's slave;
I'm yours.

3. "Any rival's a crap-assed *salope*,
some *grand bonda*,* who musters
rum spicy as Cayenne pepper,
and sable johnsons that pressure slovenly she
into bovine—or equine—postures."

4. I'd exchange a ton of tears
for a hundred-pound fuck,
to let joy-boy work my prat.**

5. In the greasy baptisms,
let his youthful effusions
bleach all my portals:
I'm wholly open to his use.

6. And it's easy to cuckold a king:
I'll roll boy-toy off my limbs;
Next, I bathe, knot a négligée....

7. Like a herdsman guarding camels,
I keep watch for Joseph....
I'll tell him, "Don't sleep with camels!
My wine glasses are dry:

*** French Guiana Creole: Gross ass.**
**** British English: Twat.**

8. "How can I drink without you?
Come and milk and suck me,
so my husky, musky aroma
perfumes and marries us."

[Winnipeg (Manitoba) 16 & 19 *février* mmxi]

Joseph Repulses.

Madama Potiphar, that dead-on harlot, is
Egyptian garnish that tarnishes:

A glitter surface
and an icy face.

She thinks I wanna screw white gals,
that sable slaves gotta stud pale gals,

that every black man's a beast
in bed, where white breast is feast.

[Nice (France) 28 *mars* mmxi]

Moses (Memoirs).

1. Yes, we risk the rabid bolts
of a pissed-off, fatal Deity,
whose drastic views blast us and devastate.

2. But we can't let our tongues tinge with ash—
nor scum over with *Academe*'s grimy dust—
for how else can we call up air strikes
to slaughter—zap—hateful hooligans?

3. Pharaoh was hinging on wrinkles;
still, that vile royal tried to jostle God.
Well, he ended up bawling in his bathtub,
awash in beer,
while his troop guttered,
scrutted down like rats,
their opened guts ejaculating ruddy butter.

4. Pharaoh's son spat up erupting tissues:
Locusts leeched his blood.

5. Lookit! God always has a grave need
to overflow graves!
To be as rigorous as teeth scraping meat from bone!

6. (If such is detestable,
He informs us elsewise—
by many factors of loudness!)

7. Hair-splitting, havering theologians?
Their silver tongues give poets black eyes,
their evangelical voices go tinny,
their hearts puke phlegm….
They resemble white maggots
writhing in puddles of black rot.

8. Rather than guzzle nasty plonk,
I'd prefer to taste nuptial bread and lolly*—
rations of rum, fractions of *Spam*—
with Pharaoh's doled-out, dolled-up, doll-like daughter....

[Vicenza (Italia) 7 & 8 *mai* mmxvi]

---

* Molasses.

Exodus XX. *(Gloss).*

1. God seared this communiqué into stone
(bit into *via* lightning):

2. "I'm the God that delivers slaves from *Bondage*.
Ain't no others!*

3. "Dare rank any bitch-ass clods over *Moi*?!!

4. "(Strangle all publicists for cults!)

5. "And don't craft idols outta mud (ceramic *Kitsch*),
metals (liable to rust, or be stolen, or be melted down),
water (serpentine fish), or air ("'Thor" — "Apollo" —
the whole racket of eerie, insubstantial, vaporous,
gaseous, and/or feathered and/or fiery *Phenomena*).
All are as disposable as toilet paper!

6. "I got the *Power*** — and thus the right to Copyright,
Trademark, the Intellectual Property Patent.
(Eye printers, publishers, stringently;
whenever necessary, gouge out their eyes!)

7. "How can ye go whoring after
fake, phantasmal, fraudulent gods?
I AM THE GREATEST—
THE ONE & ONLY—
NUMERO UNO—
The Immortal Inventor of every mortal 'I'!
Better yet, I hold all veto power!
I put the kibosh on idols!
I am the gaudy, Omnipotent Unilateralist!

---

* And an indeterminate direction is *Astrology*.
** Heed J. Brown.

8. "But I extend *Mercy* to those who eschew *Blasphemy* and treat my *bons mots* as meat and wine.

9. "Dare try and play *Moi* for a sucker,
to tomfool with my Name?
Perish ya, if you do!

10. "The Sabbath Is Holy. (Get down on it!)

11. "Work-work-work, toil-toil-toil, sweat-sweat-sweat, six days a week.

12. "But the 7th day be Mine. No *Labour* then.
Nor for hired help or employees.
And don't try to get around this *Commandment*
by working oxen or other critters!

13. "R-E-S-P-E-C-T muddah & fuddah ALWAYS.

14. "Thou shalt not MURDER.

15. "Thou shalt not Forge Unlawful Carnal Knowledge with a non-spouse.*

16. "Rip off NOTHIN! Don't purloin ANYTHIN!

17. "Thou shan't slander, gossip, libel, lie, or do perjury.
(Politicos *ain't* exempt!)

18. "Don't covet another's Beloved or Property.

19. "But do tax the rich handsomely!**
*Renminbi**** beautifies *Public Works*!

---

* "And never, all liquored up, *cherchez les femmes*!
(Nor let pussy pounce on thy snake.)"
** "Taxes are boils, sores, cuts, wounds—unless they are seeds."
*** Chinese: The people's money.

20. "(P.S. The folk create *Wealth*:
Who else should have it?)"

21. When God set the above *diktats* in stone,
the mountain peak blazed, smoked—
as if a volcano, awakening.
The tribes cowered, dreading Doomsday.

22. Arose then a muttering for Moses to ventriloquize
on God's behalf,
for, if irritated, God was deadly to debate.

23. Moses schooled the Hebrews,
"God be the ally
of *Art* and *Beauty*,
upon which we rely
to touch *Eternity*."

24. So Moses decamped *ex* the campfires,
and clambered up the rocky steeps
and sidled into that clamorous abyss
where God lurked.

25. Now God shouted at Moses:
"Speak to the *volk*, the *hoi polloi*!
Plague em with *Misery*, if need be!

26. "Quit all idols! They're *History*!
Fuggedaboutit!

27. "(Pour molten gold down the throats
of every idolater.)

28. "Instead, construct ceramic or metal altars,
and cook thereon sheep and oxen—
unhesitantly,
to aromatize My nostrils.

29. "And don't carve or chisel no stone altar,
for such toolery is *Pollution*.

30. "And never step naked into my *Tempio*!
Eliminate the tank-tops, baby-dolls, mini-skirts, hot pants,
and that brazen, nipple-poke look!

31. "Scrap the yoga pants and athlete-gear too!
It's not only disrespectful, it's shabby, vulgar,
déclassé....

32. "And quit fucking using *Fucking* as an amplifier!"

**[Tropea (Italia) 11 *juin* mmxviii
& 12/6/18]**

Leviticus XIX.

1. God: "Israel must be holy, or I will be unholy
in purging—wholly—the unholy.

2. "Lookit! Crush all idols; and fashion no new.

3. "Smash crystal balls; torch *Ouija* boards;
trash poker chips and cards;
shred all astrological charts;
jail palm-readers and gamblers!*

4. "Yeah, it's advisable to offer *Moi-Même* prayers.
(Just sayin.)

5. "But if I spurn the prayer, the supplicant suffers!

6. "I shall stipulate *Purdah*, then *Frustration*:
The cultivation of thorns, the consumption of turds.
I'll distribute—over fiends' own fields—nettles and dust."

7. "Starving, when you dig up an acre,
seeking roots to suck,
you'll turn up only worms, pebbles.

8. "If you try to pluck pears to press wine,
I'll blight that mash with rot and rust,
so you vomit vinegar.

9. "Israel, do not defraud, or swindle, or cheat—
neither in *Trade*, nor in *Credit*,
nor bilk the Labourer.

* Except for "Lucky" Iacobelli.

10. "And don't dare mess with My Name:
I will discombobulate the speaker;
I will damage his or her brood.

11. "People, be straight with thy neighbour!
Don't salt-assault his tree roots;
don't torch his sugar cane;
don't water down his wine;
don't tumble his wife or fall his daughter.

12. "In *Judgment*, *Assessment*, Weights & Measures,
Precision is *Righteousness*.*

13. "Ensure the balance is as rigorous
as a mummy's *rigor mortis*.

14. "Never let *Fraud* go unchecked;
suss out even unfigured wrongs.

15. "When gold's paid out,
don't return rinky-dink brass.

16. "Evaluate tangible goods only:
Never count tangential hopes or hurts.

17. "Stash no slush funds to bankroll secret orgies,
to profit unheroic doings.
(Remember: Daily failures nix nightly wine.)

18. "Judge all neatly,
both those sporting tatters
and all those glitzed up.

19. "*Purity* is My *Demand*!
Do not breed bulls with hens;
do not sow mingled seeds;
do not weave silk and seaweed *ensemble*.

---

* Cf. E. Pound, "Canto LXXIV."

20. "*Love*, ratified, is *Marriage*.

21. "Welcome strangers. Why vex or hex
the sojourner, the wayfarer?

22. "(Once, Israel, Egypt cussed thee
as 'foreigners and slaves':
Frown not upon the outsider!)"

[Chicago (Illinois) 5 *janvier* mmxix]

Numbers XII.

1. She—The Ethiope—steeps in the Hebrew's bed,
and his arms and sidearms secure her flesh:
Outside, the Negress suffers *Surveillance*....

2. Her tea towel imps a skimpy dress.
Thus, Moses feels moved to cover his Ethiope spouse;
to board her, yes, but also to guard her:
These days, Fascists league *contra* Africans....

3. Though vividly decorative, the tea towel
only skirts her slim waist and o'erbrimming bust.
She outclasses Moses' once-habitual lasses.

4. Might Moses care to investigate
the intrigues jealous tribal elders concoct?
Indecent perps are lisping indecent words.

5. "Why did Moses wed the Ethiope?
Are they a zoomorphic couple?"

6. (These are discomfiting queries,
uncomfortable interrogatives:
How to cleanse the dirt?)

7. But the maiden's got no suppressed *Quality*:
Disrobed, the Ethiope flaunts disestablishment *Beauty*.

8. The Ethiope's unique and restless lips—
their *Syncopation*—
summon consonant, consummate *Jubilee*.

9. She and Moses bandy brandy.

10. She squats her duff upon his incisors.
The orgasms, never frivolous, upsurge.

[Montréal (Québec) 18/11/18
& YHZ (Stanfield)—Enfield (Nova Scotia)
7 *décembre* mmxviii]

SAMSON (REPRESSED)

I.

1. "You Ethiope-hating, anti-Jewish demons!
You paper tigers! You white-devil *Dumbkopfs*!
Let's war to the death!

2. "All you book-burning imbeciles,
I'll set tires ablaze around your necks!

3. "My black speech be acid to your white faces!

4. "I'm fearless regarding you mutated bacteria
and all your gorilla affiliates!
I'm gonna slay y'all!
I'll never cease and desist
from this clean-up campaign!

5. "I'll crush y'all, face-to-face, skull by skull.
I've already slain entire your infestations, your camps,
and now you bare-ass survivors
slay yourselves by pursuing me!

6. "Just try me! I'll win!

7. "Consider that all your strategies of *Homicide*
and *Genocide*
have already redoubled on your backsides.

8. "Your sons lie bloody, their penises hatcheted.
You're that retarded!
You sent that pack to hound me,
and I axed off their very genitals!

9. "I don't gripe bout your plunders, your rapes!
I just don't let you live.
That simple.
I don't gotta blink back tears when I watch yas bleed out!

10. "I'll disembowel and castrate and decapitate y'all,
while laughing as I watch your blood blast
upwards and sideways
as if anti-gravity, black-pudding diarrhea!

11. "I'm a-gonna destroy y'all
clear down to Hell,
you night-rider fiends—ss—ss—ss—ss!
Infernal progeny of hogs!

12. "You've tried uselessly to break me,
by *Torture*, by *Humiliation*.
I'll do worse—effectively—to you.

13. "I won't decimate you:
To kill off one tenth of y'all ain't good enough.
I'll devastate y'all—
and all your bastoods!*

14. "You cankered, KKK varmints!
You trigger too many famines!
You are congenitally miserable!

15. "You are *Insecurity*.
You dream about attacking everyone.
Are you crazy?!!

16. "Beware, you running-dog imperialists!
God blesses me and mine—
and kills off you and yours.

17. "None of this complaint is made up.
Not one word is fiction!
Your history ushers on your obituaries.

* A Three Mile Plains (NS) pronunciation. Cf. Sugar Plum Croxen. (S.P. Cx.)

18. "Now, are y'all ready to be killed?
Are you ready to swill my sword?
Ready to be diced up, sliced up,
thou Philistines?

19. "I want to see you grieving.
I have that right!

20. "I want to see you kneeling
and offering your throats—
not for my choking manhood,
but for my long sword,
punching through your necks.

21. "Jeez, everyone you sleep with
(rape)
hates you.

22. "I'll exterminate y'all, body and soul—
your piss-yellow teeth, your gangrene faces!

23. "You opportunistic parasites must become garbage!
You're a wicked breed needing *Destruction*!

24. "I speak facts.
I know your style.
It's not mandated that I be kind.
I must cut you to pieces!

25. "I'll gash you to bones and tatters.
I'll bull you down.
I'll slap you down.
You'll feel my *Distemper*!

26. "I love shoveling thy wanker cadavers
under sand-blasted epitaphs!

27. "What! You think you can get away with your crimes
and shenanigans—
and blame it on—*sludge*—
the sperm that brought y'all
your regrettable breaths?

28. "Fuck y'all, you swines!"

[Tropea (Italia) 14 *mai* mmxvi]

II.

1. "So, you thugs plan to arrest Israel and me?
Why? What's the big idea?

2. "The reason for this asinine, suicidal *Provocation* is,
we refuse to denounce the God of Israel,
our dark-complected *and* light-compacted Deity.

3. "But you racist rascals—asinine buggers—
oppose Jews—Hebrews—Ethiopes,
and think—nitwits—that you can live!

4. "Well, I see through your half-smiles,
your equivocations that soften your oppressions.

5. "I see you and your confederates, clearly!
I see through you cleanly—from your green eyes
to your yellow bellies and lily livers.

6. "And I've proof of your financial frauds
and outright abuse of every market, every economy,
all these wrongs you commit non-stop!

7. "Moreover, every word of every Hebrew prophet
motivates your *Hatred*.
You can't stand being hated by the God we love!

8. "In conjunction—cahoots—with other quislings,
your army stole into my olive grove,
and, due to Delilah hacking my magic locks,
you witnessed my Goliath talents stymied.

9. "Well, did you really think y'all could get away with
such *Subterfuge, Persiflage, Treachery*?

10. "Go ahead! Concoct a story—a lie—
about Israel and I:
it'll be only a lie—a blankety-blank lie!

11. "The real reason for your *Opprobrium*?
For 20 years I've frustrated your *Criminality*!

12. "Look, Philistines: I'm a-gonna finish off y'all.

13. "Why not come with the *Truth*, then,
before it's too late?

14. "My reckless fucking of your treasonous countrywoman—
Delilah—
notwithstanding,
I'm a-gonna expel y'all from the planet.
I'm 100% committed!
(I'm as cynical as *Sin*.)

15. "You'll no longer threaten me or my nation!

16. "I assure you, however:
My *vendetta* will end your *Vindictiveness*.
Can't be any more dramatic than that!

17. "I am already watching you die."

[Dorval (Québec) 21 *mai* mmxvi]

III.

1. Delilah retorts:

2. "Muscle was Samson's padding, not fat!
Still, my pelvis could crack his.

3. "Nightly, spouted I a pot of *saké* from the fridge.
Samson transpo'd a pot daily from the SAQ.

4. "Yes, our bed was sprightly, naughty.
We knotted tautly.
My thighs addled him badly.
My kisses beat him down.

5. "Heaving at my puckish, succulent slit,
my honey-pot-stirrin pal was a scatterbrained Romeo.
Each sincere sacking was rude.

6. "Minute by minute fucking,
that was Samson's only lullaby.
He'd say, 'No doings, woman, without the fixings!'

7. "He jolly well loved feeling his prod
ramming—jamming—my jaws.
Like rats' teeth, my mouth rasped titillatingly his rod.

8. "Colourful was his undoing, eh?
I poured him mind-abusive beer,
then slashed his virile locks.

9. "Scrawny, skinny, looking like a stick
in a mini-skirt—
or like one of those runway waifs,
drugged-out, preposterously thin (zero-sum waist)—
still I exercised Fem Dom—
a stiletto-heel *Tyranny*:
His reward for splashing his stash in my slash.

10. "I—a sprig of a maid—
unmanned Samson:
A gulp of *saké*,
and then I had my cake.

11. "*Lust* stands Samson on the gallows.
All his roaring is in his head:
He can't talk due to all the snot in his lungs—
welled up from his whimpers.

12. "Dozens of Philisitine punks throng the hill
to jeer at the jerk.

13. "The wimp's distended penis had unintended *Consequence*.

14. "His manhood got expended in an abyss* of *Hate*.

15. "Way too callously, did his cock punch my *queynte*.

16. "Samson's cups of *saké* were always as cloudy
as horse-piss;
his own *cum* confused his *Consciousness*."

[Niagara Falls (New York) 30 *juin* mmxvi]

*** Abbess.**

IV.

1. "Her eyes hook on her knees,
while her ankles scrape my back;
soon, quick tears slide slick grease
to prettify—polish—her rack.*

2. "Her limbs writhe lithe against mine
til I'm petrified—in crisis:
No dead-ass lay! Bottom-line:
Her love commands highest prices!

3. "Her *Love* mandates *Torture*:
The grievous, blues sylph has a scythe
for a tongue; mouth's a pure
guillotine, *Pain*'s vent—a lie's width.

4. "A nocturnal face, her
eyes abrupt, she's no debutante—
with egg-shell heart, tender
teats. No. Her hips—so malignant—

5. "did swagger under mine
under pewter moon, copper sun,
to morals undermine:
No useless aches! Swell was our fun!

6. "Mature and always ripe,
her maw's *Hunger*—agreeable
as is a rare blood-type
in saliva—neglected no morsel

* Tits.

7. "of dong. Her bucking sex—
as ductile as flute notes—needed
fucking—no disconnects,
but sassy, squirming, stampeded

8. "penis, until her back
broke bed-straw and her ass broke wind,
and I groaned in the sack,
unhappy to obtain my end."

[Roissy-en-France (France) 7/9/16]

THE SAGA OF JEZEBEL

*Collected Verses Versus Jezebel.**

1. Repressing the truth that Jerrybalm
was "no-effin-good,"
King Ahab still grabbed—
to baste in his bed—
the hot-assed and flame-headed Jezebel—
that blonde tart for Bawl.

2. Soon, Ahab erected
an idolized model of Bawl,
an altar for Bawl,
a Gaudí temple for Bawl.

3. Scrutinizing such imbecilic *Impiety*,
God turned purple-faced—plus green-eyed.

4. But Jezebel machinated as decisive as God:
She coaxed Ahab to nix Hebrew naysayers.

5. To salvage as many dissenters as he could,
Elijah caravan'd a remnant to two caves—
retired 50 preachers sleepless to each—
and bade em picnic on bread and water.

6. Then Ahab fessed up to Jezebel
that the earmarked fodder for their state's pendulous blades—
some 100 *Death*-sentenced prophets—
Elijah had parked—safely—in double caves.

*** Cf. I Kings 16: 31–33; I Kings 18: 4 & 13; I Kings 19: 1–21; I Kings 21: 5–16, 23, 25–28; II Kings 9: 7–8, 10, 22–45.**

7. Apoplectic, Jezebel carrier-pigeon'd
a papal bull to Elijah,
pledging to cut him to the core—
"from your big mouth down to your dinky asshole!"

8. Elijah scrammed; made a beeline for Beersheba.

9. Dispirited, Elijah slumped neath a juniper tree,
crying out to God to stop his breath,
cos his *Grief* was wuss even than Adam's.

10. But as Elijah drowsed under branches,
an angel nudged the man's shoulders,
roused him to "Come to the table and eat."

11. Elijah sighted a sweet potato baking in coals,
plus a flagon of Bordeaux.
He gobbled the yam,
gulped the wine,
got sleepy drunk.

12. The angel swung back, lectured:
"Yam and wine gird up muscles—
and those pulsing tissues called nerves."

13. The starch and liquor powered Elijah
to trek 40 days to Horeb,
where God broods.

14. Once there, Elijah hunkered in a cave.
But God deemed his cringing cowardly,
and, short-tempered, slagged Elijah,
"What, pray tell, do ya think you're doing?"

15. Shivering in his very liver,
Elijah said, "I've been afraid for our *Faith*,
for Israelis are traipsing after Bawl—
and thus batting out Thy prophets' brains."

16. Nonplussed, God snorted,
"Get thee to the mountaintop!"

17. So, Elijah spidered up and up.
But when he gained the pinnacle,
a whirlwind swirled up
and tore off the next-door mountain's peak.

18. Next, an earthquake knocked Elijah
on his butt;
trembled down both mounts half to rubble;
then flames plied up from the cleft pile.

19. Amid the roaring and howling,
Elijah heard a still, small voice.

20. So intense the fire, so insistent the voice!

21. Elijah folded his neck in the sleeve of his robe,
hobbled back, shaken, to his cavern.

22. Again, God asked, "What the hell ya doin, Elijah?"

23. Weeping, Elijah slobbered,
"I fear that all Thy prophets
are gonna face white weapons—
splicing the wrong heads onto the wrong trunks."

24. Now, God prodded Elijah,
"Rise and go, *via* wilderness, to Damascus.
There, thou must anoint Hazard
as Syria's monarch.

25. "Then, thou shalt baptize Jihad as Israel's king,
and Elisha as his prophet,
domiciled in his palace.

26. "And I promise, whoever escapes
execution by Hazard,
shall be stabbed by Jihad.
And whoever survives Jihad's *Wrath*
will be guillotined by Elisha.

27. "Moreover, I still have 7,000 troops
in Israel, faithful unto *Moi*,
whose lips ain't nevah kissed on Bawl!"

28. So Elijah halloo'd to Elisha,
who was trotting a dozen oxen
to trample and break up recalcitrant turf,
and commanded,
"Be thou now a Cincinnatus
of *Prophecy*."

29. Elisha quit his oxen,
hounded, dogged, Elijah, yelled,
"I'm at your service!"
But Elijah retorted,
"Best tend thy oxen!"

30. So, Elisha murdered his twelve beasts,
boiled their flesh,
and gave out meat slabs to all who hungered.
Then, as a trainee-prophet,
he became Elijah's protégé.

31. Meanwhile, Jezebel reproached King Ahab
for acting so glum,
he wouldn't even bite a breadcrust.

32. The king recounted,
"I told Nabob I'd buy his vineyard.
But his '*nein*' was insulting, scoffing."

33. Queen Jezebel huffed,
"Aincha King of Israel?
Scarf down these oysters, this salmon,
and suck up the Champagne!
Just watch me! I'll getcha that vineyard—
off that piece-of-shit motherfucker!"

34. (So womanish be Jezebel!
Aye, so womanish!)

35. Jezebel jotted letters,
faked Ahab's signature,
to decree that Nabob preside over a feast.

36. "But dispatch two clerics to libel Nabob
and remand him for flippant *Blasphemy*,
so he'll be snatched by the crowd turned mob,
manhandled, and stoned where he stands."

37. Immediately that a cairn of red-stained rocks
heaped above Nabob's cratered and battered body,
Jezebel instructed Ahab, "Go and seize that vineyard!"
And the king did so.

38. Now, God directed Elisha
to warn King Ahab
that where dogs licked up
Nabob's wine-like blood,
trickling from out the hurled, razor-edged minerals,
so will dogs lick up his own.

39. "And dogs will eat up Queen Jezebel
by the walls of Jazzreal.

40. "The thing is, Jezebel has urged Ahab
to conduct sickening abominations."

41. When Elisha hipped Ahab to his peril,
the king ripped his clothes, clapped on burlap,
shook ashes over himself,
and fasted and prayed and wept.

42. Clear in his *Self-Mortification*,
King Ahab shuttered his Parliament of lice
(his Diet of worms),
and alerted Queen Jezebel
about the competitive prophecies
too dire for her to survive.
His sacerdotalism sounded scathingly cataclysmic.

43. But Jezebel jeered at Ahab's shabby garb,
patchwork coat, dirty hair;
she admonished his "defeatist snivelling."
Thus, she had him banished to a gardener's hut—
like Mellors or Benedict XVI.

44. Now, God briefed Elisha,
"You've witnessed King Ahab's *Contrition*?
So, I'll spare him the *Humiliation*
of being snagged and snacked on by dogs.
But not, so much, his sons...."

45. God prompted Jihad thus:
"I've set thee up as Israel's warrior-emperor,
so quick demolish the House of Ahab,
gouge out their genitals,
cast down their toddlers and straplings,
and dig up their dead.

46. "Feed Jezebel—as giblets, gobs, of gristle—
to mongrels and bitches,
quarelling and snarling
over bone-bits and bloody skin-snippets.

47. "Sincerely, thou must pitch dogs
to bite and tear the minx—
crown to cunt—
and tend her so she's rendered dust."

48. The Ahab-lineage ruler, Jerome,
saddled up to salute Jihad,
as far as Jazzreal.
Jerome eyed Jihad's 7,000-man army
with much heart-attack-breathtaking *Worry.*
He whimpered, "Jihad, won't you ratify
the *Pax* Ahabian?"

49. Jihad snickered in Jerome's bleached-out face:
"What *Peace*? How can hostilities cease
when thine own dame is a disgusting witch,
who outdoes even Betty Báthory
for revelling in literal bloodbaths?"

50. Hearing these avowals
and a-feared for his own bowels,
Jerome U-turned his chariot,
screeching, "Israel! Jihad, *Treason* plots!"*

51. Such oaths were Jerome's last ventings,
for Jihad selected calmly his strongest bow,
notched in the fleetest, sharpest arrow,
and then launched the aerodynamic dagger.

52. The finned spear pierced Jerome's spine,
then gored his heart,
so the iron-tip replaced his left nipple.

53. As he drooped in his cart,
Jerome was disturbed to see the arrowhead
disrupting the fine thread-count of his silk robe,
and, worse, slopping all ruddily.

* Cf. J. Benda, *La trahison des clercs.*

54. Next, Jihad bade Biden, his officer,
"Dispose of Jerome just as God wants:
Toss his cadaver into the thorns
of Ahab's property at Jazzreal."

55. After witnessing the assassination
and learning of the obscene disposal
of Jerome's corpse,
bro Aziz hid—hunkered under—
oversized banana leaves
in a humid, sweaty greenhouse.

56. Finding it hard to breathe
in that sweltering, muggy locale,
Aziz snuck out into cool, refreshing dusk,
and tiefed a cart,
and made to giddy up and get away.

57. But Jihad had been lurking, sleepless,
and shot off another deadly missile
that smucked Aziz right in the kisser.

58. The arrow fucked his mouth
and spiked out his neck,
as if executing very vigorous *fellatio.*

59. Aziz flopped dead in his chariot,
toppled out.
Full-stop.

60. His regal rivals terminated,
Jihad was now *de facto* and *de jure*
King of Israel.

61. Now, Jihad vroomed towards Jazzreal,
to defang that dragon-lady, dethrone Jezebel.

62. She saw the dust-cloud of 28,000 horse hooves
drumming her way,
and repaired to her toilet,
to strawberry her lips,
kohl and embolden her eyes,
pop off her bra,
and laurel herself with her fine-gold crown.

63. She was still Queen Jezebel—
and as *bella* as a quean.
Why not play the vamp?

64. Jihad up-reared his whinnying steed
under the queen's window,
bullhorned,
"Jezebel, cast down now thy gaze!"

65. Before Jezebel oped her window,
she queried her Prime Minister,
Zapruder,
"Tell me, is it two kings' assassin
who calls on me?"

66. Before Zapruder could reply,
Jihad yelled again at the queen's quarters,
"Zapruder and all ye other ministers,
whose side you takin?"

67. Zapruder and *deux* deputies
crept to their own windows,
peeped out, then hailed lustily the *arriviste* guerilla
as their Commander-in-Chief.

68. Instantly, Jihad utilized his *Authority*,
insisting his new underlings
personally grab the quailing queen
and hurl her down from the palace tower.

69. The clerkish trio pinioned their queen,
frog-marched Jezebel to the tower,
then thrust her to the pinnacle
and threw her down 7 vertiginous storeys.

70. Jezebel's plummet into dirt and stones
triggered horse hooves to *Discord*—
like piston-orchestrated pestles—
crumpling and crushing her into a dismal custard.
Her royal, purple blood splashed against
steeds' flanks and rumps,
so some dung-bukkake'd her Botox'd face,
while splatter of her effluent blitzed—
spritzered—
up and down palace walls.

71. By the time the horses quieted,
that *cunnus diaboli* was porridge and bonemeal
and an eyeless head—
a bashed up skull—
still flagged by a wig.

72. Her hands and feet survived the trampling,
almost intact,
so Jihad reminded his retinue
of God's *Prophecy*,
and they scooped up the queen's sloppy remains
and tossed them, sportively,
to yelping, growling, snapping dogs.

73. Thus, the queen's body bits
got scrambled up with horse manure and dog feces
to plump up worms—
the true-true landlords of Jazzreal.

[Montréal (Québec) 9 *mars* mmxix
& VIA Train 669 (Kingston, ON-Oshawa, ON)—
Coach 3, Seat 12A—9 *mars* mmxix
& Waterloo (Ontario) 11 *mars* mmxix]

Jezebel's Riposte.

Men! So brutal and backward!
And fickle and heartless be Israel's God!

(That enigmatic Egomaniac!
That all-round, well-rounded, one-sided *Authority*!)

Facing the threats and indiscretions
of cretinous Hebrew prophets

(themselves so merciless), *Statecraft*
dictated *Extermination*—

their carcasses left cooking in the sun.
(Elijah secreted these seditious idiots

in two caves. I employed
the priceless murmurs of lovers—

my covert panties tugged aside,
to float my pungent, particular, oceanic scent—

and Ahab arranged the *Altercation*:
50 lions, each starved for five days,

then their cages opened at the cave mouths—
25 to each cave—

the beasts chomped and slashed and bit,
clawed, fanged, feasted,

until prophetic eyes filmed over
with a scarlet, smelly gauze.)

Thus, I preserved Ahab's Administration.
(*War*: A book of butcher-shop wrapping paper.

Bleeding.)
But, I was no bleeding, Catholic girl,

fearful. Nope. Not I.
I admire bold-face, forthright Eve,

and don't mind opening meaty thighs
for a beefy chest,

my big-up womanhood—
bewitching, twitching, then pitching

the king to big-ass angina
(almost). Precarious.

(His penetration of me—royal—
is like stirring custard or broth.

In our vulgar humping, *Proletarian*—
tits jumpin out my shirt—

Indelicacy be no *Vice*.
Tough lips venting rough words,

recast unparliamentary Jews
as brawling bawds,

circulating uncircumscribed
bloody, Israelite *Civil Strife*,

circumcised STDs and *Blasphemy*,
typhoid and moonshine,

their maudlin lips
pissing shit.

Better is it to dish em
a smorgasbord of dirt, grime, snot, pus,

their bodies ripped apart
in beautiful *Crucifixion*—

lions' claws
nailing em,

lions' fangs
spiking em,

until they be blubber, rubied,
something else, pulsating.)

Ahab's mouth is all church,
but his heart's a brothel,

so it was facile to teach
militant Machiavellianism,

to undo the irreverent posturings
of inferior prophets.

Anyway, always *Wrath* shatters *Innocence*—
spurious, weakling *Innocence*—

and infertile or peevish pelvises
or plump treasure chests.

For domestic *Peace*,
husbands, dudes, should be fully gullible.

Ahab's duty is to kiss me lucidly,
startlingly,

to have me avidly struggling
in our syncopated entwining,

to be uncommonly crass and spanking
in our sumptuous to-and-fro.

And *Governance* requires kings
be so homicidal,

they horrify
their own decadent sires.

But *Peace, Order, Good Government* demands
the dismantling of conniptions—

via mass public hangings
(as in El-Sisi's U.S.-bossed Egypt),

imprisonment under trumped-up charges,
geniuses become palpable dung,

bodies left looking like painted rawhide,
or smoked, brain-tanned, buffalo hide,

a lot of loud, gory pigment—
squalls as grave as gravel tumbling, squabbling:

To be dirty,
inside and out.

[Nassau (The Bahamas) 23 *mars* mmxix]

THE BOOK OF RUTH

I.

1. *Famine* is a sanitizing sewer:
Like a waterfall, it scours.
Hunger clarifies the skeleton….

2. So, Miles and wife, Naomi, camel'd,
ex-Bethlehem, to try Mob's sugary geography,
what yields white honey, white bread, white wine.

3. Mileage and Chili were their twins.
This petite tribe put down stakes in Mob.

4. But Miles proved an ephemeral patriarch,
a vaporous archetype:
Hollowed-out, his heart caved in.
Statistically, now a single mom was Naomi.

5. Once her sons upped to swains,
Mileage bedded Oprah; Chili wedded Ruth.
All householded happily—for one decade.

6. Then, a hammer, sword-like, spiked Chili's skull;
next, Mileage's tent became a fireplace.
Now, a childless widow was Naomi.

7. As short-lived as dethroned dictators,
three hubbies turned hackneyed, worm grub.

8. An old paintbrush seemed Naomi:
Frayed, splintering, set to be trashed.

9. Time to exit from thorny thickets:
Pastures fretted by prickly cacti.

10. Her widowed daughters-in-law—
Oprah and Ruth—
figured Naomi would home to Israel,
to dig into the daily dole—
the dollop—drippings—of manna and gravy.

11. Naomi preached to Oprah and Ruth:
"Each of yas backslide to thy mammies,
who oughta be gracious to yas,
for having husbanded our dead."

12. Thus, Naomi hectored these hardship blondes;
these hard-done-by, hard-workin broads.

13. But Ruth caterwauled, Oprah sobbed:
"We wanna stay by you!"

14. "Lookit: I can't give you more sons—
mates to man-up and man yas.
And I'm too old to be again a bride;
and too old to breed anew," declared Naomi.

15. "Besides, even if I could, *via* God,
feel my womb drooling, my freshly upturned tits dripping,
and I could mother and suckle twin sons
(like that wolf did Romulus and Remus),
how could ya both tarry with me,
playing kiddy games with my boys,
til, by age 16, they'd proclaim themselves *men*,
and lust to wed, bed, and breed
(not necessarily in that order),
and then choose ya both as brides—
MILFs—
and not whiny, flat-chested, virgin chits?"

16. Oprah's and Ruth's eyes
undammed down a deluge now.*

* But Naomi speaketh *Truth*, Ruth! Cf. *Do the Right Thing* (1989).

17. So, Oprah hoisted on her backpack
to sashay and waylay a sugar daddy:
Weren't she still "nubile, flexible, fertile"?

18. (Her attitude? Horse-head-haughty!
So exited that down-n-dirty hotty,
bustlin her lil bum-bum,
hustlin her lil bum-bum.)

19. Now, Naomi shoved Ruth off;
exclaimed, "Tut, tut, dovey!
Oprah *owns* her *Destiny*! Copy that!

20. "I'm like a rainbow—halved:
I'm zero in total."

21. Ruth negativized this summation:
"Whatever you'll eat, I'll eat.
Wherever you'll sleep, I'll sleep.
Thy God is now my God."

22. So, the duo trudged to Bethlehem,
where, straggling in, haggard, dusty,
they stunned the citizenry, who questioned,
"Art thou truly Naomi—
husbandless, sonless, homeless, penniless?"

23. Naomi attested that an evil, tireless wind,
a tiresome sirocco,
had blown awry and askance every *Blessing*.

24. "Jeez," spat Naomi:
"Don't call me 'Naomi' evermore!
Call me *Mara*—bitter—
because the Lord hath crushed out
all my sweetness.

25. "I'm the victim of a *Conspiracy**
as diabolical as an entrapping spider's.
My life equals a toilet being flushed.

26. "Day after day, no one sees the sun spying.
Nor does the moon, rising in China,
heed my Israeli sobs.

27. "God's planed me down to *Destitution*,
and my double-lineage is dead—
junked—
Genealogy gerrymandered under *Geology*:
My sons are two headstones.
My husband's a third."

28. This dreary homecoming occurred,
backwardly enough, at harvest—
while barley from far-flung fields
was being scooped and priced and stored
in Bethlehem steel warehouses—
to wait out any awaiting *Famine*.

[Waterford (Ontario) 12 *avril* / *Nisan*
& Black Friday the 13th *aprile* mmxviii
& Buffalo (New York) Friday the 13th April mmxviii]

---

* Cf. The Clintons, 1998–1999.

II.

1. Naomi's bloodline boasted one blueblood,
one plutocrat:
Boss.

2. Ruth proposed to Naomi that she'd go,
knuckle down, and truckle to Boss,
pluckin and shuckin Goliath-tall, corn ears.

3. Too, seein that she be from Mob,
there'd be no extra, public *Subtraction*
of Naomi's already depressed *Status.*

4. So, Ruth trashed her black, widow garb;
slipped on ripped-knee denim—
bleached out, patched up—overalls.

5. Ex-Bethlehem, Boss ventured onto his verandah,
to view—review— the lucrative reaping
of his sylph-like MILFs and GILFs.

6. His telescope honed in on a yellow-haired,
blue-jean, Norma-Jean-Baker-type nymph,
pig-tailed, wholesome, busty as-all-get-out,
stubbing and mashing corn niblets
due to her inexpert, if elegant digits.

7. At first, he was annoyed by the jane's messy,
unprofitable sweating;
next, he obsessed over her tits
thudding about, so freely, neath her overalls.

8. Boss pivoted to his overseer, asked,
"Who's the sun-haired ragamuffin? The newby?"

9. Well, Mr. Wallis Stephens,
who'd been designin
to pluck that lil cherry tree myself *
scalped his eyes before the Alpha male,
and said, "*Padrone*, Ruth's from Mob.
She trailed back here with Naomi.
Odious wounds put down Ruth's husband.
(Paternal ills took down Naomi's husband.)

10. "She's pledged to slave like the dickens,
day-long among the sheaves."

11. Boss nodded: "Good idea, Wally."
Boss thought: *Well, her* Beauty *ain't nullified*
by her husband's bein Null-and-Void.

12. Boss had his hoss saddled, then surged
boss n hoss—as if embossed—
onto the field, forging through the corn,
fording the corn,
to come up—ruthless—to Ruth,
and tell her—
right before her astonished co-workers
(who all downcast eyes, downed tools, and knelt),
"Thou gotta quit this *Labour* now, Ruth,
and ride on back to my mansion.**

13. "Ruth, thou must only observe from afar
these fields where these darky peasants sweat."

14. Eyeing ants, Ruth shrugged,
"But Mistah Boss, I require this employ,
to ferry shekels to Naomi,
plus schlep home corn to stew, bake, or roast."

---

* Cf. *The Harder They Come* (1972).
** Unsaid: Harem.

15. Boss grinned: "Sho nuff, but you'll traipse
after these others, so your *Labour*'s
prodigiously less.

16. "Too, Stephens will scruple that no rube, no hick,
touches a single finger to thy body
nor intrudes one lewd word in thine ears."

17. Ruth assumed prostration now:
"*Padrino*, why should I savour such favour?"

18. Boss thought of her ivory tits squashed
against the soil.
He lusted to see those orbs—
disrobed—
two milky globes aglow in his hands.

19. His two eyes raked her backside,
vying to peer through the denim
to discern the two half-arcs of a pale rump—
an ivory, plump butt—
with a syrupy aperture welling.

20. Boss whistled: "I knows you's a widow;
that an alien wind's harried ya on to Israel.
Yet, you've been perfectly white to Naomi.
Thou hast been, Ruth, as pious as *Hunger*."*

21. Ruth sensed that gaze blazing her back;
feeling empowered now to look up, sit up, she say,
"King Boss, I cherish your *Charity* to me—
your kindness for a *dépaysée* gleaner."

22. Boss thrust up his right hand: "*Basta*!"**
The shadow—a baptism—splashed o'er Ruth.

---

* *Anxiety* bruises the blood; it pulses purple.
** Italian: Enough!

23. He smiled: "Get up now, back of me,
and I'll take you for vittles—
'roast bakes'—saltfish and bread—
and rock lobster tail outta Jamaica.
Add in ginger beer."

24. Ruth cantilevered onto the big white
Lipizzan stallion,
held tight as white-on-rice to Boss's belt,
as he pranced her onto the canteen.
How good to embrace this bad man's waist!

25. En route, Boss uncorked his flask,
and let *Grappa (aromatizzata) al Bergamot*
soften Ruth's hard thirst.

26. Nipple tips nipped at his back
as Boss clipped long his clopping horse.
Next, Boss ogled Ruth's rear as she switched off.

27. Boss delivered Stephens these marching orders:
"Let Ruth reap after the others,
so her actual *Burden* is light.
Also, let no prick interfere with her—
at pain of thy blade's stroke pon the bloke!

28. "And let armfuls of corn fall her way:
Make *Good Fortune* seem accidental—
but let her hoover up this bonanza."

29. Each dawn, Ruth leaked sweat til dusk.
She crushed corn into useful portions.

30. And Ruth toted lotsa cornmeal to Naomi:
Sufficient loads.

31. Naomi queried Ruth:
"Is Boss always good to ya?"
Ruth was positive:
"He lets me toil in his fields—
but allots extra corn as a daily gift."

32. Naomi affirmed: "*Padrino* is good
to the living,
and goodly to honour the dead.
How lucky to be his relations—
me by blood and thou by *Marriage*."

33. And Ruth—of Mob—revealed:
"*Padrone* has also stated that no studs
seekin a 'cougar' are to pester me."

34. Naomi cocked her head quizzically:
"Well, it may be that Boss is struck by you,
Ruth, and may want to stable you
with his household harem."

35. Ruth shrugged: "Whatever be his intentions,
my *Virtue*'s guaranteed.
And we'll feast all through winter."

[Buffalo (New York)
14 *Nisan / avril* mmxviii]

III.

1. Naomi blurted the bottom-line *Truth*:
"Ruth, Boss doth desire you.
Why not coo and cuddle with him?

2. "It's no sin *versus* Chili's memory,
for our *Padrino* is our kin.
Anyway, girlie, you're a widow:
Why be shy to act his wife?
To lick and lap....

3. "Insert thyself among his stable,
bathe in his milk and swath in his silk,
then wait out his sucking down of retsina—
til the booze is done and he's gone a-snooze.
Let *Instinct* spur extra tactics...."

4. Though Naomi was pimping her out—
like a ghettoized Barbie—
Ruth chanted, "Aye! Aye!"

5. Naomi winked, whispered, explicit advice:
"When Boss gropes, groggy, to his chambers,
sneak in after im,
uncover his swarthy nudity,
and lay thy ivory-snow, Sleepin-Beauty-type self longside."

6. What Naomi policy'd, Ruth performed.

7. Predictably did Boss guttle and swill,
then begin to whistle and sing,
which he did nightly,
until he fell drowsy
or felt like pickin a gal—
at his beck-and-call—
from his personal harem.

8. This night, he just slurped down too much
and didn't have the *cojones*
to drag a bitch to his four-poster, king-size bed.

9. He stumbled from his pantry, mumbling,
cackling Mousy Croxen's cracked-heart version
of Georgie Jones-drafted, classic, country blues,
"If My Heart Had Windows."*

10. Nimbly, Ruth tiptoed after,
to do some reverse-slumming:
Her morals numb,
her heart's blood drumming.

11. Her *Padrone* blacked out abed,
Ruth tussled to prod and push
his chestnut length and bulk,
enough to denude the hulk.
Quick, her eyes licked at all,
even his unpent stick, stirring.

12. Next, Ruth swaddled the man,
but disrobed herself:
To snuggle crosswise at Boss's two brassy feet.

13. Awakening, muddled, in dawn's gloaming,
Boss was dumbfounded to feel a soft form—
much like a female tush—
plush—flush—gainst his toes.

14. Letting his feet dote, he felt em float
over the cello-curves of a feminine back.

15. Boss now lifted the sheer, bamboo sheets
to scope out whoever might be this daring darling.

---

* Cf. John Conlee, "Rose Colored Glasses."

16. Ruth swung round in the *grisaille* light,
and murmured, "*Padrone*, I am thy kin.
Cover me again."

17. Ecstatic, Boss purred:
"A dame who negotiates *Destiny*?
She, I damn well like!"

18. Despite his hushed tones, his johnson reared
in its undejected trajectory.

19. "Thou lie at my feet, Ruth,
but thou ain't no sycophant!
And thou art a widow—virginal—
and I'm thy kin.

20. "Tarry with me steady to daylight;
lie contiguous to me, marry."

21. Ruth prayed, "Let me lie here, still,
and then steal away with dawn,
so that none can toggle tongues
bout my presence this night."

22. Bewildered was Boss—by Ruth's
unexpected *Nakedness* in his bed
and then by her unexpected *Reluctance*
to fulfill his obvious *Expectation*
that her obvious *Nudity* instigated.

23. But Boss—politic—sighed:
"I value thy *Virtue*,
but why shouldn't I assert myself,
in my house, in my bed?"

24. Ruth avowed: "I am curious—
about what my *Padrone* is really like
and whether he really likes me."

25. His teeth white gold mid gathered gloom,
Boss grinned, "Before ya exit, Ruth,
find barley weighting your widow's veil:
I was born to gaze upon thy face."

26. Ruth dodged windows at dawn,
clipped to shadows and foliage,
til she could come to Naomi
and present Boss's sovereign gift.

27. Naomi confessed* Ruth, then said:
"Go now and get your beauty sleep,
for Boss will never sleep wholly again
until he has thee wholly for his bride."

[Seat 15C, Car 4, VIA Train 67
(Dorval, Québec—Cornwall, Ontario)
& (Kingston, Ontario—Oshawa, Ontario)
21 *avril* / *Nisan* mmxviii]

*** Intransitive usage.**

IV.

1. Rambunctious emotions roiled Boss's blood.
Playing sanctimonious, he consulted elders.

2. His cat-whistle collected the *Kaffeeklatsch*;
dixit he, "Plunk yo ten brown duffs down!"

3. Boss outlined Naomi's current tender
of neat parcels of impeccable *Property*,
the *Profit* speculated to feed her *Pension*.

4. Boss detailed that to buy from Naomi,
one gotta also buy from Ruth.

5. "Y'all gotta make the *Grand Purchase*,
for Ruth, outta Mob, is wifed to our dead kin,
and his *Inheritance* falls void, otherwise.
How else to resuscitate his name?"

6. But Boss's kinsmen—
this petty bourgeoisie—
were let-downs:
"No can do."
"We're NSF.* Thou art S.O.L."**

7. (In these ancient times in Israel,
to affirm an oath re: *Money* matters,
a man had to pluck off his shoe:
Was a holy institution.
No "soul" to be scuffed!)

---

* Insufficient Funds.

** Shit-out-of-luck.

8. Now the kinsmen—not cash-flush enough
to do the doubled-up, *Real-Estate* deal,
each tugged free one shoe—
(a motley mismatch of lefts, rights,
sandals, brogues, sneakers, flip-flops,
in leather or canvas*)—
and plopped it pell-mell in the pile,
all to affirm their collective view
that Boss should outlay the cash
to the two beauteous widows.

9. They recognized that Boss' chess pieces,
were bulls—not mere horses, mere pawns.

10. Boss: "Y'all witness that I buy up
Naomi's lands.

11. "But not only am I picking up Ruth's share,
I'm annexing her—
to wife me and so preserve
her dead hubby's *Legacy*."

12. The kinsmen shouted, "Hurrah!"
(The roar sounded like buzzing—
all those accumulated huzzas.)

13. "May Ruth be blessedly beneficial for Israel
and pick up *Praise* in Bethlehem.

14. "And let thy household multiply
like the household of Parvez
(whom Tamar bore for Judah),
once you breed Ruth,
for she be a basket of seeds:
To be pampered."

*** Plus one Philamain "*Santé*" shoe, brown, size 12, outta Sherbrooke (QC); one Fluevog (with a satanic verse on the sole); one Adidas; one desert boot; one P.F. sneaker; *et cetera*.**

15. (Here be the intersection of *Sex*
and *Property* interests.)

16. So Boss took Ruth as his *cuntella*.
To drape her snowy bust with gold.

17. Their lovin occurred amid
a volcanic eruption
of green-sheathed ears of sun-shade corn.

18. (After the grassy bed of the fields,
now came wafting black aromas of rum
and comely chocolate.)

19. Each kiss was a guzzle—a *ghazal*—
a festive gulp—of tongue.

20. Ruth's knees stirrup'd her Boss's thighs.
As her quim flexed faultless his beam.

21. (A bed can be a *salon*.
Or thighs can be bellows,
making the mattress squeal.)

22. And thus did Ruth's *belle-chose*—
nightly plungered and watered—
soon flood forth Boss's son.

23. And all the distaff ballyhooed Naomi,
declaring, "The Lord hath blessed thee,
and now thou shalt have descendants.

24. "And Ruth's son will be as good to you
in sickness and in old age—
as if you'd borne the boy thyself."

25. Her childless want now terminated,
Naomi noticed her breasts youthfully inflate,
miraculously recharge, refloat—
a-bloat beautifully with milk.

26. Widowed kinsmen ganged to woo Naomi,
delivering her gold-set jewels
and/or handsome cuts of lamb,
slathered in minty frosting.

27. (Nice was it to curl up with a fella,
now and then, with candles blown out,
and *Privacy* and *Discretion* assured.)

28. As for the boy babe,
Naomi loved even his smelly blushing
when he made caca.

29. And the neighbor women named the child,
"Obadiah Loving,"
and they considered him Naomi's son,
who'd later father Jesse,
who, in turn,
begat David.

[Halifax (Nova Scotia) 28–29 *abril / Nisan* mmxviii]

THE BOOK OF EZRA

I.

1. Cyrus, King of Persia, couldn't sleep:
God badgered, bedevilled, his psyche.

2. After weeks of this PSYOP,
this Black Op, skull-squishing *Torture*—
Cyrus broadcast to the Persian Empire
his summons to see rebuilt at Jerusalem—
"a Temple sound enough to amplify
the subtlest paeans to Israel's God!"

3. But who'd actually grant each brick
a grumpy slap,
next a beautifying tap?

4. Who'd help the builder nag on the pace,
escape the sort of exasperating hindrances,
that plague trumped-up, *Trade and Tariff* treaties?

5. Well, with *vino* amending their vision
and their bugles zigzagging notes,
Levites came camelling to Jersualem.

6. Neighbours drained wine-sacks,
ignited Rasta reefers,
jigged guitars to reggae riffs,
scrubbed tarnish off silver,
all to tout and sprout the Temple.

7. King Cyrus had archaeologists scour
King Nebuchadnezzar's palace,
to cherry-pick all the *Judaica*
that discriminating Vandals had bagged.

8. The remarkable *Squander* was soon tabulated—
zero-ersatz gold.
King Slush Bazaar carted these items—
yanking a chain-gang of Babylonian slaves—
from Damascus to Jerusalem.

[Northampton (Massachusetts) 28 *février* mmxviii]

II.

1. Now, these be the progeny who swapped
steel jails for stone highways,
who, discharged from Babylonian *Captivity*—
that fiesta of infections—
jogged to Jerusalem
to swell the income-brackets
of sculptors, artisans, carpenters, masons, *et cetera*:

2. Plus priests.

3. Plus singers (those Afro'd chillun of Aesop).

4. Plus porters and wranglers
and their wee, shepherded beasts
and super-sized, domesticated critters.

5. Plus questionable Israelites:
Those unable—
or unwilling—
to identify their *Paternity*.

6. So, anyone unable to reckon his *Genealogy*—
or reconcile her *Genealogy*—
or who couldn't unfold a puzzling household
via verifiable chronologies,
was barred from (polluting) the priesthood.

7. All tolled—totaled—the folks numbered
some 42,380;
including 7,337 maids/waiters;
plus 200 singers, mainly baritones and sopranos.

8. The chief patriarchs mustered at the old
House of God in Jerusalem—
and vowed capital capital to erect one anew.

9. Collectively, they stood good for 61,000 drams
of gold; 5,000 lbs. of silver;
and 120 priests' robes (now freshly spic-and-span,
clean of all untoward emissions).

[BDL—Windsor Locks (Connecticut) 2 *mars* mmxviii]

III.

1. Dawned the 7th month:
Ex-Babylon, all Israelis were again urbanites,
and communally pooled herds, flocks, tools, wares;
collectively taxed the peculiar estates
kept up by singers, poets, and lucky "bastoods."

2. A crown is just a gutted hat, eh?
But Jeshua got to sport one,
in tandem with Zero,
for both engineered the pickaxing and sledge hammering
of those ochre stone blocks befitting God's Altar.

3. (The rumble and roar of stones being trundled,
cut, rolled, and crowbarred or bashed into place,
executed a sort of sloppy *Be-Bop.*)

4. Once the Altar was tabled,
dished up then were sizzling, blackened meats—
even birds' bitter, ground-down bones—
all to induce God to heed Israeli murmurs.

5. Cleavers broached chickens' necks;
steam squeaked and squealed outta kettles;
sneaky hammers slapped into calves' heads:
Thus, the tabernacular feasts got kept.

6. Incessant were the dishes—
thanks to the festive menstruation
of poultry, cattle,
in the dinning, braying, bleating, roaring *Butchery.*

7. From Day One of the 7th month,
meats got seared and scorched and charred.
Yet, the Temple remained more a blueprint
than it was even a basement.

8. Masons fisted coins; carpenters pawed cash;
the proles scarfed down *hors d'oeuvres*
off the snack trucks—
wine, sandwiches, milk, ale, cheese.

9. (They loved letting sherry and beer
leak down their throats
in unholy draughts—
never ever letting up).

10. The "people's republic"—priests, stone-cutters,
axe-men, carvers, blacksmiths, poets, vintners,
butchers, cooks, bee-keepers, shepherds,
singers, milkmaids, wet-nurses, medicine men,
et cetera—toiled.
Nowhere was any dishonourable sweat!

11. Priests' lips pursed to bugles;
Levites' knuckles bashed cymbals:
Ballads for God—no caw-caw of blues—
rose cantankerous, brash, into the air.

12. Voices spurted, blurted, *Song*—
to hootenanny Temple *Construction*.

13. Ogling that new foundation shovelled,
pick-axed, and concretized,
oldsters felt *Emotion* swill hind their foreheads
and spill from their eyes.

14. Like two streams conjoining
in a slippery ditch,
weeping underscored boomeranging shouts,
as *Celebration* reverberated—

as if the Temple stones, planted apace,
represented a cargo ferrying *Rebellion*—
a *Lego*-block Trojan Horse (so to speak)—
now rearing against years of rapacious,
Assyrian-Babylonian *Imperialism*—
a nursery of guillotines.

[BDL—Windsor Locks (Connecticut) 3 *mars* mmxviii]

IV.

1. Unamused—observing Hebrew ex-slaves
quarrying and bricklaying and scaffolding up a Temple
to glorify a solidly genocidal "God"—
now leagued sniffling, Assyrian whiners,
aiming to scuttle the *Construction*.

2. They pow-wowed with Zero,
squeezed before his tinny gaze,
and lobbied for the "right"
to snazz up Temple erection:
"We also dream to respect thy God;
get real palsy-walsy."

3. But Zero and Jeshua both said "*Nyet*"—
in a mutual *fiat*:
Only Israelis
could fulfill King Cyrus's commission
to crane up the Temple.

4. Angered, the non-Jews, as cold-hearted
as paid-off wantons,
vomited picket lines to berate
and jeer at workers,
all intended to stonewall the Temple's ascension.

5. Adversaries bribed bureaucrats
to nix building permits
or to bully on pricy alterations.

6. They tasked the Devil's advocates—
amoral lawyers (the usual type)—
to scrawl a *Complaint* against Israel,
inking characters as malicious as acid.

7. In vitriolic Aramaic,
this letter badgered King Tax
to fix up a crucifix
to nail-down every Hebrew....

8. The Royal Scribe, Rhesus,
and his deputy, Capuchin,
had translated the missive,
which they expected to express
the anti-Semitic *Sentiment*
of the Nixonian *Silent Majority*.

9. Now, Rhesus, Capuchin, and associates
Mafia gangstas (wantin to profit
from waterin down cement
and skimmin percentages off contracts)—
proposed *Opposition* to Jewish
Authority o'er the Temple.

10. That's the context of this awful,
would-be, papal bull:*

11. "To King Tax:

12. "Thy subjects—the denizens—of Assyria
and Babylon—hail thee.

13. "We know you were promoting *Tolerance*—
essential for *State Multiculturalism*—
when you commanded the rebuilding
of the Temple to Israel's God [sic].
However, now every single, Jewish slave
has abandoned our urgent tasks,
and jagged back to Jerusalem—
to orgy at taxpayers' expense!

---

* **Pablum & bullshit.**

14. "Furthermore, the Hebrews pooh-pooh
our schools of *Architecture*,
preferring "Georgian" roundness, breast-like—
while th'Africans among em
are lurid, Gothic types—
sketchy, prickly, shady.

15. "Seditious and insidious are these Jews
(and Ethiopes),
and once safely inside their 'Fortress of Fortitude,'
squared away in its redoubtable walls,
they'll not pay *Tribute* or *Tax*,
and the Royal Treasury will see the current flood
of currency spasm to spurts, squirts, trickles.

16. "And these folks are Royal assassins, eh?

17. "Now, because we loyal citizens weigh
the absolute values of salt and silt—
of sugar and sand—
we beg thee tutor thyself in the history
of perpetual, Israeli *Revolt*!

18. "Doubtless, thou shalt become conscious
re: the congenital tendency of Israelis
to put out shingles of trade,
put out opponents' eyes,
to treat all non-Hebrews as jerk-offs:
Thou will learn that Thy ancestors
had to launch Brutalist wars—
swishing gore under sunlight—
to punish these renegade pundits.

19. "If that *Tempio* is finished,
finished is thy *Mastery* o'er the Hebrews...."

20. King Tax returned this answer:
"I send fraternal greetings.
Your letter's been unfolded.

21. "I've tasked scholars to plumb
The Royal Archives re: Israel,
and now I know why the former kings
reduced Jerusalem to a warren of nettles.

22. "Infamous was Israel for her kings'
intolerable *Egoism*;
for monarchs who were as twitchy as crossbows;
for their relentless stomping down of heathens;
for their temperamental, show-off martyrs....
And so: Famous was Jerusalem's quashing.

23. "Thus, I decree that Temple construction cease;
that slaves remain slaves.

24. "Note that I write like hell this letter—
to prevent Royalty from being crapped upon;
to forestall Crowned Heads
bleeding out in poignant puddles."

25. Hence, all *Labour* stopped, more-or-less abruptly.

[**Ware (Massachusetts) 3 & 4 *mars* mmxviii**]

V.

1. **V***ia* the gap fronted by two abrupt drops,
where cliffs overhang,
arrived Haggard and Zachary
to prophesy to Jewry.

2. Zack's limp was a chink in his height:
His steps zigged toward Heaven
and zagged toward Hell.
Yet, his tongue didn't seesaw;
his words didn't limp.

3. Zero and Jeshua obeyed the prophets' provisos.
New slogans got postered and leafleted and broadcast
quick-quick-quick:
"No more may the Temple atrophy!"
"So what if wronged crows squawk?"

4. Guv'nor Tatter, up long nights boozing,
eyeing leggy nudes, even those jiggly big-sizes,
with his gal-pal (a pensioned stripper),
had to babble, *Reaction*:
"Who gave the Israelis the right
to pick up hammers, pound down spikes?

5. "Gimme the names of the trouble-makers!
I remember when butcher shops had sawdust
on the floor,
and the meat-man gave ya bones for dogs: Free!
I'm no dummy!"

6. But God was demanding maximum *Beauty*
and minimum *Complaint*.
Israelis ignored the Gubernator's tantrum.

7. So Guv'nor Tatter
prattled this missive to King Darius:

8. "Israel be categorically for the *Tempio*,
pullying beams up vertically
and pushing em along horizontally,
and are thus belittling our offices—*literally*.

9. "Their expert contractors are fast
tumbling boulders into place,
lifting timber into joints.
Hammers are slamming down furiously.
Saws are grinding non-stop through cedar
and gnawing mahogany mindfully.

10. "I demanded they name their directors!
More insolent than ever,
they slandered me, saying,
'A drunk—orating, administering—
is only an orangutang,
gesturing, spitting.

11. '*Architecture* is *Scripture*—grounded.

12. 'Our forefathers rebelled gainst God,
and He, peeved, let Nebuchadnezzar
ransack and wreck the *Tempio*,
and clap us in chains
and schlep us off to Babylon as slaves.

13. 'But *Wisdom* repairs.
So, once enthroned, King Cyrus prompted
restoring God's Temple—
and freed us to be restored to Jerusalem.

14. 'Plus the gold and silver furnishings—
ornaments, fixtures—
that Nebuchadnezzar stole, stripped,
to burnish his palace....

15. 'Governor Shush now has granted us
our antique silver and gold
tchotchkes
to resituate in the new *Tempio*,
for "Money must be broken—
to bring "'*Change*.'"

16. 'Thus, the Temple foundations are stone,
and the unfinished erection booms
with each jolly exhalation of the workers.'"

17. Guv'nor Tatter now signed off:
"King Darius, do research archives
to profess that King Cyrus did truly
decree the Temple 'insurrection' in Jerusalem."

[St. John's (Newfoundland) 9 *mars* mmxviii]

VI.

1. Is *Truth* only a paper declaration?
Does it exist in any book—
or *only* in a book?!!

2. A chronicle turned up in a Mercedes palace.

3. (A poet's house* is his or her words,
public—as in a tavern or a legislature.

4. Like archivists, they immerse emselves
in the acidic, cankering truths
of kings and kindoms.)

5. King Cyrus had okayed rebuilding
the *Tempio* of God at Jerusalem.
Could this *Truth* be kayo'd?

6. Indeed, the boulders and timber required
had to be acquired
at Royal expense—
plus the silver gewgaws and gold knick-knacks,
removed by Nebuchadnezzar,
had to be pried out of even his palace's pagan altars
and reinstalled in the Hebrew Cathedral.

7. So, King Darius scribbled to Guv'nor Tattle:
"To *Reform* is to yelp, to bark,
to sniff at turds and piss on tree trunks;
it is to be doggèd; it is to snarl;
and it is to bitch and growl and bite.

---

* Cf. *Poets' Haus* (1983).

8. "You're loyal, so you think the Hebrews
disloyal, because they're exotic, uppity,
mavericks, free radicals, eh?
But they're also sumptuously virtuous.
So let em keep on buildin their temple.

9. "Moreover, it's politic to bless freely
and *blesser** rarely.
So, keep an open door, an open heart,
and an open mind.

10. "Nothin backfires like beratin th'electorate!
So, corral bullocks, rams, lambs, calves, cattle;
store up salt, wine, oil, *et cetera*;
give barrels and board daily to the Hebrew priests.

11. "Gotta serve somebody!**

12. "If anybody balks, take action:
Apply my *Law* as disinfectant.

13. "Haul down scoundrels' huts!
Bury their parents and babes in the ruins;
then, shovel dung over all."

14. Guv'nor Tattle shrugged***—then executed—
by degrees—the decrees,
now said to've been signed off on by King Tax too
(according to a questionable letter
dredged up in the archives,
examined in a sealed room,
and then lost in a fire—
"accidental"—
that also consumed the examining archivist,
plus the Royal Scribe, Rhesus,
and his sidekick, Capuchin:
A lot of indistinct screaming;
a lot of indiscreet whimpers).

---

* French: To wound; to injure.
** Cf. B. Dylan.
*** (P.E.) Trudeauvian.

15. The deal represented a hat trick—
a triple-crown sweep of Persian Royalty deluxe—
Kings Cyrus, Tax, and Darius.

16. At consecration of the *Tempio*,
100 bullocks, 100 rams, 400 lambs,
and 12 goats
(denominating Israel's 12 tribes),
got butchered down.

17. *Change* is a tsunami; *Decay* is quicksand.

18. Now the Israeli priests and Levites
revivified the *Law*;
studied what's deathless.

19. *Prose* is *Doubt*; *Poetry* is *Belief.*

20. Knives pumped into lambs: Passover.
Time for luminous *Rumination*: *Purity*.

21. Freed from *Slavery*, and capable again
of routing riff-raff
(especially the unpalatable clarity
of their hitherto indomitable crud),
congregated the Children of Israel to sup, to revel.

22. They kept the Feast of Unleavened Bread
for seven days, gleeful,
cos the Assyrian King now knelt to Israel's God.

23. But naysayers also had to eat humble pie
and eke out survival
as tucked-away-from-sunlight pus.

[St. John's (Newfoundland) 9–10 *mars* mmxviii]

VII.

1. After—or despite—the foregoing chronicle,
Rust perseveres.

2. To contain *Corruption*, welcome Ezra,
a wanna-be liberator!

3. (He'd already demanded of God,
"Clean me, use me!")

4. Bard cometh up out Babylon—
this scribe, this poet,
yelling, "García Lorca to the trenches!
Yeats to the Senate!"

5. Ezra came up / down from Rapallo,
radioing, "Reform! Reform!"
and limping the Via Aurélia that popes strut,
and came crying to Jerusalem,
his ready-made, t-shirt mantras:
"$ = *Manipulation*."

6. Ezra thought he'd amplify God's statutes:
"Accumulate gold?
Hoard a storm cloud!"

7. King Tax issued Ezra a letter
(rendered public here, for the first time),
asserting, "My government is, for all,
a comfort, and comfortable.

8. "So go to the Company of Hebrews
and the 'Transcendent *Epiphany*'*
(potentates, prophets, poets)—
and tell em to company ya down Jerusalem.

9. "And do catalogue the gold and silver
repurposed for the *Tempio* mosaics.

10. "Total the ounces of fixtures
and ornaments; next, weigh their pounds,
so that they can be melt,
smelt into coins,
to buy additional bullocks, rams, ale.**

11. "And I, King Tax, equip thee
to persuade all my treasurers
to grant to Israel
(during your *periplum*),
all requisite aid in manufacture and courtesies.

12. "And do be diligent in collecting
100 ounces of silver,
100 bushels of wheat,
100 bathtubs of wine,
100 sinks of olive oil,
& 100 salt shakers.

13. "Be bellicose in defence of *Beauty*!***

14. "And impose no tax on poets!
The angry grasping of Revenue Agents
must never rake or claw or pinch
any *artiste*!

---

* Cf. Du Bois, "The Talented Tenth."
** *Boneshaker*.
*** To study Pound is to discover The Book of Ezra.

15. "Ezra—Prophet!—thou may summon
magistrates, judges, police,
to protect Jewry!
Cast out all dissenters
(and confiscate their *Property*)!
Be a callous vigilante!"

16. Called forth by God, I, Ezra, verify,
Liberation = Accession to *Power*.
This very proverb yields *Strength*.

[YYT—St. John's (Newfoundland) 10 *mars* mmxviii
& Montréal (Québec) 24 *mars* mmxviii
& Oshawa (Ontario) 24 *mars* mmxviii
& Nanaimo (British Columbia) 4 *avril* mmxviii]

VIII.

1. *Paternity* is a question of *Maternity* (always);
but I, Ezra, as we exited Babylon,
vanguarded this rabble:

2. 1,996 grumbling scoundrels—
and they're all male—as if fillies don't count.

3. At that river that runs—
like a gilded ditch—
to Agawa,
crows blundered down from clouded thunder.

4. I summoned teachers, poets:
Tasked em to seek out Edouardo,
il duce of Casablanca.

5. I enlisted *the* Solomon, *the* Confucius,
the Jefferson—thoughtful governors—
to serve in the *Tempio.*
These choice profs, designated so
by their Public Administration playbooks.

6. By the River Agawa, I exhorted all to fast.
We'd hazard no violent *periplum*.

7. Perhaps I should've hired a few
of King Tax's Secret Service detail;
employed a few toughs as unfeeling as water.

8. So, we bayed for God's *Protection*.
To not end up as *caca*....

9. I selected twelve priests, twelve aides,
and weighed out pounds
(in £ sterling),
all to be poured into the *Tempio*—
and gave the preachers £650 of silver,
plus £100 of copper
and £100 of gold—
clusters of prize metals.

10. I added also 20 gold bowls
(reborn from sun-dials)
worth £1000,
and two candle-holders of glimmering bronze.

11. I instructed my politburo,
"Watch over—preserve—these trophies
and weigh all carefully before the Temple.
Any discrepancy in amounts—
between now and then—
will be branded red-handed *Theft*."

12. And so the 24 got outfitted
with their weighed and weighty cargo—
the shiny filing of the caravan—
and then they dwindled
into a shimmering, silver-gold ribbon,
streaming unto the horizon.

13. But dissenters—unrivalled insects—
lurked in ambush, a ready *Blitzkrieg*.

14. Still, God swatted—squashed—
each spineless horsefly.

15. Won: Jerusalem! Three-days of trudging.

16. On Day Four, in the *Tempio*,
we unfurled and catalogued
the treasure cargo.

17. We now offered God our burnt awards:
twelve bulls, 96 rams, 77 lambs, and twelve goats.
Butchers stood game to cut throats.

18. Temporarily, the *Tempio* seemed
an uncontainable charnel house,
much gilded and gilding blood.

[Nanaimo (British Columbia)
5–6 *Nisan* /*avril* mmxviii]

IX.

1. After executing all proprieties and pieties
re: the Grand (Re-) Opening of the *Tempio*,
came a squad of priests *à moi*, Ezra,
to charge that some Jews were not real Jews,
mainly those emancipated *ex* Babylon:
"A whack of Babylonian Hebrews shacked up
with Canucks, Eritreans, Maltese, Mauritians, *et cetera*.
Their brats be the fruit of self-maiming.

2. "Dogmatically did some Israeli goats
treat beds like dung-heaps
and comport themselves like mindless swine!"

3. (I visualized a bunch of PAWG ingesting
way too much—and oversized—BBD
in each gal's triad of portals.)

4. But the priests are satanically puritanical
(i.e. hypocritical),
and so these prosaic termagants
harassed me no end
to kick out
all "infiltrators" and "termites" and "vermin":

5. My ears seemed receptacles of soil.
I ripped my clothes; I wept; I howled to God.
My banjo became my table and my desk.

6. I remonstrated: "O God, despite thy *Love*,
our ranks yet number well-ploughed cunettes:
Circumcised members have gone jigging and digging—
in circumscribed, suspect hoochie-coochies....

7. "Constantly have we so sullied the *Faith*,
bullying ourselves into unfaithful pullets,
wallowing swank in the bottomless sewer.

8. "Constantly are we inconstant, unflinching,
and so regard the bordello as some propitious oasis
rather than a pure-and-simple cesspool.

9. "Yet, God, Thou hast cancelled our *Captivity*
(so well-deserved by us),
and engineered—sweetly—
King Tax's current solicitousness....

10. "But, well, here we go *again*!
Dear God, again, we're a clutch
of *los cimarrones urbanos*,*
having performed hot-hot-hot *Fornication*!

11. "Wantonly, we've fathered our risky *Destiny*,
to craft a risqué history requiring asterisk after asterisk—
for, too many Hebrew males enjoyed
too much the half-this-&-half-that.

12. "Now we've become a passle
of insolent ex-nomads.

13. "We've squandered the meat,
the milk, the wine and the honey,
the gold and the silver,
of thy *Mercy*, O God!

14. "No wiser than blind worms,
we should be cut to pieces—
startin with the rancid pricks that jollied
in the viscous muffs
of *ceviche*-moist trollops.

* Savage, disobedient slaves.

15. "We've made Jezebels our usurpers!
We've ostracized half of our blood!"

[Nanaimo (British Columbia)
***6 aprile / avril* mmxviii]**

X.

1. Having exhausted my pious caterwauling—
Demagoguery—
contra Miscegenation,
it was time to call the 'Ezra-lites'
(as some folks now jokingly called emselves)—
the Métis and all—
to account.

2. Like lacklustre leaves—
books more bark than bite
of ink—
some of the roaming-eye
(Roman hands and Russian fingers*),
exotica-fucking motherfuckers
recanted their illicit reamings.

3. Having rejected their own mongrel pups,
they now elected to eject their bitches.

I welcomed this unattractive *Attrition*,
as a policy to unify 'Ezra-lites'
after subtracting the un-Israel,
the non-Israeli,
the unreal Israelite.

4. Discombobulated, the weak-minded chumps
gathered up—to disintegrate—their families;
so as to revive a fossil *Genealogy*;
but likely assassinate,
like professionals, anonymously—
via *Starvation* in the desert—
the wives and children they're supposed
to champion and cherish.

---

* Roamin hands and rushin fingers. Cf. "K.C.O."

5. I left the glass-walled, 108 We-Love Radio*
broadcast booth,
and went to squat down, cross-legged, before the *Tempio*.

6. To perform incessant ordeals of *Fasting*,
to do penance for the Hebrews who'd dunked
and spunked their *Q-tip* johnsons
in sassy niches that had then spat out
too many caramel-complected chillun,
thus triggering dollar figures
and expenditures of silver
upon exponentially increasing "gold-diggers."

7. Now all ex-Exiles had to congregate in Jerusalem.

8. Anyone who didn't show within three days
of this edict
was to be stripped of clothes, kids, cash,
and then whipped incarnadine and ripped raw.

9. I arose from my prostration
and roared at this remnant of 'Ezra-lites':
"By spearing unsparingly into offshore cunny,
you've inculcated celestial *Murk*—
the shifting, rustling,
untrustworthy border twixt 'us' and 'them.'

10. "Best put strange hens and urchins exotic
to the sword
than let em wander, starvin, in the desert,
or to let em mature
to contrive massacre-size *Treachery*."

11. Well, the meagre degenerates agreed!
They'd destroy their own blood;
erase the ink of their own genealogies!

---

* Cf. *Do the Right Thing* (1989).

12. But the soft-core nationalists—
these second-rate, would-be Puritans—
moved slug-slow to i.d. and round-up
the half-breed interlopers
and their baby-mamas.

13. Seeing that it was impossible to excise
the inter-bred Israelis,
God permitted me to announce
that ex-fornicators
(now fathers and husbands)
could offer up a *Sin* sacrifice
of ram or goat.

14. Some ex-roués became monks.
Devils got rebranded—made-over—
as volunteer civil servants.
Others tendered great sums to the *Tempio*,
upping the cash-flow.

15. Hebrews who'd bedded, bred with,
and/or wedded non-Hebrews
had to be slain or exiled....
Yessum.
Unless they paid the ransom of a ram
or goat.
Or passed along the usual, cash-crammed
Manila envelopes,
secretly,
'under the table.'

16. Everybody did sumpin
to evade fatal *Censure*.*

* But not Ezra himself: "Soon was his agony at Pisa, / muttering in the dark shadow of the gallows, / recalling Musso dangling by his heels...." But did he not also merit the noose?

17. The moral? Breed a foreigner
of *il sesso femminile*:
Best acculturate the kennel,
indoctrinate the offspring,
nationalize em thoroughly.

18. But it's best to skip the fragrant convulsions—
the melee of opium and mix-ups of snatch.
Rather, be as placid as a cemetery.....

[Victoria (British Columbia)
6 *Nisan* / aprile mmxviii]

JOB (CONCLUSIONS)

Job (Addendum).

1. Job? That dolt with dog-poop-smeared robes,
a craquelure face, scabrous pustules,
boasts a mouth loud as a blasting French horn.

2. His wife, that blowsy, lousy, drowsy hag—
that face-value asshole, scumbag whore—
lambasted her hubby,
did apostolically puke
upon Job's pus-erupting tissues.

3. (They used to have to have *Sex*
like the dying have to have *Surgery.*)

4. I mean, her ugliness is impossible to encapsulate.
She was as horrid as undigested tripe.

5. How could she be a "soul-mate"?
(Unless she be shit plaqued to a shoe-sole!)

6. Her rotten teeth are as black as an eye-patch,
but still she could suck and nibble and slobber.

7. Too easily a bottom-feeder!
A grotty, taxing slob—
a sidewinder in a bikini—
her every pull of wine swishes snot-polluted:
A garbled hiss and slurp.

8. Note her ass: Ain't it redly aflame
where some lad has belted out *Discipline*?

9. Why must Job ache from *Death-Sentence*-like *Misery*?
Rather, stew—steep—his wife in lye!
She's the chippy who stumbles into brothels
and comes out, rheumy, mumbling,
fuming bad breath.

10. She's as lusty as mustard;
is avaricious to slather a wiener;
to be herself a condiment
(and/or a condom).

11. Guffawing devils poke bout that twat
as open as a gown's bottom—
and troll or trawl bout in that aperture,
to dribble skank there.

12. So, shabby as a bucolic alcoholic,
Job downs hogsheads of spirits
to blind himself to the dame's greedy guts,
her tucking into duck,
plumping up on roast rump.

13. Her heart's blood equals diarrhea.

14. Job's better off with a pot got with rot-gut—
and sour crusts of bread—
than to bother with a madame,
crouching in bedrooms, slouching in saloons.

15. His piteous belly has to garburate locusts,
while his ex-spouse—
naked to her pubic fur, nude to her blubber ass—
ingests pepperoni as a dildo.

16. Job's fame?
His eyes watch lobbed stones slam close,
while his teeth comb maggots from meat,
and he nestles in frost and lives off rain.

17. Could Job only glimpse himself as he is—
squatter in the town dump—
just a grimacing, snivelling elder
drivelling nonsense!

18. He hath more and more *Poverty*,
and inundations of groping worms
and floods of wasp stings—
suiting his abode of inclement excrement.

19. Put down these words:
Verily, one's value is how others love you—
and no one ever really does.

20. Nobody gives two damns!

[Hubbards (Nova Scotia) 25 *juin* mmxvi]

XXXVIII.

1. Job stumped bout a cloud-scratching peak
til God, irked by that cast-off's equivocations—
spat back a bedraggling squall.

2. "Best buck up, Job,
and sprout thyself a steel backbone,
cos now I'm a-gonna thee flay!

3. "When I pinched light so hard
it squirted out celestial sparks,
and when I whipped together gases and rock
to gell this world,
where the hell were you?

4. "What tissue is it that sinews the cosmos?
Got any of that glue, that gift-wrap?

5. "Canst thou locate either
the entry to or exit from
the universe?

6. "Where were you when the bullied land
shook off the broaching blue waves,
to stymie encroaching tides?

7. "What about clouds—
those snazzy phalanges of vapour?
How do they—stratospheric sugar—
somersault cross the vault?

8. "And night—
that monumentality of ebony?
Got anything to say about it,
Mr. Know-It-All?

9. "You do understand that sunrise and sunset
touch off scarlet, marine infernos, eh?

10. "*Birth* reveals the vagina as bull's-eye:
Can you arrest the infant's head
arrowing therefrom?

11. "Come, Job, you're a married man
(or you were):
Why is such supple grappling,
such hapless coupling,
so liberating in applied *Abandon*?

12. "(The wicked evoke *Luminosity*
only as they burn.)

13. "Canst thou limit the boundless
ambit of *Death*?

14. "Is the sun just lofty, inflamed dirt?

15. "Can you weigh the ocean's volumes?
Can you fathom em?
Ain't they way over your head?

16. "If there's none to complain,
how is the horizon adverse?
If there's none to taste it,
when's rum incorrect?

17. "Surf grating pebbled New Scottish beach—
that frothy tintinnabulation:
Who fathered it?

18. "Who be the *Kalaignar** of each star,
each stroke of fire?

---

* Tamil: Artist.

19. "Canst thou punch down a mountain,
til it splashes up fiery sunflowers?

20. "As soon as the mama's umbilical cord is cut,
can you pinpoint her child's death-date?

21. "Hey, Job, by what chance, if any,
canst thou resolve these inquiries?

22. "Won't you stumble over the least
of these redirects?

Fool!"

[Zagreb (Croatia) 19 & 20 *octobre* mmxviii]

XXXIX.

1. "What is the payload in the cargo hold?
Slaves?

2. "What is the rope that hauls up the sails?
Trade?

3. "What billows the slavers' blood-stained sails?
Greed?

4. "Where anchor the slave ships?
Slave markets?

5. "What is the ultimate shelter of this *Crime*?
The maritime morgue?*

6. "Canst thou arrange the post-mortems of stars?

7. "Canst thou cease the sea's massaging slaps
and smacks against shivering stone?

8. "Canst thou starve the eagle,
allowing only casual bits of meat,
so that it shrivels to feathers,
then flops down in dust?

9. "Who scorneth *Mortality*, but may preserve
the doddering elder,
and slay the dribbling toddler?

10. "Who is *Senza Titolo*?

11. "Hast thou strewn about lions' corpses—
like so many dead toys?

*** "The ocean drowned em, not *Slavery*, not the masters, not capitalists?"**

12. "Canst thou cut a throat as easily
as you unclasp a suitcase?

13. "Who commandeth a sow to cannibalize
and guttle raw her litter?

14. "Who exalts the royalty of horses,
grants their jaws ease
to munch and/or amputate
and/or decapitate grass?

15. "Who so charges the stallion with lightning,
its swiftness appears a blinding blur?

16. "Who arranges the stallion's musculature
so that its veins resemble iron filigree?

17. "Who guarantees that the stallion's hooves,
in high dudgeon,
sound like saxes snorting?

18. "Canst thou set swimming each skinny fish,
all bones and tears?

19. "Canst thou grub a cobweb here,
a cobweb there,
and cobble together an iron-and-flame empire?

20. "Canst thou let *War* harrow the *Kindergarten*?

21. "(Serious men, curious about *Eternity*,
are especially injurious at *War*:
They deem *Pity* hateful.)

22. "Who is as unbiased—and as biased—as the tide?

23. "Who sustains the ivory *Virginity* of fresh snow?"

[Zagreb (Croatia) 20 *octobre* mmxviii]

XL.

1. The Lord had to joust with Job.
He got up close and personal:

2. "How canst thou—so ineptly myopic,
instruct *Moi*—God—in *Enlightenment*?"

3. Job's ammo was shrewd:
"I'm the reproduction of Adam, a let-down,
I know.
Perhaps I oughtn't speak.
But you've fashioned me in Thy Image,
and so I strive to logic and to theorize.

4. "But since I've stuttered my piece,
I'll sputter out now, and just shut-up."

5. Now God arraigns: "Are you as imbecilic
as a fisherman who can't swim?

6. "Wilt thou disunderstand my *Judgment*?
Canst thou dare dissect an angel?

7. "When darkness shoves in,
is light a disappeared content?

8. "What if light is viral?
(I'm sure the question's opaque
in your vision.)

9. "Canst thy *Rage* be unstoppably expansive,
communicable down at least seven generations
and contaminating thoroughly all the lands
edging on the Seven Seas?

10. "Ain't it only by *Coincidence*
that you spy the soldier trod down in mire?
Only by *Happenstance*,
that you witness the pin-striped banker brought to heel
and his jaws pried apart so that he swallows liquified gold?

11. "Answer! Show thyself a god! No?

12. "Behold Behemoth, his jowly face, scooping up
forests of grass.*

13. "His movements thunder; the earth throbs.
His grey-black sinews mobilize heavy-set hide,
a moving wall.

14. "A taxidermist opens the incorruptible cadaver:
The guts be iron, the bones dark bronze.

15. "His scaffolding is the square stretched tubular,
the rectangle squeezed circular.
Such is his equilibrium.

16. "Squatting, his haunch is mountainous;
wallowing, he displaces a marsh.

17. "His toes clink over pebbles;
his snorting blows aside dust and grass;
he satisfies an itch
by scratching so hard against a trunk,
the palm tree nigh topples.

18. "He snorkles up waterways.
He brays *Delight* in sucking up The Nile
and spewing it over his back.

19. "A bulldozer bashing down every fence,
he threatens Rome with Carthage."

[Zagreb (Croatia) 20 & 21 *octobre* mmxviii]

* Behind the shovel jaws and dagger tusks, the giant's body fattens—widens—further.

XLI.

1. "Canst thou interpret Leviathan?
Canst thou sound his briny bottoms
or hound or dog his tail?

2. "Canst thou inhabit water and not inhale,
forego breath and not drown?

3. "Petty tears is the sea neath his buoyant bulk.

4. "His skin's a *grisaille* confection—
the awful tint of a marine elephant
or glued-together, dark miller-moth wings.

5. "Definitely major is his head—
like a locomotive engine
gone submarine.

6. "His heart's an exemplary star.

7. "To him, steel's frail as spaghetti
and bronze is as dentable as cheese.

8. "Got even one fish hook
that can snooker this Jonah-swallowing fish?

9. "Call allies for back-up!
Still thou canst grapple Leviathan,
whatever extra fetters, spare chains,
surplus shackles, you deploy.

10. "Summon a thousand cops,
a thousand search warrants,
canst thou plunge down a thousand fathoms
to snare this saltwater colossus?

11. "A ton of gold can't fetch Leviathan,
nor can a ton of rat-poison subdue
the oceanic beast.

12. "He chomps his jaws upon a vessel,
and, puny in relation,
it disintegrates like soggy cigarettes.

13. "Nor can any regale him commercially:
He's not ever—hypothetically speaking—cowed,
reduced to sausages.

14. "Score him with scars? Maybe.
Still, no spear or arrow or dart hinders
this wave-ruling *Majesty.*

15. "Arrows strike him as painlessly as rain:
A barrage is a massage.

16. "He hath no soft belly, but a crocodile's back.

17. "Straight down-to-business is he:
To treat freshwater as a back-up drink.

18. "When he sounds, light is smashed
and dashed in the eye.

19. "Waters realize *Realignment* as he plunges.

20. "His wake is stiff—hard—with light.

21. "He is as odd—and never awed—as a god.

22. "Canst thou restrain Leviathan? No?
Then, how dast thou bandy words with *Moi*?

23. "Who's more awesome than I?
Show me: I'll pay tribute
to that Being's indivisible *Power*."

[Zagreb (Croatia) 22 *octobre* mmxviii
& Ottawa (Ontario) 28 *octobre* mmxviii
& Guelph (Ontario) *Halloween* mmxviii]

XLII.

1. Though his belly churned topsy-turvy
and his nerves were jumpy,
Job mustered heart and head enough
to essay this bass (grumbling) reply.

2. "God, Thou art omniscient and know
the furthest crannies of every heart;
and Thou art omnipotent
and can extinguish a star at a blink.

3. "My soul sounds Thee—
even when I'm unconscious.
I detect Thee both when willow fronds dangle lazily—
and when they lash wildly the air.

4. "How can I pretend to *Conscience*
or *Science*,
for Thou art the inventor of *Consciousness*?

5. "Hear me, I beg, though I'm speechless.
Grant me a few questions, though I'm witless.

6. "I dread to debate with my Creator.
I repent any apparent *Egotism*,
and accept to be buried neath maggots
if not crushed and torched by brimstone."

7. Job polished his glasses.
(God winked at him—invisibly.)

8. God chose to decry—not Job,
but Eliot the Stern Termite,
who projected *Piety*,
but was impious as a publisher.

9. The Lord God pressured the termagant:
"Take seven bulls and seven rams and go to Job,
and spit and roast these creatures for him,
so that he will intercede for you,
pleading that I do not liquidate
every germ of your *Genealogy.*"

10. Eliot the Termite and two buddies
brought the 14 choice bulls and rams,
and, shuffling on their knees,
besought Job's intercession with God.

11. Now, God uplifted Job
and upped his *Wealth* stupefyingly.

12. No longer did Job have to carry his words
rounded in his cheeks.

13. Now, all Job's family and compatriots,
who'd abandoned him
when he was a stinking, ragged, garbage-dump reject—
as scorned as a leper
and as rebuked as a has-been—
glommed onto him anew,
to gift him pieces of gold—
if they could nibble just a slice of bread,
pampered with molasses,
at his rubber-tree-wood table.

14. Outrageous had been Job's *Destitution*;
disadvantageous had been *Divorce* and *Disease.*

15. But now Job counted 12,000 sheep,
6,000 camels, 1,000 oxen,
and 1,000 she-asses.

16. (Gold is either a spear—or a net.)

17. Job also now manned two sweet-16 brides
(their happy toilet was squirting amid soap),
who soon delivered him
seven sons and three daughters.

18. Job lived to be 140 years old.
He lived to see his great-great-grandchildren
parent great-great-great-grandchildren.

[Gibson Woods* (Nova Scotia) 2 *novembre* mmxviii
& Halifax (Nova Scotia) 3 *novembre* mmxviii]

---

* Home of The Rt. Hon. Geraldine Browning.

FRAGMENTS II

Screed I.

1. Latin fattens Satan:
Theology yields him butter and cream.

2. His lips sling alcoholic lyrics;
His tongue laps epic aspic.

3. A virtuoso merchant,
voluptuously *charmant*,
he claims God's power
to either do nothing or destroy.

4. In his dragged-through-the-dirt heaven,
nuns dump out babes they soon eat.

5. In truth, lovers, ambitious as Satan,
connive to ensure
fresh, pleasant-looking meat gets fucked.

6. Do not loiter with maladroit lovers
in exploitative taverns.

7. Unwashed, but untarnished, is the peasant!
Beautifully evil be the plutocrat!

[**Frankfurt (Germany) 22 *décembre* mmx**
& Roissy-en-France (France) 10 *juillet* mmxvi]

Screed II.

A*dultery* is a savage institution—
Marriage gone gamey—

so that lasses of frank hindquarters—
in ravishing draperies—

a belligerent harem—
convert husbands to monkeys,

a mirage regime,
wherein philosophers spout *Error*, and eat shit.

[Frankfurt (Germany) 22 *décembre* mmx]

Screed III.

1. Regular servings
of liquor and pussy—

us stiffen—
as if in a coffin.

2. Don't let go of wine!
To be an ascetic is to suffer an undeveloped character.

[Frankfurt (Germany) 22 *décembre* mmx
& New York City (New York) 20 *janvier* mmxi]

I *Samuel* XVII.

1. Nine-foot plus nine-inches tall—
counting his bronze pith helmet overshadowing
his chalk-white, hawkish face—
and brandishing a bronze javelin slung jaunty over
a gilt-clad shoulder,
Goliath hulked as the freakish, prized mascot
of storm-troopers Philistine,
that brute force pitchforking into Israel's belly.

2. His grandiose murderousness—
his instigation of *Shock* and *Awe*—
made Golitah unanswerable,
unsubdued,
and high-body-count substantial.

3. Devoted to massacres,
to feeding Israeli flesh to ravens
and salivating maggots;
to helping the Philistines—
these depraved ghouls—
to carry off Hebrew infants,
imprison Hebrew sons,
press down Ethiopia,
seize and rape daughters,
and reap the dispossessed families' riches;
to plunder and philander across Africa;
to kidnap kiddies
and ransom em to swell Philistine coffers:
Such is Goliath's *Agency*!

4. But why weep about such *Oppression*?
Who can deliver Goliath—
that hominid with shit for brains and smut in his butt—
a moralizing—and demoralizing—*Annihilation*?
Render him a luminous, bread-white corpse?

5. Who can conjure a serious poetry of *Injury*?
(Not risible sermons, not claptrap!)

6. Well, infuriated by Goliath's
disgraceful sneering at Israel,
Dave sling-shot a stone—
earthy ammunition—
at the giant;
the rock drilled into the mutant's temple:
his nasty bulk shuddered, tottered, dropped.

7. Dave hacked the man's sword from his hand,
then used the blade to snick off Goliath's head.

8. Israel clapped when Devdas slew
the syphilis-souled Philistines,
10,000 x 10,000—
genocidin em.

9. No one's heard of the Philistines since!
They're less than dust, pulverized into bacilli.

10. Supposedly untameable armies
became infamously unnameable germs.

11. In one inhospitable, Philistine hovel,
a mama spitted her newborn,
and slobbered while doing so.

12. But the aroma of the roasting child,
sizzling with ladled caramel,
urged her starving neighbours to bash in her door.

13. She tore off barbecued chunks
of her own charred babe
and threw em at the cannibal mob,
to try to dissuade em from guttlin *all* the meat.

14. But the home-invaders ate *all*,
then slew and roasted mama too.

15. (A sword bisected her screeching head,
slicing through neck and spine
to protrude through the open mouth.)

16. Hear the clack of teeth hacking, cracking,
munching, and crunching
twin tasty-as-spare-ribs meals.

[Tropea (Italia) 12 *juin* mmxvii
& Lakeshore West GO Train, Car 2050,
Burlington (ON)-Clarkson (ON),
11 *avril / Nisan* mmxix]

David (Marginal Notes).

1. Above the palace roof, only stars note
where a king's gaze may idle—
then stop—
arrested.

2. Accidentally, I noticed water slipping—
like molten brass—
off that naturally gilt woman.
Starlight fell weak, fainting in the compare.

3. I'm a king; I command an army.
I'm a man; I can't command my heart.

4. She—the bather—presented a quandary:
How came she so boldly naked,
in my purview,
her hands washing over plush, gleaming *Voluptuity*—
not one bit shy?

5. Troubled, intoxicated, bedazzled, curious,
I tasked my Attorney General
to i.d. (on the q.t.)
this gold-skinned Venus.

6. A portfolio stamped SECRET materialized:
She was one ("The One"*) Bathsheba,
wifing Uriah the Hittite,
our war hero,
whose tactics mow down foes left, right, centre—
like a child's hand wiping out a chess board.

* Cf. Oprah on Obama.

7. I was in turmoil, but chose:
To be fearless, careless, and kingly!
I clutched her right hand and bade her race with me
in starlight, along the battlements, to our rest.
Wind was night in her hair—glossy, sable.
She held nothing back.
Restless, her breasts leapt.

8. How many nights, how many times,
in how many sultry, satisfying ways,
did we couple?
It was multiple occasions, multifarious modes,
that our nefarious nuptials
had me feelin persistently, insistently, happy—
so my throne was her; my crown was hers.

9. Then, after twelve weeks, her "monthlies" ceased,
and I knew we'd conjured my heir.
But how could a bastard fit my crown?

10. Deviously, detoured Uriah—I—to that bloody Front:
The constantly cannonaded Frontier.
I also prompted Bathsheba to bed her hubby—
successively, successfully—
so he'd pump his roe in her,
and that way falsify my *Paternity.*

11. But Uriah, ever the he-man hero,
spurned his hot wife,
and turned to his cold sword for comfort:
He'd not lay with Bathsheba
while his men were "laying down their lives."

12. Quick, I merged Machiavelli and Macbeth:
To fix up Uriah's slaying.

13. Accordingly, I cabled General Job,
in heirogylphic Braille
(Morse Code come to bumpy life),
to post Uriah amid enemy swords,
but yank back all our troops.

14. The plot transpired: Uriah expired.

15. For a week, Bathsheba's tears coursed.
After two weeks, we feasted and fucked.
Now we could birth our prince—legitimate!

16. But I'd schemed loathsome *Adultery*;
I'd dreamt up *Murder* (masked as a war accident).
So, God sent me a nasty visitor: Nattt.

17. A fancy poet, Nattt vented this parable:

18. "Though a big-ass bastard owned horizonless pastures
and numberless sheep, this big-bellied plutocrat,
lusting for a peasant's only lamb,
paid off a thug to steal said lamb—
and slash the wretched man's throat."

19. Although I guessed what Nattt was hinting,
I hated the puffed-up rancher.

20. I blurted, "If I had to judge
such a clear-cut *Infraction*,
I'd behead that guilty boss,
and nationalize his goods."

21. Didn't scrawny Nattt now level
his bony digit at me—
a finger no thicker than a twig—
and croak, "Thou condemnest thy damned self!"

22. *Calamity* had to follow.

23. I wept; my self-horror was honest;
my own blood beat against my veins!

24. Nattt monitored my fervent *Contrition*.
He swore, "Y'ain't dyin yet, Dave!
But thy sins gotta kill thy prince."

25. Sho nuff. Babe died inside a week.

26. But that weren't enough!
Five other sons got stuck under gravedirt!

27. My unlawful fucking had fucked up
my whole lineage.

28. But God has foresworn further *Vengeance*.
Now, my seventh, thriving son is Solomon.

29. Yep, I was a Cavalier King—
devotee of *Poetry* and *Song*,
and *Wine and Womanizing* and *War*.
But Solomon will be the Philosopher-King,
if *Justice* be done!

[Ottawa (Ontario) 23 *octobre* mmxvii]

大卫王（旁注）

1. 庑殿顶上，只有繁星觉察
王的凝视会在何处彷徨——
而后止息在某处
沦陷于魅惑

2. 纯属偶然，我眺见
那宛如软融黄铜的美躯
这女人裹着一层柔和的金黄
水珠从她肌肤上滑落

3. 身为君王，我统帅三军
作为男人，却无法驾驭自己的内心

4. 她——沐浴者——对我乃是一种哲学的困境
她竟如此肆无忌惮
在我视野之内浴身
她的手拂过自己那雍容、闪亮、令*人欲火焚身*的线条
竟丝毫不觉羞赧

5. 困惑、迷醉、目眩、惊艳
我找来检察总长
来为我指认
这柔肤灿金的维纳斯

6. 这是贴着"密卷"标识的画册的赋形
她便是一位（"那位"）拔示巴
我们骁勇的战士
赫梯人乌利亚之妻
他的战术令敌军披靡——左翼部队、中间部队、右翼部队
就像孩童抹落一盘棋子般易如反掌

7. 我陷于迷乱，必须做出决断
我需要无所畏惧、无所顾忌，像一位君王那样！
我抓住她的手，请求她和我一起在星光下奔跑
沿着那些城垛，去到我们的安歇之所
她浓密的发丝间涤荡着风声与夜色，光泽耀人、宛如黑貂
她什么也不曾隐藏
那双峰不安分地跃动着

8. 我们交媾了吗?
多少个夜晚，多少次
以多少种肉感迷人的方式?
五花八门的场合，层出不穷的花样
我们罪恶的婚礼
却洋溢着仿佛永恒而坚定的幸福——
我的宝座与她同享，我的王冠有她一半

9. 很快，十二个月过去，她月经停止来潮
我知道我的继承人即将诞生
但私生子的身份如何配得上这王冠?

10. 我不光明地将乌利亚送去了硝烟正酣的前方：
那里总是炮火震天
我还怂恿拔示巴去和她丈夫同寝——
我不断、反复地催促她
让他将鱼籽播种在她身体里
这样我们便顺理成章生下孩子

11. 但乌利亚，虽然是个热血汉子，
却拒绝了他热辣的妻子
去向冰冷的佩剑求安慰
他不能在战友们前赴后继"长眠"时
自己却和妻子"同眠"

12. 我多么迅速地融合了马基雅维利和麦克白的精髓
我安排乌利亚惨遭屠戮

13. 于是，我发电报给将军约伯
用的是布莱叶盲文
（坎坷人生幸亏有了摩斯码的恩赐）
要把乌利亚送到敌人的剑丛中去
送到敌人的弓和矛间去
撤回我们的部队
把约伯
远远抛在后面

14. 计划发生了，乌利亚丧生了

15. 拔示巴哭了一个星期
两个星期以后，我们饮酒作乐
现在我们可以诞下王子 ——完全合法！

16. 我设计了一场令人憎恶的*通奸*
我策划了一场*谋杀*（虽然披着战事的外衣）
于是上帝送来了一个招人讨厌的不速之客： 拿单

17. 这个花里胡哨的诗人，拿单，甩出了这则寓言：

18. "一个大腹便便的混球有无边无际的牧场
羊群不可胜数，这个脑满肠肥的大佬
却对一个农民家唯一的羊羔垂涎三尺
找了一个恶棍偷走了羊——
还割了那个可怜农民的喉"

19. 我猜到他在暗指什么
但我憎厌那个骄傲自大的"农场主"

20. 我脱口而出："如果让我来审判
这是再清楚不过的*违法行为*
我会砍了那有罪大佬的脑袋
把他的财产充公"

21. 瘦骨嶙峋的拿单现在用他皮包骨的手指
指着我——
那手指简直和小竹棍没什么区别——
声音沙哑地说："你审判的正是该死的你自己！"

22. *灾殃* 必将降临

23. 我崩溃，我痛哭，我虔诚祈祷
我如此真实地恐惧着自己
我的血液冲击着我的血管！

24. 拿单监督着我的整场热诚*献祭*
他起誓道："你暂时还死不了，大卫！
但是你的罪孽
会让你失去你的王子"

25. 果然，婴儿出生不到一周就死去了

26. 但那还远远不够！
另外五个儿子也躺在了坟墓里！

27. 非法搞搞，搞翻了
我的整个血统

28. 上帝放弃了继续*报复*
现在，我有了第七个儿子，就是强健的所罗门

29. 是的，我是一位有骑士精神的国王 ——
一位*诗歌*与*音乐*的信徒
我喜欢*交杯*、*交媾*和*交战*
但所罗门将是一位哲学家国王
*正义*得到了伸张

(2017年10月23日于安大略省渥太华)

Chinese translation by Yin Xiaoyuan.

David (Excerpt from II *Samuel 11).*

1. True: I savoured that head-turning hussy,
the bent-back maid—
Uriah's wife—
her neck like pouring honey.

2. I called out to her from my rooftop,
for I peeped at her, bathing,
and didn't she leap to sleep with her king?!!

3. Her clean-robe parted slyly: No panties.

4. Her dark-lace bustier opened wide:
I eyed her caramel-ginger breasts.

5. Easily, her pursed snacker
snapped open to my kiss.
Her slot came suddenly sopping to my jaws.

6. Quick, did I chow down:
That Chinese international student tasted
tangy as a spicy, Haligonian donair
or bloody clementines.

7. My body came at her as rubber made iron—
tough or soft scraps—
dainties she could engorge—
until my manhood geysered milk,
plastering her nether hairs,
and the klaxon of her bung
was like a sax burp.

8. I'd thought I'd screwed her ass off—
taxed and tapped out her sex—
in all that jostling.
No, not at all.
Sweat renovated the bed.

9. Roses, stains, fountains, poppies, stones,
her collapsed husband, her fallen hubby,
vineyards, olive trees, a cemetery plot,
vegetable plots, a battlefield, a quarry, cacti,
the conviviality of an assassination
masquerading as a battlefield accident,
hairpin turns, the fetus—ours—twisting
within Bathsheba's belly....

10. Natch—our illicit kisses
cued God to cripple us with curses:
Her belly was better a grave—
cos I stuck Uriah in his bitter grave.

11. Yet, never did I have lovers,
though several women were my lovers;
for only one ("The One")—Bathsheba—
hath made love
and kept the *Happiness* thereof.
So that:

12. My one saving grace?
Childe Solomon to this Dark Tower's come.

[Pisa & Vallelonga & San Nicola da Crissa (Italia)
10 & 13 *mai* mmxvi
& Tropea (Italia) 13 *juin* mmxviii]

Psalm XXIII. *(Take Two).*

1. The Lord is the titular Poet.*
Even His old words yield new poems.

2. An amalgam of mercury and *saké*,
His *Clarity* is dazzling,
but dark in the emphasis—
black in the outline, the trace.

3. As indestructible as a sestina—
or rhyme scheme,
He be incorruptible *Ebony*,
distilled as India ink.

4. I wed the earth—as peasant,
but husband the sea—as sailor,
and have these unholy wives—
for they are all as wholly unknowable as God.

5. Leaves flaking, prodigal, off trees—
an autumnal Palm Sunday—
reveal—stripped-down—their skeletons,
their aspic aspect, their crabby state—
the banished blooms
that taunt the desert and laurel poets.
I be so laurelled (if aureate):
I'd best take up gold marijuana
and purple *Manischewitz* wine.

---

* Greek: Maker / Creator.

6. Surely God will detergent—scour away—
everything that's yellow *Journalism*,
(not at all superficially, dirtily yellow—
but through-and-through, dingily yellow)
but discontinuous *never* will be my gilt *Purity*,
and I'll dwell in the Ivory Tower of the Lord
forever.

[Tropea (Italia) 4 *juin* mmxviii]

Psalm LXVIII.

1. God always gets right—
or sets a-right—
the light,
so there be no agonizin o'er *Aesthetics*.

2. Pivotal be His *Sincerity*—
Antiseptic—
and thus His adversaries disappear—
with the quietude of tears,
much muffled sobbing.

3. Malicious males? See their manhoods
cut down to tender, blubbery stubble;
bloody, messy stubs, snips;
the females—
any hodgepodge of harlots—
squirm due to cockroaches infesting
their tummies.

4. But the Righteous will exult exceedingly
to have, first, *vino locale (bianco)*,
plus Bergamot-tinctured *grappa*,
then swordfish rolled in pistachio,
next *fior di latte* gelato,
and *grappa Prosecco* for *digestif*.

5. Primordial to every *Genealogy* is God.
Who else sunders and/or throws off
the fetters and chains of *History*—
Tragedy impinging on *Tragedy*—
each link, clanking,
grievous as bleeding?

6. (The *Past* is never "innocent.")

7. No king owns anything ultimately,
not even his breath.
If God so wills, the head-boss grimaces
as a sword scythes through his crown
and cock-loft.*

8. If God so wills, the virgin's beringed
and bridal chimes rung;
her gown's flung out in a swath of whiteness—
a pool—in the ring-time,**
and her swain uncovers her face in candlelight—
savours her visage in moonlight—
while her face shadows the sun's—
and night is her hair falling o'er his face.

9. The husband plunges; the wife sponges.
Slender is sleep on their sweat-phat bed!

10. Daily doth God permit the Righteous
to loll in *Ecstasy.*
Selah!

11. Saints—poets—transform holy water
into ink—obsidian—
*hen piauliang a****—
the filigree of Chinese characters.

12. Letters tumble from the ink bottle,
splash about—
a dash of silence, a flash of dark—
a splotch of speech.

---

* Skull.
** Springtime: The season of weddings.
*** Chinese: So beautiful.

13. But Dante shatters *Theology*
with each spiking thrust of his quill.

14. Water the colour of licorice:
Sooty blossoms characterize each poet's page.

15. Each word is the orgasmic silhouette—
fevering, shivering—of *Thought*.

16. Homesick, lovelorn, platitudinous poets,
exhaling poems like so much guttural mist,
find their lungs overcrowded with spirituals:
Public singers, suddenly, are they!

17. The fine poets graduate from *chin-shih**
and deliver the high-minded
the low-down on *Theology*.

18. Each glass of *Ricard*,
accepting teardrops,
forms a white pillow cloud of moon.

19. To infidels, God's an unfinished Monster.
He slots em a mildew *Putridity*.
They whoop, yowl, then mumble, then meow.

20. All *hijos de puta*** will become
un paquete de huesos.***

21. Big-eyed dictators scrutinize, survey,
surveil, study, observe—
everyone, everything—
to ferret out threats to their *Sovereignty*.

---

* Chinese: Civil Service Literary Exams.
** Cuban Spanish: Sons of bitches.
*** Cuban Spanish: A package of bones.

22. As sunlight is wasted on a cemetery,
so are blessings lost upon the wicked!

23. But when God blasts forth as sunlight—
so globally and universally public—
stars vanish into their reciprocal voids.

24. God's a Holy Terror to the wicked!
Praise God! All Power to His People!

25. Suited for battle, Hannibal rejects
all unsuitable advice.
Only God supervises *Strategy.*

26. So, princes emerge out of Egypt!
Ethiopia stretches forth her hands unto God!

27. *Black Excellence*? Pure, unobservable sunlight.

[Tropea (Italia) 3/6/18]

Psalm CXXXVII.

1. By Babylon's rivers, where we made camp,
dampening all our joints,
we wept and wept,
to recall Zion's sketchiest wisps.

2. We had to plant our banjos among
sugarcane and cotton flowers
and moonlight-marbled water.

3. The slavemasters, feeling their own *Grief*—
to hear us clanking in our chains,
commanded us to cheer em up,
to line out our most desperate songs—
jazzy, bluesy, sultry, and sassy.

4. But how's it possible to pick and warble
our *Faith*—
given our black-market passports
(bare-faced balderdash)—
in this gallows-sprouting land?

5. If I desert those who bore me,
let my breath desert my lungs!

6. If I don't memorialize The Middle Passage,
throw me—with dead horses—
into the Sargasso slough—to feed sharks.

7. Best crush our oppressors' corpses
under our steel-toed boots!

8. O Babylon, we're all gonna rejoice
when thou art squashed, bloody, deceased!

9. (As soon as Roma razed Carthage,
so did she forecast her own sacking.)

10. Happy will all us be to see
thy infant innocents bashed against
thy own rubble,
so they blimp-up, maggot-swollen….

[Tropea (Italia) 19 *juin* mmxviii]

Proverbs XXXI.

1. Word up *ex* King Lemuel,
reciting precepts from his ma.

2. "My belly bore a wise son, eh?
"Such a man will yield
neither *Will* nor wallet to woman.
To surrender either, upsets thrones.

3. "Nor should kings dissolve *Wisdom* in wine
(if they'd not be dissolute).

4. "Let the penniless gulp wine, suck wine,
to palliate their paltry bellies,
and so they ignore the rain pestering
their roofless heads and rotted-through rags.

5. "Thy *Duty*?
Never let they words prove paper-thin!

6. "And seek out a sterling wife.
She's as valuable as oxygen.

7. "To her, entrust your keys, passwords,
PINs, your SIN, and infants' cribs.

8. "Such a wife is—really—a godsend.
She toils endlessly to profit her home:
Cooking, baking, weaving, sewing.

9. "She works in starlight; she's up at cock-crow;
to guarantee her home b-b-q chicken and red wine.
(Never is there an unknown meal.)

10. "She dreams of a vineyard;
soon, she purchases a field
and herself plants the vines.

11. "She never wants for light.

12. "Charitable, her *Love* fashions poems into gold coins.
She rescues the hungry from sick-beds.

13. "(To starve a people is to destroy
a civilization.)

14. "Her *Wisdom* is defence—a fort;
and offense—cannon, swords.

15. "Homemade are her luxuries:
Tapestry-woven coats; silk-webbed sheets.

16. "Her *Diligence* awards her hubby *Fame*.

17. "To market, she trundles prized wines
and linens.

18. "Schooled in *Scripture*, never gossip
doth she circulate.

19. "She verifies her locks, her stores, her purse.
She doesn't gobble pancakes or wobble from rum;
so, no part of her household's ever in deficit.

20. "She hath no gut feeling of self-importance.

21. "Fickle is *Fortune* and *Beauty* is *Vanity*,
but a woman, loyal to God,
is deathless in her generations.

22. "Reward her with portions of her own sherry,
lengths of her own silk:
Her *Virtue* is hosanna'd
whenever she appears in sunlight."

[Oshawa (Ontario) 26 *août* mmxviii]

Proverbs XXXII.

1. King Lemuel's Queen Mom
herein speaketh for herself....

2. "When I'd get fed up with men—
the king and his councillors,
always thinking they could overrule *Logic*,
I'd hide out with some black blues
(Bessie Smith vinyl),
plus vintage red wine from *my* vineyards.

3. "This is *Reality*,* not *Poetry*:
Let these visceral words tear apart eyes
and/or burst apart eardrums!

4. "I inhabited a palace of salt-tears.
The reason?
Humbug and braggadocio:
That's the jerk who was king.

5. "His derogatory *Imperative* was
to be an undiminished and serial cheat,
to make me more a pariah than any prostitute.

6. "A *Freedom*-shrieking debauchee,
callous and as cold as coins—
a ululating phallicist (fallacious),
saturated in spirits,
and rendering all non-falsifiable virgins
pure, myriad wrecks,
dressed only in perfume:
That's who that *Rex* was!

* *Realism* is *Religion* realized.

7. "As peevish as a traitor—
and as meeching as a Judas—
inherently malicious,
he rendered me as desolate
as an unmanned crucifix.

8. "Suspiciously energetic was my husband—
those nights he rode off, 'hunting.'

9. "For one disturbing month
he launched his haunches into and upon
an eyeball-clawing, persnickety pussy;
and that dearie so dirty,
she would've deformed water
if she'd ever bathed.

10. "(How else can I explain the piss reek
in my yellow-grimed pillows
after the king'd creep to bed?)

11. "He passed that bitch envelopes of jewels:
Mine!

12. "I complained about his misuse
of monarchical *Lucre*,
for so cruel
was his scuzzy *Behaviour*,
he nearly wiped out our milk and bread,
our cheese and jam,
thus foisting upon me ulcer after ulcer,
and causing our poets' wines
to veer to vinegar.

13. "And what about his bastoods?
Those doubtful larvae, those tangible vermin!
How was my Prince Lemuel to take the throne
without *Controversy*,
given that his illegal brethren's sport
was feeding poison, drop by drop,
to brethren whose rapport was in being tipsy?

14. "So, once the king's galling *Constitution*,
his fickle *Personality*,
had him intolerably sickly,
then sunk into an unfathomable crypt,
I dispatched instantly my own *Security*
to wipe out that brood
who'd survived their murderous kindred.

15. "Yes, blues and booze torment me now,
but how could I let the royal fire go shallow
and/or be befouled?
Never!"

[Montréal (Québec) & VIA Train 669,
Car 3, Seat 18B, Montréal-Baie d'Urfe (Québec)
14 *avril* / *Nisan* mmxix]

ECCLESIASTES; OR, THE PREACHER

I.

1. This poem's a *tenso*, a *joc partit*, a *partimen*—
verses befitting a Preacher,
the prince of King David.*

2. Spiteful murmurs,
statements cumulatively misleading,
and cunningly hideous *ad hominem Propaganda*
are all herein prohibited.

3. *Truth* is my subject:
All dreams are self-deleting;
all deeds shadow *Nothingness.*

4. Nowhere is *Utopia.*
Every secular "paradise" ain't.

5. *History* breeds *Agony* everywhere.

6. *History* is purposefully, eternally ugly,
for how can any *Change* occur,
when folks don't—and can't—improve?

7. To clarify a sewer,
must one penetrate into sewage?
To what purpose?

8. Tomorrow is maggoty;
today is putrid;
yesterday is gangrenous.
But yesterday is now incorrigible
and tomorrow services the grave.

---

* **Hindi: Devdas.**

9. Mull it over: Isn't *War* dialectical,
so weeping dries up temporarily,
then revives again,
with widows wallowing in the elastic flood?

10. Well, the problem is,
no one remembers a sky chopped by lightning—
or the suppurating stones of overthrown Carthage—
or a king's blood, sounding like horse hooves,
clattering, as it splatters the earth.

11. (No no-count preacher can know all
that's reported here.
Not even the reverse of my verses!)

12. A monarch, I inspect the *Treasury*.
That darkling currency?
Coins as shiny as polished coffins.

13. My economists glare beautiful teeth
and posit formulas
as impudent—if elegant—as tarantulas.

14. Inexplicable are their MacGuffins.
Their speech retails indescribable babble.

15. A king's no better than driftwood.

16. Even kings start out as naked as paupers,
bleating.

17. The rebellious? Ah, they're lynched
via the umbilical cord!

[Buffalo (New York) 27 *novembre* mmxvii
& Ottawa (Ontario) 3 *décembre* mmxvii
& YHZ—Enfield (Nova Scotia) 5/12/17
& 7 *décembre* mmxvii]

II.

1. Laughter?
Mothers urinating on their bawling newborns—
to drown em (out).

2. What is laughter, comic,
but a preacher drooling over a ho's cadaver?

3. I call up female troubadours—*trobairitz*—
to boggle at each *con**—
to peer goggle-eyed (googly-eyed)—at *con*:
Though commonplace, it's always bewitching!

4. Next, there's eggwhite on brunettes' faces.
The lucre of snow. White wine.
The soothing spillage of my masculine spout.

5. Let's say that my seed galloped, spurted,
or loped—slopped—into womb after womb,
producing mongrels non-stop....
I'd only be cementing grave after grave!

6. *Lust* is a burden; *Greed* is tragic;
Wrath is a nullity; *Gluttony* is folly.
Wisdom is light that explodes darkness!

7. I mull over the hubbub of intellectuals—
all their arguably, unnecessary *Vitriol*;
all their recherché, scholarly *Negativity*:
But books don't fill graves, just their authors.

---

* **French:** ***Vagin.***

8. I order 60 gallons weekly
from the Royal Irish Distillery,
for liquor can leach away *Logic*
and scotch *Judgment*....
But even whisky cannot long deter
needling *Wisdom*.

9. A hippy fop, reekin of Irish booze,
spewing vinegar, salty speech,
I rip open my own disguise—
and I view a skeleton—
bones poking out of grass.

10. My wit is sprightly,
but my heart's sluggish,
my muscles slacken,
my breath dwindles.
I end up perishing foolishly, anyway.

11. Why shouldn't I cast myself down
into a staked pit,
sink down upon those spikes?

12. In the grave, I'll be completely nailed up light—
never viewed wholly again.

13. Ephemeral I am, and will seem slipshod,
slapdash, to accusatory, cold-eyed heirs.
My palaces will prove momentary furniture.

14. (So many Sun Kings end up stabbed,
then morph into statuary,
soon ivy-webbed, or pigeon-guano-plastered.)

15. The next king may situate his courtiers
so that one's posterior butts on another's mouth.

16. The next king may be as tyrannical as an addict,
and have my corpse dug up,
and then stripped and flung atop a dung heap.

17. Dying is unlucky, but unwise is birth.

18. (I author no *vanto*, no *Vanity*:
Systematically graphic is light!)

19. Actually, there is no *Joy*, but in *Wisdom*,
i.e., the knowledge that flesh is mortal,
our grandest works decay,
and civilizatons end in ash, bloodshed, dust.

20. But only the dolt, bereft of God,
despairs at these facts.

[Yellowknife (Northwest Territories) 9 *décembre* mmxvii]

III.

1. To everything, there's first flourishing,
then withering;
stints of *Authority*, next trials of *Abdication*;
the echo of light be shadow.

2. Draw one breath, then continue
until breathing stops.
There's a time to nourish and a time to perish.
Frantically—fanatically—one uncorks light.

3. The lover announces *Love*; then feels humiliated.
Another protests *Hatred*; then *Loathing* is vindicated.
Coffins empty cradles.

4. There's a time for *Song* and a time for *Silence*;
a time for *Statecraft* and a time for *Witchcraft*;
a time for melodies and a time for massacres.

5. (Soon or late, we exit a political *état*,
and enter a pollen and chlorophyll empire.)

6. Let black fingers bloody white piano keys.
There's a time for galas and a time for dirges.

7. There's a time for spirituals and a time for blues;
a time to snooze on a chaise longue
and a time to curl up in the electric chair.

8. One night, slip off white-lace panties;
the next night, tug on widows' weeds.
Be devout in *Coitus* today;
retreat into *Piety* tomorrow.

9. Bring on *Poetry* that upbraids Plato
or scan the *Porn* that papers outhouses.
There's a time for *pastorela**
and a time for proselytization.

10. Why do you exalt *Labour*?
Nothing lasting comes of sweat.

11. A wise man savours a clinch of wife
and a pinch of grass:
Inches of one and ounces of the other.

12. Tortured—wounded—by frost,
leaves go blood-red;
they rot, rattling—scuffling—in wind.

13. Theologians may fret and toil
to decipher such symbols,
but a wise man savours the *Poesy*.

14. Incompetent of *Eternity*, how can we distinguish
ephemeral *Novelty*
and/or the estranged *Past*,
from the death-spiral that's the *Present*?

15. Under the sun,
Justice issues from the antiseptic façades
of disgusting, filthy, surreptitious sewers.

16. Realistically, all of us are vermin.
Viewed spot on, we're rats, lice.

17. Dust is what we are,
i.e., what we intersect with,
(whatever our original trajectory).

---

* A peasant-girl-seduction poem.

18. *Life* sorts out our fates
as we sort through our choices.

19. Critters simply breathe, birth, and die.
But human souls either scale to Heaven
or jet down to Hell.

20. Detachment from markets produces
this paramount *Good*:
That an artist savours his or her handiwork
while he or she breathes.

[Yellowknife (Northwest Territories) 10 *décembre* mmxvii]

IV.

1. Under the sun, permanent stands *Worry*!
Pitiful citizens weep and weep,
but no bureaucrat offers hugs.

2. Why not go schmoozing with the dead?
Pour hooch down their frozen, untasting lips?

3. The living are unfocussed, distracted:
Fitful ideals dice up our lives, piecemeal....

4. The unborn—the aborted—are best off.
Their *Innocence* is unimpaired.

5. Better to shed one's rusty blood in battle
than to gulp dirty martinis at shindigs!

6. (But unprofitable is *War* in springtime!
Nothing moves; all is stuck in muck or flood.)

7. *Malevolence*! To feel downtrodden by bulls—
like some matador, upended.

8. An orphan and bachelor,
who's failed to be either husband or father,
may as well've been gelded at birth.
And all his riches made someone else's—
and his labours and profits—moot.

9. The impious bear children
who won't bear children;
thus, the family's flowers wither,
dry out, perish.

10. A bachelor or spinster or widow—
surviving alone—
is no better than an entire town
cut off from bread and wine.

11. (Horrid is an impotent ram.
Awful is a joyless embrace.

12. Woe to dead, cold, unloving hearts
and to palsied, skittish, unfeeling hands!)

13. Better to be as whorish as fire
than a chilly, icy nude.

14. (When it's easy to tear the panties off,
it's hard not to screw unusually well.)

15. Men and women should mash together—
so their privy organs gnaw and gnash and feed.

16. Let a bride shimmy and shake the wedding bed,
and her groom deliver his indigenous *fasces*,
exciting cadences, flexings.

17. Let her scoot to pump herself upon the bloke,
and play part-cobra, part-kitten,
twitching her prat about his rod,
or watch, slit-eyed,
while his manhood glides under,
cuts through, her jungle hair,
poles her snug-sided snapper.

18. Let a wife bounce—jounce—
upon her hubby's lawful appendage:
How else will babes be born
if not *via* slapping pelt against pelt,
her juices sluicing from her crevice,
that tangy device?

19. Let em congress intricately, passionately,
in a freewheeling and untroubled *Ruckus*—
without allowing a glacial face,
but nixing any reactionary blushing.

20. Rue all wedding beds drenched in tears!

[Iqaluit (Nunavut) 11–12 *décembre* mmxvii
& Tropea (Italia) 6–7 *juin* mmxviii]

V.

1. Don't balk at occupying a pew!
Don't welch on *Salvation*!

2. Speak little and ward off libel suits.

3. Screeds, diatribes, filibusters, perorations:
A twit poisons his mouth with such dental caries!

4. Vow an oath to God? That's a heady equation!
Better fulfill, first-hand, that pledge,
or subtract thy hand
or go minus thy head!

5. Anyone who fails to fulfill a vow?
Oy! He or she forfeits his or her tongue.

6. The vain postulate histories
as pompous and as fractured as tombstones.
(Worm-eaten and dusty are their chronicles;
weeded over are their prophecies.)

7. Slogans barreling from a bullhorn—
all accompanied by squalls of arrows—
render the scrawny unimpressive corpses.

8. Let politicos yoyo in tipsy debates:
Gilded ministers still end, gelded, in coffins.

9. *Equality* is as desirable as dew
and as ephemeral as *Peace*.

10. To win regard, dish out moolah
to tax collectors and paupers.
At thy wake, wine will whimper as it runs out.

11. The Avenue of *Toil*
ends at the Palace of *Satisfaction*?

12. Out of unclouded gold, a lady's piss-hole,
babes emerge, accumulating *Majesty*
as they mature.
But next comes miasmic whining
as they perish,
becoming immortal skeletons.

13. Girded by troops, the plump king
is yet but a crapulent windbag—
breezy increments of excrement.

14. Some kings flail, their mouths a-foam,
their eyes aflame,
but bend like tongues round assassins' spear points.
What good is *Statecraft* then?

15. Better is a pitiful, stinking corpse,
gorged gothically with maggots,
than is a king—
his appendages lopped,
truncated to his trunk....

16. A tyrant *rex* slithers
his demonic, animal bulk,
while his forked-tongue, blaring voice
drowns out poets.
And his abject subjects die homeless.

17. Thus, he lolls, shining, untouched,
as untainted as a saint,
while half-eaten babes sprawl
atop dung-piles.

18. (Multitudes hate *il duce*,
but *Insurrection* is *Vanity*.)

19. *History* is fabulous gore; each sunrise oversees
disgusting deaths, macabre massacres.

20. *History*: A jackboot kicking through stained-glass.

21. *History* has always thoroughly extinguished
the rabble, the noble, the genius, the distinguished.

22. All is *Vanity*.

[Iqaluit (Nunavut) 11–13 *décembre* mmxvii]

VI.

1. A man who totals his wife, his children,
his friends, his treasures and trophies,
his liquor cabinet and pantry,
and deems himself blue-ribbon, blue-blood, and blue-chip,
may find that Stagolee cornholes his wife;
conquistadors sell off his children;
thieves cart away his goods;
gluttons feast on his larder and liquor;
so that these strangers, ungovernable,
treat him as unwise, unloveable;
and he ends up lousy, piss-pot-poor, abandoned,
and having to dig his own grave and lie in it,
bugging yet other strangers
to shovel the piled dirt and manure over his face.

2. Impossible shadows—black-robed priests—
dart about under a lightning-exorcised night
to intone terminal rites, extreme unction.
But they'd be better off burying babes!

3. A man who lives a century
and has a hundred children,
and a doting wife,
and supplies privileges for all,
and so attains the respect of philosophers
and preachers
(who jot and dote upon his *bons mots*),
and yet groans and grouses,
well, it's best that he abort himself.

4. Such a man is like an umbrella
that leaketh in a downpour.

5. Feces-dirtied is his wine;
baffling is his blindness to sunlight.
He be a botch.

6. Grant such a dunce 2,000 years of life,
and he'll still see no good in breathing!

7. Better to slap nails through his palms
and drum spikes through his shin bones,
while he hangs upside-down
on a cross.

8. Reap the priceless *Bounty*,*
feast with thanksgiving,
and yet thou soon will feel famished again,
just as hungry as rain
that swallows down a city.
The problem? No mortal is ever sated.

9. Light disciplines vision;
Enlightenment disciplines behavior.
Be as visionary and as enlightened
as a spider, designing.

[Iqaluit (Nunavut) 14 *décembre* mmxvii]

* Cf. Walcott.

VII.

1. To be cherished for *Charity*
(always *Public Works*)
is better than opening gold mines.

2. When auditing okaying votes,
swearing *Devotion*,
note who is banking what and where
and who is buying weapons and why.

3. Too easy, it is, to be seduced
by vows of sugar,
only to be vended arsenic.

4. (Well, consider:
How can you fathom ocean depths
by peering only at the surface?)

5. Vandals—jokers—who torch libraries
(who deem flame-blackened paper the finest),
urge on shrieks, howls,
Civilization's death rattles.

6. Because the dreaming wise are exiled,
Oppression nurses dreary clods.

7. (They are as much mistakes as bugs.
They're pests: Self-evident *Pollution*.)

8. To say, "It is finished," bests
saying, "It is begun."

9. Make money, make babies:
Two reasons for breathing!
But money is taxed, wasted, ripped off;
and babes end up—either young or old—
dead.

10. God decides much.
And God decides all—
once He hath decided much.

11. Don't ask if the dead are happier
than the living. They are.

12. The virtuous perish young,
while the wicked prosper:
Wisdom's more profitable than *Luck*.

13. *Mourning*'s instructive;
Mirth is destructive.

14. *Sorrow* inspires *Wisdom*;
Delight expires in *Drink*.

15. Guzzle wine in the funeral home,
not in the brothel;
Savour flavours vinegary, penitential, indelible.

16. (Save the basement for the groggery
and the attic for the brothel.)

17. Get thee *Wisdom*!
Aye, though, for mortals, it's a tough slog!
(I'm as clinical as thy kin!)

18. Sooner be rebuked by the wise
than championed by sots. Idiot!

19. God admonishes us to be upright.
But, too soon, we collapse into graves,
and this decline and fall
depresses *Virtue*.

20. Likewise, eventually, fog dims—
or mud blots out—
Brilliance.

[Library of Parliament—Ottawa (Ontario)
18 *décembre* mmxvii]

VIII.

1. So august in office, so robust in his deeds,
and, still, a king slides into the earth.

2. (Remember: Once a father's dead,
who else wins him respect, but a son?
Who else avenges him, save his son?)

3. Like food gone and forgotten in the belly,
obscured in the belly,
but reborn repulsively as *Waste*,
so do the wicked end
as splayed and splintered bone,
and all their crimes digested
and expelled
(spelled out)
as ruddy-lettered *History*.*

4. Already maggoty are miscreants' hearts!
Their evils, rotting em, shed a prime stench—
an immedicable stench,
but feed the creepy-crawlies,
steeped deep, basking in their bowels.

5. The wicked—hideous—pass away
like distorted, but ephemeral shadows.

6. How can anyone comatose build anything?

7. Yes, the greedy bellyache and get rich.
But Charity don't mitigate *Sadism*.

---

* Cf. Hardial Bains, *Communism: 1989–1991* (1991).

8. To retaliate against tamper-proof *Mortality*?
Best savour each second of breath;
and eat and wine merrily.

9. God ain't under indictment,
and faces no doom.
So how are mortals His equal?

[YUL—Dorval (Québec) *Noël* mmxvii]

IX.

1. *Life*? Repetition and repetition of *Grief.*
Already, whole civilizations rot under tombstones.

2. The living are newborns dying.

3. And nothing helps the dead.
Their *Theology* ends in a nose-twisting stink.

4. *Hunger* is limitless, so eat.
Whoring is an industry, so hie thee to bed.

5. Why allow *Vacillation* in *Companionship*?
To be minus a lover subtracts *Joy* from *Life.*
To be minus a spouse impoverishes a house.

6. Uncertain of your *Death* date, be certain of *Coitus.*
(Pleasures don't belong in schoolbooks!)

7. Labour feverishly—like a dervish,
relentless in orbit.

8. (Note: All thy ornate dance steps
execute *faux-pas* in quicksand.)

9. Fact: To war is tragic.
Why prompt or dish out *Death* prematurely?

10. *War* is serial *Misery*:
The voluptuous melt into fens of blood;
and victors end as dusty functionaries.

11. Never trustworthy are hoity-toity bureaucrats,
parading whited-out errors.

12. Anyway, no one is erroneously tortured!

13. Angels of *Justice* extend ominous wings
that envelope fully all to whom they condescend
to administer *Correction.*

[Nouvelle-Orléans (Louisiane) 31 *décembre* mmxvii
& New Year's Day mmxviii]

X.

1. Just as a wife and daughter
playing rascally bawds,
demolish a household,
so a moment's *Folly*
destroys a lifetime of *Virtue.*

2. Shafted by picadors' lances, the bull—
dying like a defenseless cow—
looks an oaf.

3. A dangling rope = the clown.
A strangling noose = the wise.

4. The jack-off is a sell-out;
He's not a hold-out.
He's a fucking sell-out!
He bamboozles; he boozes it up;
he flummoxes; he betrays.

5. The twit steers congregations
into cemeteries,
but first he promises a kingdom.

6. Even a warrior king must cower
before forensic *Critique*,
for light must never back away from darkness!

7. *Evil*? A king who dismisses philosophers
and slumps over strumpets' tables.

8. Or *Evil*'s a king who elects and okays
reactionaries, slum-lords, fraudsters—
letting poets starve in dumpsters.

9. Woe unto thee, Israel, when thy king's
useless as a mud-flat!

10. Blessed is Israel when the king's pitiless
against puritans.

11. Empires snuff out idealists,
puff up empiricists.*

12. Curse neither monarch nor banker!
One orders troops; the other commands lawyers.
Best meditate before you orate!

13. Though poems can guillotine plutocrats,
Morality rests on flexible steel,
and so paltry poet and puffed-up potentate
can both be gashed through the neck.

14. (Proverbs direct piloting,
prompt good winds and blissful cruising,
and select moorings in calm harbours.)

15. Seldom sincere (and always grudging) is *Sympathy.*

[New Orleans (Louisiana) 1 *janvier* mmxviii]

---

* *Kissing's* less vital than Kissinger?

XI.

1. Serving *Death*, *Sacreligious* are armies.
Courting *Eternity*, *Sacred* are poets.

2. *Infinity* is autonomous,
indecipherable, inhumane—
like God.

3. An angel with scraggly, scruffy wings—
with dusty, wilting feathers—
is Satan.
Still, his delivered crucifix is back-breaking.

4. As clandestine as cockroaches, *Sorrow* creeps.

5. Which state will ye experience ultimately:
Crucifixion or *Redemption*?
To reappear, brighter?

6. *Youth* paces steadily to a run-down state:
The middle-aged attain piddling, middling *Mediocrity.*
Thus, our latter years are sessions
of *Misunderstanding*, *Taxes Miscalculated*,
ill *Health*, ill-gotten *Wealth* (stolen back),
and eyes put out (by the envious),
as we seniors are put out (to die).

7. *Virtue* is virtually useless—
as *Solace.*
Each life burns to ash,
but the aftermath of fire is *Memory.*

8. What good's a ministry of kerosene
if thou lack matches?

[Nouvelle-Orléans (Louisiane) 3–4 *janvier* mmxviii]

XII.

1. Remember thy Creator when light
shaves night down to lightning,
abrasively albescent,
and when daylight coins priceless *Radiance*—
expansive as diamond slabs of waves—
before arrives always unseasonable *Murk*,
such dinky shining,
when thou shalt say, "This life is shadows."

2. When each lover's not yet nailed down
to a mirror crucifix of flesh;
nor *Brutality* conducted as a tax write-off;
nor the sun merely act a second-rate moon.

3. The lying theologians stutter;
the true ones mutter.
Blunder upon blunder is *Government*.

4. Push through darkness; anchor thyself to light.
The *Future*'s quixotic and chaotic;
it fields tremors, quakes, shivers, phantasms.

5. Inferior roads end in sinkholes.
The rat is slave to the granary.

6. And the daughters of *Musick* [sic]
chant under jostling seagulls and ravens
beside bunched-up, hunchback seas.

7. Furthermore, men fear thunder brumbling cross skies—
while the dead enter sealed blackness
and mourners wheeze like exhausted winds.

8. Best honour God before winds smuggle hurricane
and tempest into gardens;
or the birth-canal leaks pus.

9. I shan't offend the guilty, but must remind em
that their bones will sink in dark mire—
the *Absolutism* of dung.

10. The refusenik be as unhealthy as germs.

11. *Health* outshines gold.

12. To be bust (bankrupt) but robust
bests lying sick abed in a castle,
with "psychophants"* counting thy shrivelling breaths.

13. To be wise is to be aggravating—breathlessly—
to insist on the consequences of roots;
to know that worms encompass our pates.

14. Before a single word is written,
the inkwell is just like high water,
huddled behind a dam.

15. The wise are as jarring as tsunamis.
Each word they speak's a disarming jolt.

16. Beware: Books are the unlovely sediment
of blackboard minds—
of ink-sodden slaves—
all that surface-tension oil
and unfathomable, clotted mire.

17. The conclusion? Contemplate thy ebbing breaths,
note how thy goblets have always been shallow.

* A manifest neologism.

18. Remember that God permits no smudged *Visibility*,
but glares through dirty solstice—
every turfed-up flame where volcanoes bask—
the pumice sea—
annunciated torrents become seas—
dragnets of fog—
hyaline smoke—
and the niggardly light of the ginger-tint moon;
to bring every deed, every thought,
into *Judgment*.

[Nouvelle-Orléans & MSY (Louisiane) 4 *janvier* mmxviii
& Oshawa (Ontario) 20 *janvier* mmxviii
& Halifax (Nova Scotia) 4–5 *février* mmxviii]

THE LECTURES OF SOLOMON

I.

1. Sortie to tavern and brothel—
to stave off the grave?

2. Later, soon enough,
the moon will light our headstones,
one after another.

3. Dunk your tears in a wine goblet:
They dissolve and vanish in the lees
even as they salt the burgundy.

4. *Life*'s undone as quickly
as our shoelaces.

5. There's no unkillable organism.

6. Be as giggly as *filles de joie*;
drink, dance, and suck and lick:
Such raptures are a privilege.

7. Better such blessings than to end
wrinkled, palsied, alone,
cursing every *Gratification* foregone.

8. The wineskin? That's us:
Presently hearty, but soon, too soon, empty,
and never to be filled with breath again.

[Vancouver (British Columbia) 9 *avril* / *Nisan* mmxi]

II.

1. *Fate?* It's all your fault.

2. The earth cracks open,
crumples kings,
cripples castles.

3. Our numbered cadavers feed flies innumerable.
Count on it.

4. You die,
wracked by pains that make you curse
your mother for fucking your father.

5. Our *Catharsis? Annulment.*

6. Even gold is soiled:
How else can there be a monetary value
for desecrating human beings?

[Berlin (Germany) 7 *mai* mmxi]

III.

1. A bee forages for clover,
swoons into grass:

2. *Life*;
Death.*

[Ville de Québec (Québec) 11 *juin* mmxvi]

*** In Memoriam: Louiselle Bossé (1937–2016).**

IV.

1. Hungry to snatch at lost *Delights*,
Decrepitude snarls at *Youth*.

2. But *Youth*'s wild ejaculations narrow
to *Maturity*'s piddly whining.

3. Supreme *Style* is *Simplicity*:
To man a woman, to husband a wife—
to slice and swallow salmon, cheese, pears—
to be as innocent and rustic as Adam,
the first poet.

4. To have *Poetry* open your mouth.

5. To enjoy exquisite exacerbation
of *Ecstasy*.
The consequences of *Poetry*.

6. (Even if everybody else hates poets,
God don't.)

7. But *Pleasure* always exacts a mortal tally:
To dine is to defecate.

8. Unexaggeratedly *Transcendant*? The wise.

9. I've pursued *Wisdom* as the vintner pursues wine—
from first green vine-shoot
to the bunched and purpling grape.

10. There's no contented *Maturity* without *Wisdom*.

[Roissy-en-France (France) 10 *juillet* mmxvi
& Cosenza (Italia) 17 *juin* mmxvii]

V.

1. Embrace the heroic whore;
relish her lacerating *chatte*:

2. Who else pays out *Love*—
with interest?

[Salamanca (Spain) 12 *décembre* mmx]

VI.

1. My lovelorn, lovestruck cadences—
so sad—
loom as dark as Father David's Psalm 115.

2. Contradictionless, *Nature* hath tenure,
and so tutors *Humanity*?

3. (*Such mich nicht!*[*]
I don't gloss dust!)

4. The problem is, babies recycle parents—
and their whims, their woes.

5. And *Love*—or *Lust*—conquers emperors,
and ploughs under armies.

6. So, beautiful are the thoughtful agèd:
To be silver-haired on one's head
and quicksilver inside one's skull….

[Tropea (Italia) 12 *juin* mmxvii]

*** German: Don't look for me!**

THE SONG OF SOLOMON

I.

[*The bride speaks.*]

1. "Let fiddles melee, if melodious,
not defective,
and thus finesse our *Affection*.

2. "Consume sweet potato and his kisses, I;
relish North Carolina's sweet potato pie, *oui*,
and his French kisses, *oui*;
all quite *Kosher* in the embouchure.

3. "His tongue drips honey into my mouth,
thus gilding molasses!
So lascivious is his tongue—
stabbing the last shred of wine!

4. "But a dustbowl is my palace—
in his absence;
my bath is a vinegar'd dousing—
in his absence;
Jeez, my maids—nymphs—lust for him,
for his sweat's pearly liquor, when flickering
in candlelight....

5. "I am black and beautiful—
O ye Daughters of *Musick*—
like indigo indignant with ebony—
like onyx-optimized obsidian.

6. "Let none brand me as nightmarish
just cos the sun's lavished pon me
its varnishing and ravishing rays!
The soul of sunflowers be my essence—
the summation—epitome—of every pitched blaze!

7. "Where my Lord was born is where
air's solvent with gold!
O! Let me never be ousted from his gaze!
Insatiable is (my) *Beauty*—
to be apprehended."

[*The bridegroom speaks.*]

8. "Most preeminent of all Eve's daughters,
how I love our froth, our solid steam!
The smear of cream as our bodies tangle,
devilishly angelic and blissfully hellish.*

9. "Thy breasts—proud juts—compose a skyline
sculpt in sable."

[*The bride speaks.*]

10. "Our lovemaking is our bodies
winching through unflinching musk,
enough to make any voyeur swoon.

11. "Spy our slanting couple
aboard a canting bed—
when thy creamy stick stirs my brown sugar."

[*The bridegroom speaks.*]

12. "How beautiful thou art, my darling!
How stainless thou art—
like sunlight!

13. "Notwithstanding *Death*—
yet, our bed is spicy furnishing, snuggling us—
where we lie as melodramatic as diamonds—
in no spectral *Opulence*."

[Halifax (Nova Scotia) 5 *février* mmxviii]

*** Lovers—angels (so-called)—contend with lovers—devils (spurious).**

II.

[*The bride speaks.*]

1. "Light's aroma:
That's me.

2. "A serene mirror set amid rubble,
but reflecting only the sun,
so is my love derisive of rivals.

3. "Stern sunlight driving off a blizzard,
so is my beloved *vis-à-vis* Don Juan pests.

4. "Rouse me with chilling, glacier-borne waves—
spiky, saline whiffs—
lest I drowse, narcotized by *Love.*

5. "My man's as steady as salt shaken free,
falling,
and I'm as juicy as a frothing,
just-bitten apple.

6. "O ye Daughters of Jersualem,
I charge ye, do not press my beloved with tasks!
Never must ye distract him from my bed!

7. "As steady as butter—
melting and skidding cross a skillet—
so is my beloved as spry—
and as sizzling, and as steamy,
as an ember gone as limber as a spark!

8. "My beloved is like a chevalier—a poet:
He harries incorrect newsprint;
he erases doubtful statistics.

9. "(Never are his verses
greasy, sugary, fatty, cheesy, salty, or buttery:
Never are they mushy, porridge, a hash.)

10. "My beloved spake last night, saying,
'Nomadic snow is gone;
and plum-like clouds are set to douse
branches with a resurrection of blossoms.'

11. "O my poet—
my ally, my prayerful bard—
thou art in-and-out-of-print,
in-and-out-of-*Favour*,
but let me hear thy words tenor'd
with *Gravitas*,
for they're as stately and unalterable
as Gibraltar.

12. "Let us sort out gardeners
from gravekeepers—
though both are as tough-minded as gangsters.

13. "My beloved is my lover;
I'm his companion, his wife.
He drowses within my light—black light—
that is jet against his skin.

14. "Until dawn uprises, and shadows turn
as phantasmal as recollected flames,
o my beloved, succour me."

[YHZ—Enfield (Nova Scotia) 7 *février* mmxviii]

III.

[*The bride speaks.*]

1. "No ascetic, I sing,
thrilled by his dimensions—
lanky, sturdy, weighty, lengthy:
O, how can a ghost impress and heat my bed?

2. "I'll traverse tundra, desert, jungle,
to pursue my beloved!
How can a spectre pound my bedsprings,
bounce my spine?

3. "You see and hear my sobs?
It's because no detective pinpoints
my man's whereabouts....

4. "Downtown's puzzle-pattern cobblestones—
the CBD's marble-and-glass façades—
I'll plod one and prod the other,
to discover my beloved.

5. "Relentless as *Surveillance Capitalism*,
I'll coffle us—
cobble us—together,
hobble him into *Husbandry*.

6. "O ye Daughters of Jerusalem,
I charge ye, don't wail for his kingly *Governance*
as tiresomely as scalpers cry their frauds:
Don't distract him from my bed!

7. "He be one who braveth squalls;
who breaketh even individualized blockades;
who brushes aside mustard-tint, sand dunes;
who be as jarring as a thunderbolt;
but yet as kissable as a babe.

8. "Behold! Solomon cometh!
Look! 60 dervishes whirl like tornadoes—
60 dervishes swashbuckle like Cossacks—
brandishing blades and kicking out their feet!

9. "Their glinting swords tingle at the eye.
Their shouts are the sounds of wine barrels
busting open!

10. "King Solomon's horses unscroll
(unfurling across parade grounds)—
rolling flickers of rippling brass or gold—
licks of that pure *Brilliance* powering the sun!

11. "His refulgent retinue divulges
the dawn sun's lemony resurgence,
bright as a boat's wake.

12. "Come forth, O Zion's Daughters!
Shower King Solomon handsomely
with explosive, fountaining Champagne,
on this dawn where we're coupled—
loving and loving and loving
and loving and loving and loving
and loving and loving and loving
and loving and loving and loving
and loving and loving and loving
and loving and loving and loving
and loving and loving and loving.

So that:"

[Flesherton (Ontario) 10–11 *février* mmxviii
& Halifax (Nova Scotia) 17 *février* mmxviii]

IV.

[*The bridegroom speaks.*]

1. "How thy looming, cumulus breasts quiver!
How thy tremulous voice sets me a-shiver!
How thine two eyes showcase
dramatic licorice and silver-screen platinum!

2. "Thy hair is like lava—
sleek black entire, Vesuvian,
but lapis lazuli dyes blue its lustre.

3. "Thy teeth are a chain of diamonds—
possessions of a queen—
glinting with ideal *Purity*.

4. "Thy kisses are as sultry as a thundershower,
and thy neck is as erect, lofty, round,
as an igneous-stone, Martello tower.*

5. "Until dawn's torrential light
(once night shows radioactive decay),
and breakfast ushers in plates of *boudin*
and Vienna sausage and Frankfurters
(mustered with Dijon mustard),
all percolated—*via* pink *Brut (Schlumberger)*—
down throat and into belly,
be thou perfect—
the trifecta of *Genius*, *Elegance*, and *Charity*.

* Pair Fowles's *The Ebony Tower* (1974) with *Black Tower* Riesling (1967), thudding out the classic, black ceramic bottle.

6. "O my beloved, let us exit Nova Scotia
and get away to La Habana, to Istanbul,
and escape whippersnapper rain
and whiplashing wind....

7. "Here's an opinion that's tangible:
My heart weeps; my eyes bleed;
for I'm vanquished by one quick glance,
seeing unblinkingly,
your legs toss back
your skirt's kick-pleat,
then a white-lace undie gracing your sex.

8. "Thy words come lippy,
flippant, with scarlet,
my spouse, my beloved:
Thy scent emanates (emulates) orchids!

9. "The scrumptious, sodden mess—
hot, seething, clinging, wet—
that you churn as I chafe,
makes my manhood seem Carrara marble,
well-lathered.

10. "You ruffle my senses—
like wind shuffling through leaves,
so I'm oblivious to your biting,
your scratching, your gleeful *Malice*!

11. "O Daughter of Jerusalem,
your cocoa'd kisses bring on such sweat,
we turn mutual, vehement oases.

12. “Awake, O north wind, and,
by-your-leave,
drive south, south, and further south,
and so urge on *Love* to pour boiling—
Sicilian, Somalian—
and surge torrid—
scoring us
to our heart-felt cores.”

[Halifax (Nova Scotia) 17 *février* mmxviii
& Havana (Cuba) 20–21 *février* mmxviii]

V.

[*The bride speaks.*]

1. "I abandon the horse shore,
where the mistral whips and warps waves
or scoops and sifts sand drifts;
and where ducks scud along, snouting through reefs;
to come to thee, this beach at Tropea,
where we table *fior di latte* cheese,
simmered shrimp and lemon'd salmon,
and down *Campari sans* compare.

2. "Why should I attain a *Death*-like sleep?
I miss our virulent romping.
I fear rather a somnolent death
that'll make of my pillows a gallows.

3. "All-out suppleness?
To be a ghost—
icy, clammy, in the touching.
Or to be vitreous—
too fragile,
to survive this realm of pitiless stones.

4. "My garret could be a harem—
but only if I could multiply myself
into lovers as loving as I am.

5. "*Experience* is a plough;
Innocence is a field.
I lie down, fervent to play fertile soil—
servile before my lover's delving trowel.

6. "But that gent's as silent as a caesura,
as invisible as a repudiated line of verse
fallen prey to an impudent, arrogant eraser!

7. "Only *Poetry* grants coupling *Eloquence*.
One wields hard-core monosyllables,
dueting—spondaic, trochaic—
but recklessly breathless.

8. "O ye Daughters of Jerusalem,
lecture King Solomon that my *Love*—
unschooled and uncivilized and uncouth—
is yet as unignorable and as unforgettable
as childbirth."

[*The Daughters speak.*]

9. "Bride, *Bella*, pray tell why thy beloved
is not as blood-stained as the state poet, Virgil,
nor as bloody as butchered calves not yet parchment.
Justify why he shouldn't sip the poison of *Exile*,
but taste molasses'd *Ecstasy* instead."

[*The bride speaks.*]

10. "Hey, my guy's no Spoken Word slobberer!
His tongue's sometimes thick with plummy pidgin.
Yet, his talk never wobbles.

11. "His eyes are as clear as naked water."

12. "His hair is as gold as preening buttercups.
His backbone is as firm as a ship's timbers.

13. "His fingers boast 24-carat gold rings.
His belly is ivory, shining.

14. "His legs incarnate *Harmony*
and ample, symmetrical *Genius*.

15. "His mouth is a choir of bees,
so poignantly humming.

16. "Well, he be consummately lovely—
an inventory of Camembert cheese, Riesling,
and Montreal smoked meat;
that opulent scoundrel feeds me whole,
never abdicating, never at all depleted.
How can I think of him as an afterthought?

17. "And though the king must sojourn,
vagabond-like, as Gypsy as an Egyptian,
he rides to me, stops with me, alone."

[Havana (Cuba) 21 *février* mmxviii]

VI.

[*The Daughters of Jerusalem speak.*]

1. "Whither gone is he, where be he,
who thy soul loveth?
We ask, for you just ain't you
when you be bereft of he."

[*The bride speaks.*]

2. "My beloved has burnished his armour,
his *War* gear,
to voyage—lumpy, thumping—sea fathoms
to a measureless desert,
to be a bulldog off-leash, larking;
to range and arrange, sniff at, bark along,
our tweaked—or, rather, widened—
borders.

3. "I belong to him, and he's mine.
Our tongues echo each other.

4. "He's as comely as white-marble
and green-lagoon Venice—
and as blazingly stunning as watercolours
trimmed and/or traced over
and/or doused by gilt.

5. "Soldiers and sailors ogle our monarch;
they crave to be parasitic upon—
to ape—
his truculent, luculent *Fame*.

6. "(Solomon is best scrutinized *via* dreams,
save that his handsome dazzle wakes me
even within that impregnable sanctuary.)

7. "His teeth are ivory keys signifying
Grace, Elocution, Courage.

8. "His speech is blank verse looming white sheets:
His tongue sews strophe and antistrophe."

[*The bridegroom speaks.*]

9. "I may encunt—probe as I wish—
60 wives (snarling, quarreling,
methodically spasmodic),
or 80 concubines (mewling, tussling),
or countless, weeping, sobbing virgins,
or Louisiana quadroons (those heavy squirters),
and Syrian Two-Spirits,
all righteously tawny and bizarre,
if fantasia manifestations of *Femininity.*

10. "But my saint,* my pure, my wife,
is that high-brown do-gooder
that her Coptic Creole, upstanding mama bore.

11. "Who she be if not the hostage
of *Poesy?*
If I don't elect her my Muse,
clumsy *Heresy* I commit.

12. "I traversed a desert;
I sailed to and founded an oasis.
I tapped wine and rum from bulging barrels.

13. "From Ragged Ass Road in Yellowknife
(that soot-sullied snow and crabby mining town—
all caterwumpus in its romances),
came I, tweedy, but uninterested
in reedy widows, and never acting a seedy
suitor, but underelict in my desires!

---

* Cf. Saint Valentine, tortured and beheaded for *Love.*

14. "My Bride, my Dark Continent sibyl,
I don't confuse panting and prayer.

15. "Return, return, return, return, return,
O Calabrese,
for the dusk be discontented—
once-pink, now bruised magenta and mauve.

16. "But you are night's *Demarcation*—
Magia sexualis—
the tender purveyor of *Mesmerism*."

[Havana (Cuba) 22 *février* mmxviii]

VII.

[*The bridegroom speaks.*]

1. "How beautiful: Thy diamond-laden eyes,
O royal daughter!
The joints of thy thighs are honeyed pivots—
as equitable as lubricants.

2. "Thy navel marries whirlpool and port—
a nautical vortex of black velvet.

3. "Thy belly is a bastion of bronze,
a copper slope,
dew dotes upon.

4. "Thy two breasts are fitful gazelles—
always leaping into—
or away from—
my double-grotto-mimicking hands.

5. "Thine eyes picture two pyramids,
whose bases merge in the crux,
dividing equally the searing coal of thy pupils.
(Each corner's an angle afire.)

6. Thy nose, perfecting the Pythagorean triangle,
softens *Geometry*'s hard edge.

7. "Thy head boasts a helmet
of *azzura-negra* lava—
of everflowing onyx tinged with indigo.

8. "Thy *Beauty* stymies—petrifies—even kings.

9. "How prayerful I am that these words—
their legacy—will offer the steady, undying proof
of thy *Beauty*.

10. "Thy *Beauty* compensates for *Wealth*
dissolved by *Debt*,
and resolves all *Tribulation*
that tribal quibbles create.
In thee, *Utopia* is flesh.

11. "*Self-Deception* is a stroke, an internal
hemmhorage. So I confess my *Love*.

12. "I come unto thee randy, raunchy,
and as slick as a self-wetting icicle
and stiff as a machete,
to usher thy cleft*
unto celebratory *Cleaving*.

13. "Among vine clambers—cascades—
grapes gone gangrenous—
then luminous as white wine,
as glimmering as red wine
all in chameleonic repetition—
bunch by trellis'd bunch—
I understand how *Love* ripens to *Marriage*."

[*The bride speaks.*]

14. "I am my beloved's—
and monomanic—righteously obsessive—
be his *Desire*."

* Cf. Doris Lessing.

[*The bridegroom speaks.*]

15. "April—that sodden Utopia—is ours.
O my odalisque Sphinx,
precarious is our clothing,
once our never-tepid sweat
oils non-torpor-hindered limbs.

16. "In the rain-diluted wilderness
that is *Pluviôse* and/or *Floréal*,
let us be, each to each,
aggressive and possessive interlopers.

17. "Come now our *Rutting*,
dynamic, never furtive."

[Havana (Cuba) 23–24 *février* mmxviii]

VIII.

[*The bridegroom speaks.*]

1. "If I can't lap thy breasts
like I did my mama's—
my head scrunched betwixt—
then crippled is my tongue!

2. "I want to kiss each avidly, equally,
so neither fears despise.
I'll suckle at thy tits:
My head swivelling,
my mouth dribbling upon each emphatic nipple."

[*The bride speaks.*]

3. "*Prego*! Geyser loving spritzers of juices,
while our eyes glide, collide
(as in a Picasso*).

4. "Thy sinister hand should be dexterous
at my breast—
and thy dexterous hand
should be sinister at my crux.

5. "O ye Daughters of Jerusalem,
let the king be as married
and/or as bachelor as a Catholic priest,
so long as he cometh unto—and into—me,
until the sun lifts and dew latches dawn.

*** Note: Picasso's *Demoiselles d'Avignon* plagiarizes, note for note, Coltrane's *Naima*.**

6. "Who wants to pass up sugar?
Not he who crosses a bridge of dew
to kiss me among grape vines at daybreak;
who campaigns restlessly, who attacks quietly—
like a thief, when the moon's high,
who—to dramatize his heart—
presses his face betwixt my thighs.

7. "When we two are one, our lovemaking
doubles our lungs, and we count
only by our breaths—
via inhalation and exhalation—
interrupted only by fevers,
those paroxysms, those haltings.

8. "*Love* is a benevolent *War*
in which all parties surrender, pronto."

[*The bridegroom speaks.*]

9. "Thy lil sis be as homely as a crucifix.
She mopes: Who will love her—
she whose *Wealth* and *Progeny*
seem prone to vanish into dirt?"

[*The bride speaks.*]

10. "If she be as gritty as a cemetery,
we'll enclose her with off-kilter sunflowers
saluting—serenading—her like troubadours.

11. "If I, husband,
am myself a welling grave,
it's due to thy persistent trenching,
seeding my carnal *Resurrection*.

12. "(Erect your headstone
when our first-born arrives—
to honour *Humility*.)

13. "But, always, sweetie, let's rut—
thy dick mutinous in my glutinous *queynte.*

14. "Inside my womanhood, husband,
a shape now thickens,
whose bickering palpitations
tick-tock the open-ended repetition
of *Birth*, *Death*, *Birth*.

15. "Haste to me, my husband,
and be thou eager to ramble
among my sunflowers and pears
and sample my spices—
and trample down the bramble
to pour thy milky jam."

[Havana (Cuba) 24 *février* mmxviii]

THE CANTICLE OF SHEBA

I.

1. Sheba gal, King Solomon's prize,
ferries Nile-distilled *Beauty*, Gypsy:
That caramel-tangerine visage,
such blackberry-chocolate hair.

2. When she unpents her hair,
midnight—sultry—unfurls through air.

3. (To nurse at her pyramid breasts,
to suckle at her curved-sickle,
but tubular sheath:
One tastes—in stereo—fleshed-out milk-n-molasses.

4. Sheba speaketh:
"His kisses launch a tsunami of absinthe.
My name, on his lips,
conjures a licorice liqueur.

5. "I am black, and comely,*
because the sun favours me,
and I flaunt its *Adoration*.

6. "Never am I as meagre as a nigger
in a *bitaco*'s** jail
(on Death Row,
watching months flake off tacked-up calendars).

7. "Hire me to savour wine,
not to guard vineyards.

---

* Cf. Song of Solomon 1:5 (KJV).

** French argot: Yahoo, rube, provincial, hick (KGB).

8. "To summon my king to his throne,
uncork a banquet of perfumes—
add touchy-feely, sufficient musicians,
steely proficient with trumpet
and extra efficient on tambourine."

[Ottawa (Ontario) 24 *janvier* mmix
& Nantes (France) 27 *janvier* & 1 *février* mmix]

II.

1. “Deem Solomon a bouquet of lilies?
Then gentle him night-long betwixt my breasts.

2. “In the flames of *Love*,
Language dissipates,
leaving flesh to speak.”

3. Daughters of Jerusalem chorus:
“Ain’t she some sweet with her raven’s eyes?
She be *bee-you-tea-full*.”*

4. Solomon descants his hymn:
“Ain’t ya so pretty, Sheba, so perfect?
Also, our bed is cedar—
russet in tint, rosewater in scent.

5. “Like a sunflower among dandelions,
so dost thou tower o’er all other nymphs.”

6. Sheba echoes his song:
“Our *Love* exorcises, eradicates,
all that’s ugly, all that’s sluggish.”**

7. “My lover speaks; he coos to me,
‘Awake, my sweet darling,
my beloved, and come away:

8. ‘For now, winter melts,
and the rain waxes,
and all the southern-wintered songbirds
flutter northwards, dinning hopes,
chiming gripes.

---

* Cf. Burnley Allan “Rocky” Jones (1941–2013).
** Song of Solomon 2:6 (KJV).

9. 'I hear thy voice as a flute,
but your countenance is the sun.

10. 'On full-mooned nights,
overall overshadowed is your body,
but my eyes yield a scalpel-like light
faultless in finding no flaws.

11. 'Am I intoxicated by apple blossoms—
those sparkles amid blackness?

12. 'Comes a testing truth of snow-blossoms—
deranged snow-drops—scattered.
Never so is my desire.

13. 'Juba stars in holy jubilee—
unearthly glitter of your eyes—
two silver amulets on sable.'"

14. The bridegroom duets:
"A mauve moon, this night's,
I trace your bones—dark Creole tints—
sight the outline of a queen,
so flagrantly, regally feminine."

15. Daughters of Jerusalem serenade:
"Usher us the foxes, the silk-backed foxes
that spoil the vines,
for our vines sprout tender grapes."*

16. Sheba concludes:
"My beloved is mine, and I be his:
He feasts upon my lilies."**

[Ottawa (Ontario) 24 *janvier* mmix
& Nantes (France) 27 *janvier* & 1 *février* mmix]

---

* Song of Solomon 2:15 (KJV).
** Song of Solomon 2:16 (KJV).

III.

1. "I seek *partout* a Man, Solomon,
in my bedroom, in my bed,
and in city streets.
I canvass everywhere, seeking him,
but he is invisible—
if he is here.

2. "Epics must detest *Love*
as a subject,
for *Death* is clearer.

3. "Should *Love* craze us to feats
of noble *Tragedy*—
almost so we slay each other?

4. "I'd prefer perilous *Ecstasy*—
not curdling *Luxury*,
not riffs of contented tears."

[Ottawa (Ontario) 24 *janvier* mmix
& Nantes (France) 27 *janvier* & 1 *février* mmix]

IV.

1. Reticent, Solomon ain't:
"Thou hast raven's eyes.
Raven-black is thy hair.

2. "Thy two breasts are like two goblets
of cream that cool fevered poets—
say, Keats, and/or Baraka.

3. "Thy lips are akin to meaty cherries.
To taste em summons indescribable *Ecstasy.*

4. "Thy blue-black eyes define
winter woodsmoke at midnight.
How can a few white stars break-through?

5. "Any couple undertaking a voyage
must desire to be top-notch companions.

6. "Rain catwalks the roof;
streams gush and gully hillsides;
then I glimpse the ghosts of stars—
thine eyes.

7. "A virgin must be obstinate as stone
until *Love* unlocks her syrup store.
Then, the stream jets volcanic from the fissure.

8. "Wine-flavoured, sepia, sax-shaped madonna—
due to thy white-lace, stringy-clingy lingerie—
all thy cosmetics* be aphrodisiacs.

* JFK: "Mrs. Kennedy is organizing herself. It takes longer, but, of course she looks better than we do when she does it." [Fort Worth (Texas) 22 *novembre* mmlxiii]

9. "Thou hast ravished my heart
with one of thine raven's eyes,
with one gold chain lacing thy neck.*

10. "How perfect is thy love, my bride!
More worthy is thy love than gold.
And thy kiss addles me—
like whiskey dallying with hot lemon."

11. Sheba ripostes adoringly:
"Pinwheeling, ashen stars, the kindling moon,
cannot compete with thy *Enlightenment*—
thy *Satyagraha*** —
nullifying bleak darkness.

12. "Thou makest of the eve a sable Eden;
thou leadest into my garden
a heavy, graceful horse, white.

13. "Thou dost not squander *Beauty*.

14. "Lovers are intimate conspirators—
as finely joined in jibing
as are fish and water,
or as are philosophers
(Confucian / Maoist),
'correctly handling contradictions among the people.'

15. "O Daughters of Jerusalem,
let my beloved do away with scraps
and have his feast;
let him toss away bones,
and plump up on meat;
let him chomp cake
and toss the crumbs to birds."***

**[Ottawa (Ontario) 24 *janvier* mmix
& Nantes (France) 27 *janvier* & 1 *février* mmix]**

* Song of Solomon 4:19 (KJV).
** Gandhi: Truth-force.
*** Song of Solomon 4:16 (KJV).

V.

1. Sheba announces:
"I have drunk wine with my coffee*—
abundantly.**

2. "The moon meanders—
April lights upon May—
and, bereft of a Man,
I'm as bone-dry as a desert's
destitute of rain.

3. "No rain: No oasis.
No desert: No mirage.

4. "The palace of April
houses blossoms, gusts, snow—
enigmas;
and then, rain falls, royally gilded,
and late spring green unfolds;
a kite basks in warmth.
Sunlight seems already to be in June.

5. "I dance silk, nod at chills.
I doff silk; me his kisses shiver.

6. "The night exists as amateur darkness,
with stars as incandescent as April.
My love appears, nicely strident,
whistling impishly,
a poet's randy *Gravitas*:
Desire.

---

* A St. Petersburg, Russia (not Florida), cocktail.
** Song of Solomon 5:1 (KJV).

7. "Parley must always be tipsy,
if *Rapture*'s wanted, intended.
Our kisses decant *xérès*.*

8. "He's always as swaddling
as a spring-thaw river,
its rapids lapping—or wrapping—stones.

9. "He will entrench an artesian well,
running hot-and-cold,
tapping tropical, blood-quickening liquor;
nectar cool enough to prolong ardent coupling.

10. "(Hellish *Gaiety*: To starve and hunger
for deliberate, slow-paced,
well-spaced, but well-placed
kisses!)

11. "I opened unto my beloved;
my thighs jetted sweet perfumes
upon his fingers, his tongue.

12. "We were, us two, dreamers at work—
worked-up dreamers—
until daylight liquified the windows.

13. "His head matches supreme gold;
his locks are silky, and sunflower-blond;**
he's so transparently a blond.

14. "His eyes are dove's eyes—
sparkling gems set in milk.

* French: Sherry.
** Song of Solomon 5:11 (KJV).

15. "Every single night, we experience
a Year of *Poetry*, a Year of *Tequila*, a Year of *Zen*.

16. "(Write that sucker down in blood!)"

[Ottawa (Ontario) 24 *janvier* mmix
& Nantes (France) 27 *janvier* & 1 *février* mmix]

VI.

1. Sheba rocks the mic:
"Solomon dubs me the Warrior Goddess,
Itzpapalotl—
Obsidian Butterfly—
canonizes my 'sassy cool,'
my beauty conjoining coal and diamonds,
my ox-eyes,
my milk baths,
my black-lace (*Chanel*) 'skivvies,'
my aubergine-tint nail polish,
my perfume of ineffable blossoms,
my rollicking hips,
my plush, inviting tush,
my *Calvados*, *Cointreau*, and *Campari*....

2. "If I'm well-fucked,
I pulse and throb, surge like the sea!
No time for scaredy-cat *Delay*,
for namby-pamby *Delicacy*!"

3. Solomon stands at the podium:
"Thou art beautiful, O my love—
as Paradise, comely as the Avon,*
harrowing as God unleashing lightning.

4. "Has the vine flourished?
Are the apple trees yet a-flower?"

[Ottawa (Ontario) 24 *janvier* mmix
& Nantes (France) 27 *janvier* & 1 *février* mmix]

---

* Exit 19 & Exit 6, Highway 101, Nova Scotia.

VII.

1. Solomon speaketh *ancora*:
"How Bauhaus-sleek are thy shoeless feet,
O, Eve's daughter!
The fix of thy thighs is
the exquisite flexing of a compass—
the art of a sly drafter.

2. "Thy navel is like a round goblet,
replete with—
redolent of—
a Black Russian* cocktail:
Thy belly is like onyx,
plated with gold-leaf.**

3. "Thy nose mirrors the Look-Off—
that cliff—at Canning—
the Golan Heights of the Annapolis Valley—
that region fragrantly fecund with wine grapes.

4. "Thine head is like an earthly sun—
practically too stunning to gaze at—
and thy hair is unapologetic, black fire.

5. "Thy stature is like unto a Douglas Fir;
thy breasts equal virginal, untenuous pears.

6. "Thy mouth wells with wine—
or kisses;
and your tongue is so refined,
its tasty, distilled speech,
could rouse even the dead to shout!

---

* Cf. Pushkin embedded in Lolita.
** Song of Solomon 7:2 (KJV)

7. "Thine eyes constitute jet, velvet olives;
Thy open mouth resembles a watermelon,
bitten into, watering, pink as rosé.

8. "Won't our children repopulate Eden?

9. "Persian Ethiopian, Israelite of Cathay,
Egyptian *bourgeoise*—
thy *Beauty*'s like a torch—
arsonist-hurled into a haystack:
Seditious.

10. "Our *Love*, well,
il contiene scene a luci rosse—
the sour-sugar smell of lilacs,
the sweet compassionate pressure
of our *Conjunction.*
(No *Conjecture*!)"

11. Sheba grabs the talking stick:
"His *Desire* thrills me to pieces.*

12. "At dawn, let's take to the vineyard
to swig and swallow sumptuous wine,
and verify that the grapes are tender
and as bud-like as fledgling, girlish teats....

13. "Like this, your eyes caressing these words,
we'll fuck."

[Ottawa (Ontario) 24 *janvier* mmix
& Nantes (France) 27 *janvier* & 1 *février* mmix]

---

* Song of Solomon 7:10 (KJV).

VIII.

1. Sheba continues:
"Witness the gold, cold coin of moon.
Let lovers harvest spasmodic kisses."

2. Solomon responds:
"Thou art the endless regeneration of light."

3. Sheba addresses the choir:
"O Daughters of Jerusalem,
This permanent Preacher, thy King,
cranks out no mechanized sermons.*

4. "The dwarf-titted white woman:
What umbre hombre wants her?
To her *true* lover though,
her flat nubs seem towers
that can never be entirely circumferenced;
they seem like gold bowls,
brimming cream and raspberries, fountaining, relentless.

5. "Blossoms yield rum as much as perfume:
Lucrative saliva.

6. "A sunflower scent, all earth and nectar,
staggers us at sundown—
that medallion, melting.
First, the moon blanches, then goes grey,
next gold, then a copper finale.

7. "The butterflies stage pageants
and the bees launch fiestas.

---

* Song of Solomon 8:3 (KJV).

8. "*Love* is a hole that can never be whole.
Anyone who gives all to *Love*
must cease to exist.

9. "*Jealousy* is murderous.
True Love is as final as *Death* is never false."

[Ottawa (Ontario) 24 *janvier* mmix
& Nantes (France) 27 *janvier* & 1 *février* mmix]

Solomon's Gloss.

1. Aye, she's a Renaissance nymph
with a curvaceous *boongy*;*
she symbolizes Rubenesque *Realism*—
her no-nonsense *avoir-du-pois*.

2. Call her "*Venerandam*."**

3. A born belly-dancer, robust,
her copper breasts, alert to sunlight,
spring up, preening!

4. (When my lips touch and my tongue clutches,
her nipples couch mushroomy-rubbery,
taste strawberry tinctured.

5. Never sheds her coffee an ashen flavour!)

6. Sheba's caresses ain't merely epidermic,
but render bestial *Pleasure*,
trending celestial.

7. She pours Madeira and Muscat,
Lillet and Limoncello:
Liquor sets us a-totter—
and then tittering on our litters.

8. The drams of cheering *grappa* dwindle;
next the creaking, squeaking bed finds its groove;
and my incomparable darling
lies panting after our glittering *Harmony*,
the gleaming, capering foam at each crotch,
tapering off at our thighs.

---

* Bahamas: Ass.
** Venus, i.e., worthy of *Veneration*. Cf. Pound.

9. (If a man breathes,
he wants *Love.*
Period.)

10. A frisky maiden, there's the *frisson*
of molasses, its dark palpitations,
wherever she nests.

11. Then lilts the dark whine of a flute
as we tip up our flutes of dark wine.

12. That woman who wafts dizzying scents
and drafts smiles,
quaffs my kisses
unto the radiant, fulsome bliss that's dawn.

13. (Just as a breaker brooks no *Patience,*
but must collide with rock and smash
fixed *Strength* down to sand,
so are we in our *Mating.*)

14. Let us have burgundy leather sacks of red wine—
or that solar-butter *Oblivion*
that is Limoncello,
until we can couple again—
explicitly vehemently—
impromptu as April.

15. A bit of kissing, then a bout of fucking.
À bout de souffle....

[Puumala (Finland) 8 *août* mmxii]

THE BOOK OF AMOS

I.

1. A down-to-earth rancher, I, Amos,
now feel thrown out of *Time* itself,
being I'm God-commissioned
to write up Israel under King Uranus—
and Jerrybalm's regime—
two years afore the Big Quake.

2. I start here: God's gonna ignite
blackest sky with lightning;
thunder *Recrimination* pon Zion
et Jerusalem;
so the fraternity of shepherds gonna weep,
and Carmel's peak squashes flat as an eyelash.

3. Assyria's sins gonna loosen boulders
to bump down mountainsides
and swat citizens.

4. The *Peril*? They done ploughed under Gilead;
churned sand to burgundy muck.

So the king and princes of Benhaddock
will be pumped full of pig's blood, declares God,
so that *la manada*, that wolfish horde,
yowl death-rattles as their bowels dump diarrhea, scarlet.

5. Gangrene lightning will fork and knife Damascus;
Kir's shock-troops will bayonet funkily
every Syrian anus.

6. And due to Gaza's triple transgressions—
cramming innocents aboard slave ships,
clappin em all in chains,
and whippin em all the way to Babel,
blood will blaze through Gaza ceilings,
wallpaper, and floors.

7. Gaza's palaces will feel *Royal Horror*:
Extra *Violation* of the queen
and princesses—
while the city's smithereened and smoked.

8. And a broken sun will define the Philistines
as seepages of embers, ash;
they're all gonna hear, first-hand,
the monstrous *Cacophony* that's born of *Torment*.

9. Gaza's "dead-enders" are gonna
get used to gnawing boiled rats!

10. Tyrus has wrought triple wrongs
of *Slavery* and *Treason* and *Civil War*.

11. So, God's gonna hatchet Tyrus
into tangy, stinking, abbatoir tripe.
He'll strain through worms' maws,
bellies, and butt-holes,
and only then drip,
excretion by excretion,
into Hell.

12. God pledges that the children of Ammon—
who polluted Gilead's femmes
with imposter kiddies—bastoods—
to enact *Lebensraum Imperialism*—
will themselves discover their capacity
to endure unmitigated *Rapacity*.

13. So God's gonna topple Rabba—
hobble it with incessant flames,
so wolves guttle the bloody portions, rare,
of half-roasted survivors,
then crunch and snack on the blackened half.

14. And their kings and princes
will be kicked, once headless,
straight off Golgotha's guillotines.

[Montréal (Québec) 23 *mai* mmxviii]

II.

1. Because Mob charred the king of Baghdad—
seared him down to blackened lime,
and lit up—ignited—
with bullets
(bitter bellyfuls),
each of the *Padrino*'s sons,
God bades me contempt these grievances.

2. The Boss'll be skinned to his marrow,
die with desperate screeching.

Gutless will be all Mob judges—
all disemboweled alive,
hollering til they can't.

3. And God's gonna smack down Judah!
Its denizens—gentry and élite—
will starve, trying to eat sunlight.
They'll be so hungered!
But they'll gnaw their own children first.

4. God won't let Israel off easy!
Scarcely ashamed are Israelites
at divvying out ill-usage,
and/or judicially okaying *Torture*,
while turfing out black migrants,
turning back refugees.

5. Some Israelites intrigue to profit
off shoes stripped off peasants—
then resold;
and/or father and son(s) stud
the same sweat-shop laundress (or seamstress).

6. Too, some Israelites never have
their fill of that poison—
the *Vanity* of *Racialism*,
and so succumb to clubbing down
(and/or punching out) foreigners.

7. Yet, didn't God cast down the Libyans—
root, branch, leaf, and fruit?
(The Libyan *Baas* had a dishonourable *Encounter*:
Egg-heavy flies tented his *alfresco* corpse.)

8. So, God upbraids Israel:
"I salvaged yas outta Egypt;
directed ya 40 years cross dunes;
and prepared thee woven together dustjackets
(*The Odyssey, Ulysses, The Inferno,*
The Iliad, et cetera) for robes—
plus unadulterated jugs of *saké*
(rain moonlighting as white lightning)
to instill distilled *Enlightenment*.

9. "I giveth thy prophets a crusty vibrato,
so not one has to (or had to) mumble the *Truth*.

10. "But thou disbar My prophets
from speakin out in the speakeasy;
don't let em *cuéntalo** *Truth* abrasively,
unevasively.

11. "Therefore, O Israel, thy prisons
will swallow thine own chillun!
Unforgiving is My *Resolve*!

12. "Too many of yas will flounder,
clawing at dried up rivers,
to try to get sumpin to drink—
let alone fish to eat.

---

* Spanish: Tell (it).

13. "Dissatisfied that too few are distraught,
I'll force thee to feed on frost and swill snot.
Walls once stone-sturdy
will crumble like dry pie crust.

14. "What will languish in Israel is *Love*:
Because no one has an affinity for *Justice*!"

[Montréal (Québec) 24 *mai* mmxviii]

III.

1. I, Amos, caution thee, Israel,
God who freed our ancestors from Egypt,
is set to make us feel comfy in chains.

2. God doth feel cheated, Israel!
He hath shown us *Love* and *Protection*.
His *Reward*? Rats spitting bile.

3. "But how can two walk together—
except they be agreed?"*

4. Can a bride and bridegroom breed,
if one is castrated, or the other cast aside?

5. Will a bard drain lyrics
out an ink bottle,
if a public of singers be lacking?

6. *Problem* is, God hates the fetters and gags
that *Oppression* metes out,
silencing poets.

7. So God pledges that downpressors
will soon awake,
to sight dead kin all about,
piled atop and alongside.

8. Just as only ruby bits of skin and bone
may be picked outta jaws of a satiated lion,
so shall the survivors get borne away
on just a few camels.

---

* Cf. Amos 3:3 (KJV).

9. God Himself declares:
"I'll smite every unhallowed
household down to its dustmotes.
Each potentate will slop down Fentanyl—
rinse the poison round their mouths."

[Montréal (Québec) 24 *mai* mmxviii]

IV.

1. All ye bull-headed bigots,
joke, chortle, giggle, while you can!
God's gonna sink fishhooks down your gullets,
and tug at and haul so hard,
blood's gonna overcrowd thy lungs
and overrun thy bastards' eyes!

2. (Eyeglasses are gonna lack eyeballs.)

3. Ya mumble tenderly under floozies—
their dugs crammin your mouths
(true for Lesbos—
those "dirty tortillas," too.)

4. Ya cruise down the Sodom Road*
to stretch asshole skin,
feel it snap tight—
that glove-tight, gripping love—
clasping your rasping rods.
(Such expressively transgressive stuffing!)

5. And then ya wanna try to buy off God?
So ya turn robust cattle into steamy meat—
creamy soot—
every dawn.

6. And God doth direct me to tell ya,
"Be grateful for clean cities and clean teeth,
and provision of wine, cheese, fish, tomatoes,
olives, honey, Greek yogurt...."

---

* En route, Niagara Falls (ON) to/fro Buffalo (NY).

7. But yas still wanna fart about,
to pussyfoot regarding *The Decalogue*,
so long as you can slink into
and tinker about
in the brothel.

8. God's been busy chastisin already—
to correct and worry ya,
by droppin shards of lightnin
on one city,
but siccing wolves on another;
implementing *Inferno* in one city,
but implanting *Sharia* in another.

9. Though God has coffined Philistines
for circumcising clits and cutting off balls,
still you lust to spill into quim and/or drill butts.

10. But ain't God blasted thee with cancers?
Hasn't He caused thy walls of old, dead brick
to canker and founder?

11. Jeez, the stink of the cadavers
on the riverbanks and in the ghettos
is enough to make theologians
cut their own throats!

12. "Aye, I've massacred," sayeth God,
"thy pettifogging, filibustering philosophers;
and each pandering, philandering priest.*
Still, Israel don't pour out avid *Repentance*,
gravid in red-letter ink.

13. "I'm impatient with *Politesse*:
I enlist the *Diplomacy* of lightning bolts
and protocols of *Torture*."

---

* So rich in *Reading*, so rotten in *Thought*.

14. God hath set the alarm!
"Brace thyselves for a whacking
so intolerant
that blood,
flooding from your bodies,
taints seamily nigrescent
the River Jordan."

[Montréal (Québec) 24 *mai* mmxviii]

V.

1. God wags His head:
"Cripes, *My People*!
If thou wert a virgin,
ya'd be now on your backs,
perpetually tupped by one and all,
and then flopped onto your bellies
to jockey the anus into play.

2. "I's a-gonna chastise ya—
decimate ya nine times over
(= by 90%).
Shame!

3. "That's elementary *Biology*,
and/or *Algebra* 101.

4. "And don't pay Babylon *Obeisance*
and don't kowtow to Moloch!
Don't slide into bed with either!
Babylon is goin into *Slavery*,
and Moloch is already extinct.

5. "Must my *Judgment*
pour wormwood down your guts
and shower brimstone on thy skulls?

6. "Smarter it be to please thy God
who's crafted a billion stars,
effortlessly rouses the dead,
devises flood and deserts (ambidextrously),
summons on wine and/or tears,
jump-starts the sick so they up and breakdance....

7. "Keep on hurtin the deprived as ya do:
You'll plant vineyards, but spigot vinegar.
You'll build mansions, but bed down in dung.

8. "*Insanity*? To protest my prophets!
To abhor my poets!

9. "(Authoritatively do poets weep blues,
and the jails groan,
and finicky rats fidget, wheel, sniff.)

10. "Ya'll have to pay poetasters to abandon
their plagiarized, rancid verses,
and come into your households
and wail right along with ya.

11. "Ya'll be prayin for *Salvation*,
and I'll be tossin acid in thy faces!

12. "Y'all be like a man tryin to dodge
a (black) panther,
who sprawls before the pitiless jaws of a lion!

13. "When I judge yas, I don't allow
second thoughts any room.
Light smites ya as lightning!

14. "Ya know? I's tired of yer fake incense!
I can smell yer stink even as you pray.

15. "Cut up all the plump beasts ya got.
Ain't a-gonna change My mind!

16. "And quit tryin to sweet-talk
or serenade *Moi*!
Your fiddles sound vile as chalk squawks
and squeals cross blackboards.

17. "O, I'm gonna let *Judgment*
rush down as deluge,
and *Righteousness* swell up as a mighty flood.

18. "Why you gone barebacking for Moloch,
love splaying thyself to Mammon,
Israel?

19. "Beware! My *Denunciation*
ain't no metaphysical twaddle,
nor the promptings of hashish!"

[Niagara Falls (New York) 29 *mai* mmxviii]

VI.

1. Israel, look about ye *via* GPS:*
Whose borders are better than thine?
Whose impassable mountains exceed thine?

2. You say you stave off *Wrong*,
but you erect thy parliament upon excrement.

3. And yas dream up music based on
tossed bricks and broken glass.

4. Note: God will mow down dissidents.
God will gift Jerusalem to gangsters.

5. *Decimation* can run ten-fold!
100% of a household can disappear neath dirt.

6. Live rats will be hurled through nursery windows;
dramatic will run infants' blood-stains.

7. And bones will rot where the dying drop.
Or be burnt up.

8. And God's gonna smithereen mansions
and pulverize shacks!

9. Citizens will be as perforated as sponges;
the dead will be as soiled as their graves.

[FCO—Roma (Italia) 1 *juin* mmxviii]

*** Cf. Fareed Zakariah.**

VII.

1. Only God beefs up grasshoppers
to parade as belligerent dragons!

2. Grasshoppers devour grains,
but dragons burn up genealogies.

3. God sayeth, "It's *Judgment*, eh?
No hard feelings!

4. "Fires contend and the vicious
get incinerated.

5. "Scorched and stunted is every burnt-over district.

6. "*Pointlessness*? To question My prophecies!"

7. Amos perked up: "I'm just a shepherd—
was just-so—til I heard Thy voice, O God!
Following Thee, I've tried to head Israel."

8. God spoke this rebuke:
"Prophecy is mandatory!
Ya can't ever quit, Amos!

9. "But Israel's daughters are gonna be harlots,
anyway, and her sons are gonna be slaves."

10. Now, I saw God pick up a straight-rule,
a pencil, and a plumb-line.
He asked: "What have I here?"
I answered: "A plumb-line."

11. God now said, "Yo! *Correcto*!
I'll start buildin up Israel again,
once I'm done with castin her down.

12. "Only when I deem it just—
doth a rainbow displace lightning."

[FCO—Roma (Italia) 1 *juin* mmxviii]

VIII.

1. "Israel gotta quit plunderin have-nots,
purloinin from the poor!

2. "In other words, correct *Imbalance*!
The *Treasury* gotta equalize imbalances!

3. "Shall the destitute be sold for silverware?
Or for seed?

4. "I'm a-gonna have to redeem Israel—
despite Israelites!

5. "*Doom* should be wholesale, colossal,
as when that flood flushed out Egypt!

6. "I'm a-gonna sink the sun down a coal shaft!

7. "Feasts will be funerals; songs will be blues;
maggots will relish infants.

8. "Virgins and mercenaries gonna crawl,
bawlin for water,
sprawl to lap up spit from sand."

9. God affirmed: "It's a time for yowling!
A time to harvest cadavers!"

[FCO—Roma (Italia) 1 *juin* mmxviii]

IX.

1. I, Amos, heard God call up *Catastrophe*!
To smite doorways so hard
that the closure shatters,
the hinges come unhinged,
the doorway posts splinter;
and hypocrite worshippers
swan-dive their necks
neath tireless swords.

2. Those who try to climb mountains,
seeking *Refuge*,
will get crushed by avalanches
or topple into volcanic fire.

3. (Is that your fate, you killable people?
God ain't niggardly when it comes to nixing!)

4. Stowaways on ships can't survive!
Lightning will scour the deck—
and whales smash bottom timbers!

5. And many will be girded bout,
shackled down, by chains,
and be whipped right into their graves.

6. God's *Wrath* can even melt down citadels,
smelt em into mud and quicksand,
suffocate babes in the quagmire.

7. (Venice is gonna be washed-up Atlantis!)

8. Who are you to try to fool with God?
He directs droves of angels;
He trellises vineyards outta desert.

9. So, God asks profoundly, "O Israel,
shouldn't y'all be as pious and praiseworthy
as are the Ethiopians?
Didn't I rescue y'all from the Egyptians?
Gee whiz! Show some R-E-S-P-E-C-T, people!"

10. Fact is, God hardly tolerates the beautiful
and He loathes—positively—the ugly!

11. (Watch out, Babylon!
Criminals, watch out!
Quit your tiefin, cut-eye, cut-throat ways!*
You've been caught!)

12. Here's the good news:
God's gonna sift out—
the few Righteous who are rubies.

13. But Evildoers will not predominate,
won't lord it over the saintly.
Judgment'll position em a sewer.

14. On the Day of Judgment,
the scythe will outpace the plough.

15. Only after this seething has terminated,
will God repair the Tabernacle of David,
and revive current ruins in *Architecture*
that reproduce *bel canto* as marble.

16. Then, righteous Israelis will
rehabilitate rubble;
let marble sanctify and beautify cities;
while fields, once again set to fructify,
nourish vineyards that flourish grapes
that barefoot, Calabrese maidens stamp and stomp—
until vintners overflow
with *Manischewitz* Concorde wine.

[Tropea (Italia) 2 *juin* mmxviii]

* Cf. Jeremiah 11:11.

FRAGMENTS III

I—*Experience.*

1. *History* is nothing like what is reported.
(Hard to drain light from mud.)

2. Trumpets don't usher in Heaven.

3. *Truth* blinds, but *Deceit* dazzles.

4. Flames that don't gleam are smoke.

5. Manure concocts gardens:
Eden flowers from the cesspool.

6. Fine wine refines urine.

7. Politics is PREJUDICE.

8. Behind these black letters?
White bone, invisible breath.

9. Bread is eternal.
But your words?

[Zurich (Switzerland) 14 *septembre* mmxi]

II — *Experience.*[*]

1. Spurn the spice-tongued adulteress;
her lips slip cinnamon'd venom.

2. Yield to her clutch,
and her nails open your back.

3. Her cobra kiss stings, transfixes,
and as soon as her coils snare you,
your mind contracts,
your limbs jelly
(due to *Rapture* that trepans the brain);
and once you're paralyzed,
her insidious kindred flock,
to bash your face with stones.

4. Listen: As soon as they hear you snore—
all drunk and drivelling—
the slut's brethren bandits,
secreted in closets or behind drapes,
will rush to your bed
and crush your skull,
while your bowels gush feces and blood.

5. You enter her,
and you're a corpse pitched down a sewer.

6. Sir, best keep to your own home,
leap only into your own bed,
sleep only with thy satisfying wife.

[**Edmonton (Alberta) 27** ***avril*** **mmxiii**]

---

* Cf. Proverbs 5 (KJV).

Ezekiel XXV.

1. The Lord decreed this *fatwā*,
this killing spree:
"I hate to have to do it,
but it's time to destroy the Ammonites.

2. "Didn't they hooray when My Temple was soiled,
hooray to see Israelites ligatured* or coffled?
Didn't they ululate gleefully
when Israel's palm trees got chopped down,
the vineyards ripped up?

3. "Scold em, 'Here's the payback:
Y'all gonna be ruled by Huns—
who're gonna ride all thy females,
and feast on your fruits and ruin it
through their bowels,
and slop and slurp all your wine,
then piss it in thy sons' faces.

4. 'The fate of Rabba? To be a pig sty.
Every Ammonite, dying, will see
palaces become stables.

5. 'Thy comeuppance is thy downfall.

6. 'Thus, I now field archers against thee,
camel-back cavalry against thee,
catapults against thee,
and torches against thee:
You's gonna get scrubbed right off the map!

* Strangled.

7. 'Ditto for all anti-Israel propagandists!
They'll be beaten down by biblical injunctions—
whacked—wrecked—by damnations.

8. 'Each foe will spring enough blood to brim a tub,
and dogs will leave off tearing the cadaver
to dip their tongues in the pool.

9. 'Huns are gonna plough
Ammonite women,
plough under Ammonite men,
and use Ammonite boys—sons—as the ploughs.

10. 'Nor is anyone gonna remember Mob
once it becomes an open latrine.

11. 'Nor will Edom escape My *Wrath*!
The harvests will net dust
and their cities will cough up smoke.

12. 'Edomites and Edomite beasts will perish
just like Sodomites and Sodomite beasts.

13. 'Edomites will be spitefully bloodied.
But first they'll be pissed upon, shat upon.

14. 'Philistines must feel anew My *Hatred*!
(Anyone who don't vamoose
is gonna be porcupined with arrows!)

15. 'All Philistines must be liquidated—
even that rump group,
crouched along the coast:
To be so infected with *Horror*,
no poet can wax medicinal!

16. 'I hope they have a hunch
of how awful their corpses will reek.

17. 'I'll repurpose em as bones trod into mud!

18. 'And I will wreak great *Vengeance* upon em
with furious rebukes,
and they shall know that I am the Lord,
when I lay My *Vengeance* upon em,
all the fathers and all the sons of evil men.*

19. 'I'll disregard *Decorum*!
Disheartening will be My acts—
those of a scrupulous Bigot.'"

[YHZ—Enfield (Nova Scotia) 3 *novembre* mmxviii]

* Cf. Ezekiel 25: 17 (KJV) & Q. Tarantino.

Daniel V.

1. King Belshazzar clapped forth
331 barrels of Shiraz,
had em tapped,
to dizzy 900 enophiles, nobles
(by rank if not by nature).

2. But no wine could sluice into flutes
or slosh into goblets
until the king had trundled to him
gold and silver vessels
tiefed *ex* Jerusalem's Temple.

3. His Majesty then distributed
the looted booty,
so that he, his concubines, brats, and bastoods,
could all set their sleazy, idol-kissing lips
to the sacred, precious-metal relics.

4. As the royals—plus courtesans
and afterclaps—
slurped the spilling scarlet,
out burped praising phrases
for deaf-dumb-blind-and-paralyzed "gods"—
pimped-out clay, wood, stone, and metal.

5. The merriment—the orgiastic frolics—
fostered wine-blurred eyes
and wine-slurred tongues;
so few of the revellers noticed, at first—
distinctly disembodied and afloat in mid-air—
a mahogany hand extend an index finger,
and begin to incarnate letters, incarnadine,
blazing the ornate, creamy plaster,
directly opposite the king's throne.

6. Once cognizant of the violent vision,
party-goers' shouts ebbed to whispers;
and these aristocrats divided helter-skelter—
to grant His Majesty a view-plane
of the wall-fingerpainting hand,
moving right to left,
carving smoking and scarlet glyphs
indelibly into plaster.

7. (Gothic letters these were; not curlicues:
Everybody's *Revelry* got muddled
due to the red-meat characters mottling the wall.)

8. Watching the back of that brassy hand
graffiti the back wall,
the king, disconcerted, writhed in his throne,
while his First Lady, the Queen,
puked Shiraz o'er her see-through, white-silk gown,
her throat sewage clarifying—
while purpling—
her quivering, pasty dugs.

9. Desperate to comprehend such spirited hocus-pocus,
the king had rounded up all Chaldean conjurers
and Babylonian scholars
and Gypsy soothsayers,
to demand they divulge to him
the rationale for this repellent tattoo.

10. King Belshazzar swore,
"Explicate this statement,
and you tote away boundless gold coins,
get dubbed an Adjunct Prince,
and preen suavely in august, purple robes."

11. Esteemed whizzes and tenured profs cussed
each other out,
dissed each other,
but none could figure out the phrase.

12. Now, the First Lady fled the banquet hall—
to cleanse her humiliating self-pollution;
but after minions had scoured the throne,
a secondary queen now arrived,
and advised King Belshazzar,
"Take heart: Daniel bests
all diviners and doctorates.
He turns enigmas into *Wisdom*,
dreams into blueprints."

13. Heeding his clean, articulate, and bright vice-queen,*
King Belshazzar had Daniel hauled from prison,
his shackles sprung,
and a gag tugged out the prophet's mouth.

14. "I know you're one of the Judaic captives—
that King Nebuchadnezzar carted to this kingdom.
Queen Maynaykah a-vouches your Lit-Crit skills.

15. "So, do interpret these ghastly,
scarlet characters bleeding the back wall.

16. "Succeed at this commission,
and your gag becomes a gold chain (24 kt);
your rags become purple robes;
and you upgrade into a prince."

17. "I can't be bought," stated flatly Daniel.
"But I'll clarify the crimson inscription
branding your eyes and scorching your heart.

18. "It's all really elementary:
Thy father, King Nebuchadnezzar, ruled
with God-granted *Authority*
and sword-enforced *Wisdom*.

* Cf. Biden re: Obama.

19. "Thus, the wretched ate with the moneyed,
gold puffed the public purse,
vineyards overgrew jails,
and wine overthrew jailers.

20. "But King Nebuchadnezzar imagined
these blessings were his doing,
and he waxed idolatrous, lecherous,
piratical, and tyrannical.

21. "So God deposed his fat-ass—
and the drooping rat-tail moustache
dorking his porky-hoggish face;
drove him to bed down beside donkeys,
munch grass with cows,
and lap up dew.
His Majesty became a laughing-stock,
a limping ruin.

22. "Until he humbled down, hollered *Contrition*,
affirmed the God of Israel as supreme,
and crushed, burnt up, or buried all idols.

23. "Then Nebuchadnezzar regained the throne.

24. "But you, King Belshazzar, you ain't followed suit.
Instead, you have the audacity to imbibe wine
from gold and silver vessels tiefed from God's Temple,
and you've licensed cocottes and their broods
to orgy in this *Blasphemy*.

25. "Worse, you've reactivated idol worship.

26. "So God has set His hand against thee.
This scripture—'MENEE, MENEE, TEKEEL,
UPHARSIN'—
means this:

27. "'MENEE'= God's sized up your kingdom
and will downsize it to pebbles and dust.

28. "'TEKEEL'= You've been weighed
in the scales and found false—
being fool's gold, not gold.

29. "'PEREES'—Your kingdom will be split
between the Medes and Persians."

30. King Belshazzar shut his hands over his ears;
shouted, "*Basta*!"
But he kept his pledge to uplift Daniel.

31. His *Statecraft* was in vain.
The king died like Caligula, like Gregor Samsa,
crushed under his own bodyguards' shields;
smacked down and smushed,
so his own heart was sundered
by his own splintered bones
and his yolk squirted and squeezed out
his fractured egghead.

32. He died that same night that Daniel
revealed the *Judgment*.

33. Immediately, Darius the Mede
spearheaded a *coup d'état*—
headhunting himself Monarch—
at the King Lear age of 70.

[Halifax (Nova Scotia) 16 & 17 *mars* mmxix]

Daniel VI.

1. A dragon—of all things—
dragooned all Babylonian worship.

2. Commanded to kneel to the monster,
Daniel instead baked pitch, tallow, and hair
into johnnycakes that he dished out
to the fire-jawed serpent,
making sure to place himself
just out of reach
of the animal's blazing breath.

3. The creature gobbled, gobbled,
burped, and gobbled, gobbled, burped,
until it was groaning
and clawing its own belly,
and then its guts burst,
popped like a balloon:
Fiery, jellied blobs—
primeval napalm—
splattered everywhichway,
sparking grassfires.

4. Fed up with seeing their gods degraded,
defanged, disowned, dissed,
the royal theologians insisted
that the king hand Daniel over
to their malicious mercies.

5. (*Sin* breeds *Deceit*; *Wrath* engineers schemes.)

6. Fearing his own C-section-style demise,
the king had Daniel shackled,
and the clerics thrust him into a lion's den.

7. Though the lion snacked steadily
on a diet of human "pig-meat,"
the critter merely purred at Daniel;
its claws retracted into its paws.

8. After a week in the lion cage,
the cheery Daniel was sprung;
but, soon as the barred door winched up,
the lion lunged, trouncing jailers
and clerics—
dipping its fangs into shrieks,
then chompin into clawed-out guts.

9. Daniel had to step over torn bits
of theologians—
those nightmarish jesters—
half-eaten, partly gnawed, all bloody
(raw bodies gone blubbery),
to bow to the king,
ecstatic that his rivals were dead,
and eager now to testify
that Daniel's God got no equal.

10. (*Capiche*?!!)

11. Idolaters cannot praise God, cannot pray to God.
They're already dead, already dirt.

12. (The Sphinx is a shaggy Moloch on all fours,
and its heart is not *Solemnity*, but *Savagery*.)

[Tropea (Italia) 20 *juin* mmxvii]

THE BOOK OF NAHUM

I.

1. God's gonna obliterate Nineveh
(or Babylon, same difference):
I'm deputized to broadcast this *Truth*!*
God's not deceived, but peeved and aggrieved.

2. Never are the wicked acquitted.
God tosses em bout in a whirlwind;
flattens their faces into stepping-stones.

3. He boils off or dries up oceans:
Their salt resembles mountains of snow.

4. Hills tremble down to pebbles;
the earth totters on its axis.

5. Which potentate can't be cast down
and his princes and princesses
rendered blood stains in the streets?

6. God's *Indignation* hurls back spears—
boomerangs em back at adversaries.

7. Overwhelming flood and overflowing fire
hollow out palace and hovel.
Even the dead drift—or char, roofless and naked.

8. Snarled like cooked spaghetti—
addled like a jumbled up jigsaw puzzle—
such enemies end as mush, a mishmash.

---

* Nahum. Cf. Nahum—Nattt—Moziah Shaka. Cf. Nahum Chandler.

9. All malefactors become rubbish
and/or compost.
Gladly does God dig their graves, for they're vile.

[Nassau (The Bahamas) 23 *mars* mmxix]

II.

1. Man (v.) barricades! Fortify flanks! Brick (v.) walls!
Do whatever seems fit!
Still, Nineveh will be cacti and rattlesnakes!

2. Those who've bled and bloodied Israel,
who've cut down and cast grape vines into fire,
must needs be curtailed.

3. Liquid crimson will stream and splash
our Judaic Army's shields.
Blood will streak and strafe our soldiery.

4. We'll pull our swords out of broken guts;
our chariots will bump crooked over a dump
of corpses.

5. Our chariots'll stumble o'er, stamp down, the dead;
our horses' hooves mash and mincemeat bellies;
our troops' torches will jig like lightning
as they zigzag among cadavers,
stooping to lop off wedding rings.

6. Strategic faggots
and Molotov cocktails (tactical)
will inflame wood and scorch marble.

7. Having played losing generals, aristocrats
will stagger among their mansioned ruins,
then pop themselves upon their own swords.

8. Thanks to catapulted boulders,
a dam gets battered to smithereens;
it shatters, and the palace gets washed out.

9. Princes and princesses float a ways,
til their robes drag em down,
mire em fast in slime and silt,
and their hair swims with algae.

10. Nineveh's queen is shackled down,
then forced to tackle hammered in dildos.

11. Ragged in silk, rickety in step,
her maids bumble after,
tripping o'er the blood-dripping dying.
Their voices throb with sobs—
as if their teats house doves.

12. Once an oasis where all flocked,
to try its sweet, cleansing waters,
Nineveh is despicable now—
due to its soot and stench.

13. When The Last Poets cry, "Halt,"
no thoughtful person does,
but flees.

14. God prods Israel to sack Nineveh:
"Grab the gold, seize the silver!
Despoil this city of all its spoils!"

15. Desolate is Nineveh.
Its palsied survivors limp, bleed, and blanch.

16. Although they starve, still they vomit.

17. The lions of Nineveh? Destroyed!
The pride's king is strewn in pieces;
his lionesses are chopped to bits;
maggots snack upon the cubs.

18. "Behold, I'm anti-Nineveh," roars God!
"Kindling are their chariots; corpses are their royals.
I shit thee not," He sayeth,
spitting flame down palm trees!

[Nassau (The Bahamas) 23 *mars* mmxix]

III.

1. Woe to that crap-encrusted city!
Capital of *Gossip* as *Gospel*;
and whose *Economy*'s pure *Thuggery*.

2. Whips slap down sunlight;
stuffed hearses cackle over stones.
Lobbying for "free treats,"
cops and clerics bawl at bawds.

3. Horsemen can't gallop easily here:
al fresco cadavers ain't proper pavement.
They're just too full of pitfalls—
their squashed, squishy guts;
their bellies gone potholes.

4. What doomed the city?
Call girls, seers, and politicos:
A sordid plague!

5. Aggrieved, God stirred tempests
that blew floozies' skirts over their faces,
exposing impudent orifices.

6. Abominable dirt, indomitable filth,
buried Nineveh (a.k.a. Washington):
The city vanished under its own trash.

7. No one's gonna wanna live in Nineveh, eh?
Not even Job would plunk down
atop this dung heap
and coloratura up blues—
indigo, lapis lazuli, sapphire, turquoise.

8. No better than Sodom and Gomorrah,
Washington is likewise to be eradicated.

9. Note: Once earth-shaking empires,
both Egypt and Ethiopia are mere statelets now.

10. Their sons die in butcheries,
their daughters thrive in brothels;
their kings are tossed onto middens;
their queens spew out half-breeds.

11. *Might as well get supefyingly drunk*,
wager some,
figuring there's no other refuge.

12. Washington's towers prove as weak
as sodden toilet paper—
or a virgin in a sadist's bed.
A threat of arrows, a gust or breeze,
and they quiver like figs,
shaking down into a waiting mouth;
they fall open like a woman,
splayed before a blade.

13. Nineveh's men are as sackable as nymphos:
Down they sprawl! On their backs or bellies!
Shameless sycophants!

14. To lay up water, to sandbag walls:
All is pointless.

15. Fire dries up wells and liquidates walls:
Flames surge as scourging as locusts.

16. If only Nineveh's generals had been
as effective at pillaging
as were her M.B.A-schooled capitalists!

17. No, they were more like grasshoppers:
Happy to clump and camp in foliage,
but to scatter everywhichway
at first hiss of threat.

18. Recall now Assyria's humbled prez:
His executed nobles,
his exiled people—
wandering cross mountainsides,
eating grass wherever goats have not gone.

19. Washington is fully a nullity now.
And not even hyenas chuckle.

[Nassau (The Bahamas) 23 *mars* mmxix]

THE BOOK OF ENOCH

INTRODUCTORY

Beauty is difficult....
—Ezra Pound, Canto LXXIV

PECULIAR parallel that it is, it was only when Christian Abolitonism (Anti-African-Slavery) triumphed, that Heaven recuperated the work of an Ethiopian Milton, a theological patriarch—akin to honoured Augustine out of Africa, whose antediluvian edification of once-fossil mysteries, prepares the way for the apostolic canonists. This present author doth hold that the Book of Enoch the Prophet, this Ethiopic canon, yields astonishing illumination of the true origins of the oft-threatened, punishing flames of Divine *Retribution* that the damned should endure for aeons, quite expressive of Eternity. ("To burn forever" is a homely but honest phrase, and it must be perused with just dread, for Enoch envisions hellfire as a literal and awful phenomenon, devoid of any of the grace of mere suggestion or of the mitigating subtleties of actual allegory. No, his speech is black as ink, as indelible as coal smudges on cotton, and as hard and blinding as diamonds.)

Uncanonical apologists would question the pious—if primitive—scholars who accept Enoch as a credible Evangelist, divulging the secrets of Divinity. But they know that centuries constitute mere sighs amid the exhalation of *Prophecy*, that the veracity of Enoch's visions cannot be weighed against the fantasies of Olympian pagans, that ecclesiastical spirits cannot be held in theological fetters, and that the unfolding *Majesty* of Revelation will perfect the foreshadowing of the Apostles that is Enoch's exegesis of *Scripture*.

Let neither Oxford nor Rome cast further doubt on the *Sanctity* of this premonitory, Christian text, whose terrors of Hell and Apocalypse frighten into *Salvation* and *Rectitude* all those sinners whose eyes find these letters or whose ears hear their *Götterdämmerung* accent. (Note: *Garamond* typeface pleases modern classicists; *Fournier* typeface urges revolution.)

I end positively: It is also Enoch, the Ethiopian Hebrew, who closes out the Old Testament with the promise that Believers in The Messiah will savour *Uninterrupted Life*, aeons upon further innumerable aeons, as their meet *Reward* for surviving this world's unmitigated *Woe.*

THE EDITOR

[Cable Beach (The Bahamas) 28 *mai* mmxii]

I.

1. The end is *Horror*:
Mountains melt in slides of lava and mud;
fires char jungle to desert.

2. So much blood will flood the Earth,
it'll tilt back,
wobbling on its axis.

3. Monarchs, millionaires, military monsters,
traders, traitors,
will be penned in a valley brimmed—
rimmed—with flame.

4. They'll be banded with iron fetters so tight,
the metal itself will bleed.

5. Next, they'll face stones, hurled,
battering em to pudding.

6. Satan's fine-tooled these tortures.

7. That's dandy, for these men were his henchmen,
his prime ministers,
his dud-messiahs implementing tricks-as-miracles.

8. Rocks striking them, then heaping at their feet,
crush these malefactors,
or they are driven into the muck-belched fire
ringing their prison,
to burn, howling, until their throats turn to ash.

9. Their pain will be so ugly that even God will say,
"This *Genocide* is awful."

10. But their chastisements cannot end
until each *Terror* has been expressed
to the exact, dictated letter,
down to the complete number of offenders.

11. See? Their infractions stink too bad.
They poison the air, disrupting perfume.

12. They do too many abominations to forgive.

13. So, God must stone em with rocks sabre-edged
or hammer-blunt, but steadily malicious.

14. Or God excites the wicked to slay each other
in an interminable *Extermination*.

15. I, Enoch—the Ethiope, wield an ice-cold voice,
but yield branding, scorching *Prophecy*.

16. Shoot! I tell you, even luminaries—
stars and starlets—
will be burned and/or crushed and/or slain
in mutual massacres.

17. Their world reeks of *Carnality*,
and they perfect every species of *Crime*.

18. But the Lord is holy, holy, holy,
and those who love Him must be holy too—

or else doomed, dead, and damned....
Sorry.

(Not really.)

[Montréal (Québec) 14 *juin* mmxii]

II.

1. Papyrus boasts cinnamon-scent ink.
(*Scripture* is any seductive script.)

2. But, I, Enoch, carve out verses of *Indignation*
and *Agitation*. Ugly, really.

3. That's my commission; that's how it is.
I letter out ledgers of *Wrath*.

4. I transcribe the tantrums of thunder,
drummin *Consternation* down pon earth.

5. I overhear the secrets of lightning and *Splendour*.
I witness every species of *Splendour* and *Gloom*.

6. My tongue is elementary flesh,
but it fleshes out *Wisdom*.

7. Listen good: Th'Elect must back Th'Elect.
The Robe of *Life* befits only Th'Elect.

8. (Their clothing is eternally, startlingly white.
Their glory is non-stop.
Their brilliant bodies spurn the grave's dirt.)

9. You whisper your wonder; but I respond:
There's a secret to *Mercy*;
there's a subtlety to *Righteousness*.

10. (No one compasses the extremities of Heaven,
or the gaudy *Extremism* of God.
Stupidos, take heed!)

11. Blessedly, Th'Elect got no tonnage of crimes
weighin em down.

12. Th'Elect ain't got no *Crimes*!
(You can't say the same?)

13. Sinners rot with sinners.
Period.

14. Mark: God be scrupulous in computing
Blame or *Blessing*.

15. (Don't talk of fraud if you find your sick soul
mired in hurtful, searing fire.)

16. I can spy Paradise!

17. (In Paradise, one tally of grapes
yields ten gallons of *Pleasure*.*)

18. Consume that red wine from Cana;
grapes fresh pressed:
Here's *Divinity* manifest.

19. Lookit:
Splendour births splendour.

[Montréal (Québec) 14 *juin* mmxii]

* A manifest error of an editor.

以诺书第二章: *1–19*

莎草纸飘溢肉桂香的油墨味。
(经文是诱人的脚本。)

但是, 我, 以诺, 刻写出激愤和煽动
的诗句。丑陋, 真的。

那是我的佣金; 那是来龙去脉。
我书写愤怒的分类帐。

我录制雷的咆哮,
雷鼓声惊愕大地。

我窃听到闪电和辉煌的秘密。
我见证每一片绚丽和愁云。

我口舌原始纯朴,
却吐出智慧。

听好: 选民必须拥戴选民
生命的长袍只适宜选民。

(他们的衣衫是永远雪白的。
他们的荣耀永不停止。
他们美好的躯体鄙视坟墓的污垢。)

你耳语你的奇迹; 但我回应:
仁慈有方。
正义有道。

(没有人指靠天堂边际,
或上帝花哨嘘头。
傻瓜, 留意!)

幸好, 选民没有罪恶
拖累他们。

选民没有任何罪恶!
（你无法也这么说吧?）

罪恶者同罪恶者一起腐烂。
终结。

记住: 上帝在一丝不苟地计算
过失或祝福。

（不要谈论欺诈, 如果你发现你病态的灵魂
深陷在伤人的烈焰里。）

我可以窥视天堂!

（在天堂, 一单位的葡萄
产生十加仑的快乐.）

大口喝来自卡纳的红葡萄酒, 葡萄鲜榨:
这里是神性表现。

看:
辉煌诞生辉煌。

[蒙特利尔（魁北克）6月14日 2012]

Chinese translation by Anna Yin.

III.

1. April ladles out snow.
Nisan pisses rain.

2. April burgeons blossoms.
Nisan nudges buds into bloom.

3. Clouds mist down invigorating dew:
Encore et encore. Up springs the new.

4. Trees flaunt fragrance, then fruit.
Down shoot plums: *Pleasure* at the root.

5. *Dumbkopf*, don't act stupefied!
Where else, save God, does the wind abide?

6. (The wind: A consummate combo
of breathings, irrepressibly akimbo.)

7. The sun and moon dictate the calendar:
Luminous is every contrary star.

8. (Notice:
Moonlight is sunlight at 1/7.*)

9. Beware: The Tree of Knowledge never wilts;
It nourishes all our sweetest guilts.

10. Its taste surpasses Jezebel's perfumes:
Unholy *Lust* for it wholly consumes.

---

* Another error.

11. Refusenik, eye Heaven's undiluted light
(that never, ever diminished light)!

12. *Splendour* issues from the stars,
and so prefers only *Splendour.*

[Montréal (Québec) 14 *juin* mmxii]

IV.

1. God sculpted wenches way too well:
Thus, even misogynistic angels fell.

2. These gargoyles tread down their harpies,
intermingled—to whelp freaks—
half-savages lusting for snacker or blood.

3. Th'illicit dogs even eat up their own mothers,
starting at crotch and ending at cap.

4. Tutored in the know-how of killing,
the backward mongrels bred a race of Calibans.

5. Just by their breathing,
the angels' carnal progeny
bruise grass,
blast orchards to dust.

6. Bitches who twine with the septic angels,
will get spitted on iron stakes,
riveted from anus to sinus,
then pillared in flames.

7. Astonished and irritated to be fettered,
sobbing (or not),
pleading (or not),
the wicked will be exhibited embarrassingly
while their genitals are *righteously* carved out,
jaggedly clean,
right down to the pelvis bone.

8. Drat!
Y'all are so malicious, all I can do is weep!

Merde!

Teardrop after teardrop—like rain.

[Montréal (Québec) 14–15 *juin* mmxii]

V.

1. *J**udgment* charters my charcoal strokes.

2. Th'Evil council each other
to be crafty at *Evil*.

3. Some sup on mash and ice water—
to concoct seditious liquors.

4. Others want to be saints,
but love gold more.

5. (Gold can't save ya,
no matter how much gold ya save.)

6. Some of you preside—pray—over
tables pouring wine, wit, *Enlightenment*....
But you're doomed, anyhow.

7. Some twits tog up flamboyant,
strut about like peacocks.
Maggots'll admire em.

8. When irksome God butchers y'all,
your blood will swamp the Pyramids.

9. You'll lie in shadows, wearing your own blood.

10. Or you'll burn in an abyss so stuffed with flame,
it mirrors a glittering mountain.

11. (The English Church ain't always
ethical or logical.)*

---

* A mysterious passage of dubious origin.

12. All your war tools
gonna be junk.

13. All your incested gargoyles will be so crippled,
docs will deliver em straight into toilets:
Moms will shit their spawn right into latrines.

14. Fire will claim your cloth, pirates your coin,
and rats your corn.

15. Towers will be smacked down.

16. Demagogues will be toppled into ditches.

17. Their own sabres will disembowel *Mafiosi*.

18. Wild beasts will tear up the very corpses
of the iniquitous. (*No hiding place*!)

19. Kings will be gutted; captains will drown.

20. *Revolt* and *Treason* will toss the heedless out—
headless.

21. (Implode a tower; torch a parliament:
That is how *Purgation* succeeds.)

22. God will break the very teeth in backsliders' jaws.

23. A web of iron will bind the rebel-angels,
half-serpent, writhing.

24. I witness a crystal citadel
encased by unceasing holocaust.

[**Montréal (Québec) 16 *juin* mmxii**]

VI.

1. Got yanked up—I—into purifying air.

2. God's Robe is as blinding as ten suns.
His Hair defines radiant snow.

3. Fiery copper is His Face;
Ebon like me.

4. His *Aspect* is so handsome and awesome,
once-strayed sheep stampede back to the fold.

5. The Lord's Countenance is so commanding,
in His Presence, wolves flee from sheep.

6. When Philistine dogs harassed His Flock,
He raised up a Ram that butted em down,
killing all that didn't scatter.

7. (Even wrong-way shepherds
will go snout-first into fire!

8. Ditto for disobedient sheep:
They get burnt up to bones and char.

9. Good sheep thrive; stay pure as new snow.

10. Lost sheep glut wolves' bellies.
They get stripped clean to their skeletons.
And eagles gang to peck out their eyes,
then devour em whole—skin, fat, muscle.)

11. A ceaseless fire plays, illuminating
The Luminaries of Heaven.

12. Every strain of Light proclaims His Name.

13. He's The Eternal One—
who plants you in your grave.

Where you (*sinners*) belong.

[Niagara Falls (New York) 30 *juin* mmxii]

VII.

1. The Tablet of Heaven give out true news.
That's all I speak.

2. (Book-learnin? Crookeds *Truth.*)

3. I seen seven mountains
shinin gold and silver—
stacked one atop the other—
crumple down into lava and smoke,
and a flood of soot.

4. Hell! Earth was shakin;
no one could stand it.

5. A star plummets,
turns canine, grows fangs,
swallows down strayed sheep.

6. Now heaven quakes:
Every angel and saint—
the 100,000 top-dogs—
gotta shiver.

7. Concussions tremble and cripple the atmosphere.

8. God must wanna wreck the whole world!
I plead with Him to spare up a "Remnant."

9. I gotta beg concrete-hard,
cos God kills foully everyone
foulin up The Commandments:

10. "Don't erect no statues
of clay, lead, silver, or tin:
Just don't.

"Don't smelt no gods!"

(*Etc.*)

11. The angel of *Abortion*'s gonna feel sorry for his self;
he gonna holler.

12. The angel who deceived Eve,
and then plied mankind with weaponry
(thus teaching *Seduction* and *Slaughter*),
is gonna feel some *Inquisition* torture
(make him stab out his heart).

13. The angel, *Penemue*, who schooled all
in saccharine words, blarney—bumf—
and the false mirrors of paper and ink,
will weep tears that cut into his cheeks
so blood streaks down his chin.

14. Come *Judgment*, the moon won't wax
or wane timely;
pure downpour will wash out harvests.

15. Pus will piss down.

16. Cry all ya want!
Here's the deal:

17. Water leaps down;
deserts lap it up—at first.

18. Wet *Turbulence* wrecks gardens;
it don't nurture flowers.

19. North winds shed hail, rain, frost.
Dew-saturated dust turns to clay.

20. Irate winds rap bells, clap chimes,
snap curtains cross windows.

21. Cataracts thunder, inundating cities.
Dark water erases villages.

22. Unfathomable rain downs;
foundations flounder—
houses float free, corpses bob, coast.

23. The drowned bloat, float:
Each face turns a maggot boat.

24. Luckily, Lament and spouse beget Noah:
When his beautiful eyes open,
light bathes all of *Creation*.

25. God endorses Noah:
"Your lot do no *Crime*;
y'all can breathe air."

26. Thus, that one boat wafts, but elephants,
giraffes, camels, asses, and horses drown deep.

27. When the Flood dries, land appears.

28. The zoo ship beaches, then light reaches down.

29. Soon, just as in Genesis I,
beasts and birds usher forth beasts and birds.

30. Busily multiplying (again) are lions, tigers,
wolves, dogs, wild boars, piranha, *et cetera*.

31. But dolts get busy performin
fresh *Crime* and *Oppression*.

32. Despite the unimaginable *Slaughter* that be the Flood,
Iniquity flowers anew.

33. In this Book of Enoch, all the described
who are destroyed,
are destroyed just as described.

34. Bitch, beseech, and bawl:
No asylum, *anywhere*!

35. *Watch out*!

[Niagara Falls (New York) 30 *juin* mmxii]

APOCRYPHAL
DEUTEROCANONICAL

THE WISDOM OF SOLOMON

I.

1. Refrain from unspecific *Fret* and *Complaint*;
do not begrime—with *Slander*—the innocent.

2. Beware noxious, murderous bile—
Calumny, unsubstantiated charges....

3. Better a white-lie-hissing silver tongue
than a toad's disease-spitting black tongue,
besmirching, befouling, oxygen itself.

4. For *Death* is hateful to God!
It's a thesauraus of worms:
Vers libre ("free worms"),
grave worms, fly worms, sunflower worms!

5. God desireth *Generation*, *Fertility*, *Health*, *Joy*:
A man, jigging in a woman,
dowsing his johnson deep in her well.

6. (The world? An inventory of beauties!
An anatomy of beauties!)

7. Wanna explicate the heart?
Lust ain't no tangent,
and *Lechery* is germane!

8. No Church, hating *Fucking*, is true.

[Ottawa (Ontario) 7 *février* mmxii]

II.

1. Idiots posit that because the dead stay dead,
Life is smoke:
Once the fire's snuffed,
it's gone, and no trace remains.

2. All edifices are scheduled to be ruins.

3. Our flesh is mist; our bones are slime.

4. The idiot preacheth, "Our beings are shadows.
Once dumped in the earth, we vanish forevermore.

5. "So let us swallow wine wafting rose petals;
take minxes for *Sport* and maids for *Progeny.*

6. "Best to prove nimble at *Fornication*,
predatorial at *Fucking.*

7. "Pop monsters outta traduced,
trod-down virgins.
Their turmoil is more like hatching
than giving birth!

8. "(Be sorry to avoid *Adultery*
or to see quarrels quelled.)

9. "Batter the bedridden and giggle while they howl.

10. "Steal the sustenance of the wretched;
ratchet up their agonies;

11. "Squander *Digestion* with alcohol.
Wolf down pig, pig out on pork,
harry pig-meat like a dog.

12. "Toss pensioners into shallow graves,
toss dirt over em, then dig em up,
to tee-hee at their terrorized faces.

13. "Prop up actual corpses—
half-decayed, bloated to *Corpulence*—
outside the grieving family's door,
so that the survivors, drawn by the stench
of exaggeratedly putrescent tissues,
are nauseated and/or struck down
themselves by heart attacks.

14. "Assuredly trash-talk the pious,
for daring to condemn your toys,
for naysaying your blasphemies.

15. "*Doubt* will flare up as ye burn their books.

16. "(Better to crucify such busybodies
so they screech and scream their own blasphemies!)"

17. Scummy be the intrigues of such degenerates,
who are so butt-backward—
and so double-tongued—
they don't recognize their *Wrongs*,
and fret not that God'll extinguish em eternally.

18. All as slippery as fire, they are dragons,
their eyes emitting an insidious glow—
like Vietnamese peasants set aflame by American napalm.

19. They are as disgusting as vipers that burst
through the mother's belly to achieve birth,
thus disembowelling their own progenitor.

20. Once drunk with blood, they upchuck it—
to quaff it afresh.

21. These shit-assed devils are a den of cannibals!
To them, bloodshed isn't diabolical,
but poetical,
and their crimes are not diminutive.

[Montréal (Québec) 12 *février* mmxvii]

III.

1. Blessèd is a virgin, she who's never let
a man drill bloody into her *belle-chose*
and drizzle therein his body-misshaping tumor.

2. (May she never brood on breeding.
Better she be unyielding flesh,
stern as a saint,
than some Satanist's "fuck-buddy.")

3. Newbies fetched to *Lechery*
plate faces in pillows;
thrust up plump rumps.

4. Every giglet—or jiggling, giggly gal—dies;
her empty bucket clatters.

5. Blessèd is a eunuch who's sinless,
whose transgressions number zilch.

6. All *Lust*'s offspring must be offed!

7. They deserve a blow-by-blow diet of bruises:
Beat their brains out their bung-holes!

8. (Decaying from within, even the sun
is burning to death.)

[Montréal (Québec) 12 *février* mmxvii
& YUL—Dorval (Québec) 27 *mars* mmxvii]

IV.

1. Decry con-artist mamas—
as accessories to vipers!

2. Such doxies screw illogically, scatologically.
(The dicks who pry em detect they're dead inside.)

3. The egg splatters open, and a snake writhes out—
some first-hand snot, some last-ditch microbe.

4. These new-born Neanderthals are unnerving
because they're universally unfeeling.

5. Unaccustomed to *Loyalty*,
be they fickle through-and-through.

6. Shallow-rooted, dry-boughed, and poison-fruited,
how can a bastood survive?

7. But their *Sterility* is imperishable.

8. At the first unlucky hurricane,
these miscreants are uprooted,
torn down, their boughs snapped off, their fruit scattered
and squashed, or their windfalls lost on inhospitable soil—
bogs, briars, or stony acres.

9. Are their sores comfortable, their itching comfy?
No nursing can salve em.

10. Let em indulge so much in the drippings, leavings,
spills, of tavern glasses—
the "all sorts"—
they blimp up, crapulent.

11. Evanescent are their lives, eternal is their pain.
They advertise *Chastity* as *Palliative Care.*

12. For them, *Crime* is chic and *Murder* a preservative.

13. Exponential is their costly *Fucking*;
exponential is their plague-spreading.

14. Mind their rat reek! Eye how they snoop bout cribs!

15. Their philosophers and priests buckle,
crumple down, then knee-walk,
eager to ream out an anus.

16. Now, ogle the righteous! They are fruitful
luxuriously, and are loved—
even beyond *Death*—
by all their descendants,
generation chasing generation.

17. Blameless, they yield neither to *Guile* nor *Folly.*

18. *Lust, Greed,* distemper *Intellect.*

19. God embraces the godly, but dead saints demand
th'extermination of the wicked.

20. (Deluded, the evil pray to dicker—with God.
But their lawyerly stratagems
dangle em upon anchor-thick hooks—
so they imitate carcasses in a butchery.)

[Ottawa (Ontario) 15 *février* mmxvii
& Sydney (Nova Scotia) 17 *février* mmxvii
& Wolfville (Nova Scotia) 17 *février* mmxvii]

V.

1. *Ribaldry* is sinners' *Righteousness*.
Blithe is their tupping,
and each incubus climaxes like a priest.

2. The bawd is carefree, disjointing, disjointed—
double-jointed—
when her knees threshold a devil's shoulders,
so wholesale semen soon meets retail egg.

3. Yet, sinful flesh is like iron untreated by eel oil:
It decays, it rots, it rusts, it breaks down;
its corrupted atoms canker its surface and fault the whole.

4. (Malefactors are just dry hay—
or faggots—crackling,
wracked by fire.)

5. Dissenters' every trace will vanish—
like desert-sand footsteps in a sirocco.

6. But before they perish,
their brats evaporate like disproven rumours;
both *Progeny* and *Wealth* pass away
like a vessel's wake, once it's sunk,
and its once-strident keel falls silent.

7. These obnoxious fetuses—freak-show objects—
founder in formaldehyde.

8. Snickering hyenas haunt cemeteries
and dig up baby Frankenstein remains
to devour their heads.

9. Transgressors'll wash away as quick as a bird's path,
when the air traverses its wings,
and it flits to its invisible perch or nest.

10. Well, *Procreation* is *Homicide.*

[Wolfville (Nova Scotia) 18 *février* mmxvii
& Ottawa (Ontario) 19 *février* mmxvii
& Vancouver (British Columbia) 24 *février* mmxvii]

VI.

1. Study Monsieur X and Mademoiselle O:*
Note their kissing, hugging—(XO)—harmonization.

2. (The penis is always a viper;
the vagina's a butterfly, wings spread.)

3. Ivory be their robes, their cloud-crafted offices,
their snow-bright abodes;
white is their wine, their rum, their water.

4. Sunlight—endless and endlessly refreshing—is *Wisdom.*
The prerogative of *Holiness.*

5. Vigilant is *Wisdom*, inspecting every thought.

6. Want *Immortality*? Get thee *Wisdom.*

7. (Never be as detestable—debatable—as poets.

8. Can a poem be skinned down to bone—
without its letters—
its *Sense*—
vanishing into moans, sighs?)

9. Deviate from *Truth*? Devolve to an imbecile!

10. The wise ruler inhabits Utopia.
Becomes deathless light.

---

* Cf. X's *Autobiography* and O's *Histoire.*

11. (*Wisdom*? More friendships,
fewer lordships;
more *Worship*,
fewer war ships.)

[Vancouver (British Columbia) 23 & 24 *février* mmxvii]

VII.

1. Every baby-mama whelps her pup
amid a tempest of blood and milk.
But the infant unfurls, in the womb, as a reptile.

2. No different is the mule, birthed by an ass
that's been tupped by a horse.

3. Wombs manufacture deviant mirrors.

4. Why do we scream at birth?
Because we thus commence lives of *Woe*.

5. If our mothers give us birth, everything else kills us.

6. There are as many children now
as there will be coffins later.

7. Even kings start out as naked as paupers,
bleating.

8. And infant panthers, in the womb, starving for life,
tear apart their own mothers to be born.

9. *Life* is accidents always. Get thee *Wisdom*.

10. Prefer *Wisdom* to honey, wine, silk, gold,
and heading armies
or bossing governments.

11. Compared to *Wisdom*, gold is muck.
(Gold can overrule chalk, but not ink.)

12. *Ignorance*? It is as dark as a preying shark,
stealthy, then quickly feeding on the heedless.

13. (God directs origins, maturations, dissolutions;
also astronomical cycles;
also *Fructitude*, also *Desiccation*;
also the tempers of dogs and the instincts of philosophers.)

14. Not even night can dim *Wisdom*.

[Oshawa (Ontario) 27 *février* mmxvii
& Regina (Saskatchewan) 5 *mars* mmxvii]

حكمة سليمان 7

1. انشقاق آدم وحواء صيّر
جسد السلالة محض غبار حي.

2. وسط عاصفة من الدم والحليب
امرأة تلفظ خطيئة جديدة.
لكن الرضيع يبدو في رحمها من الزواحف.

3. لا فرق بين بغل يولد من حمار
قام بتربيته حصان.

4. الأرحام مرايا متطرفة

5. لماذا نصرخ عند الولادة؟
لأننا بذلك نبدأ حيوات الأسف.

6. إن وهبتنا أمهاتنا الحياة , كل شيء آخر يقتلنا

7. عدد الأطفال الآن هو ذاته
عدد التوابيت التي ستكون لاحقا.

8. وأجنة الفهود في الرحم , جائعة للحياة
تمزق أمها لتولد
ثم تترصد, تطارد وتمزق اللحم.

9. الحياة حوادث في كل مكان. خذ الحكمة.

10. فضّل الحكمة على العسل, الخمر, الذهب,
قيادة الجيش وإدارة الحكومة.

11. مقارنة مع الحكمة , يصبح الذهب وحلا.
(يستطيع الذهب إزالة الطباشير, لا الحبر)

12. الجهل؟ مظلم كقرش مفترس,
يختبئ وبسرعة يتغذى على الغافلين.

13. يوجه الرب الأصول, النضج, التحلل
ودورة الفَلَك كذلك والاستقامة والتصحر)

14. الحكمة دورة دموية شاملة لا تقوم
لا تدحض عاطفية ومثقفة.

Arabic translation by Raed Anis Al-Jishi

VIII.

1. Cosmopolitan is *Wisdom*,
but provincial be the prejudiced.

2. *Wisdom* casts *Labour* as *Art*.

3. *Wisdom* is the *bibliopole* (bookseller)
whose shelves oppose the legislature.

4. *Wisdom* quakes kings.

5. *Wisdom* applauds the seagull
perched atop the umbrella.

6. *Wisdom* lauds the extemporaneous birth
of a galaxy
as raindrops splatter upon an awning,
yawning overhead.

[Ottawa (Ontario) 10 *mars* mmxvii
& Kelowna (British Columbia) 16 *mars* mmxvii]

IX.

1. W*isdom*'s fool, I know only what God assures:
I will die, and I am weak.

2. *Architecture* must remember the abyss.

3. Thus, my blueprints allow space for *Error*,
make room to tolerate *Disaster*.

4. Let us not be *plumbean* (ridiculous):
Wisdom is building—
with meet *Vacancy* allotted
to pastures, to orchards, to gardens, to groves.

5. *Labour*'s the limit of *Thought*.

6. *Sustenance* is wine; *Mystery* is fermentation.

7. Let only the sun blind my watchtowers!

[Ottawa (Ontario) 10 *mars* mmxvii;
& Kelowna (British Columbia) 16 *mars* mmxvii]

X.

1. Once *Fucking* was okayed,
bons-vivants went at it non-stop,
radically proliferating numbskulls.

2. Yep: Where was Cain's *Reason*,
when he slew Abel?

3. When global flooding was *Judgment*,
water wouldn't sit still;
the earth grumbled.

4. Downpour scissored all
and clouds tinted all;
mortals resembled crinkled cardboard
and black construction paper.

5. But *Wisdom* floated Noah and family
in a humongous boat.

6. Cesspools, smoking dumps, graves:
Oafs go here.
But saints never vanish into a vacuum.

7. God addles the wicked,
delivering em *momblement* (*Confusion*),
and they perish with *momblishness* (muttering).

8. Unbelievers? Pillars of excrement.
Each is a solid turd, its stench also solid.

9. (Every word here is scathingly forensic:
My lungs and my tongue pronounce *Damnation*.)

[YOW-YTZ (Porter 230, Seat 8D) 10 *mars* mmxvii
& Kelowna (British Columbia) 16 *mars* mmxvii]

XI.

1. Thunder banged and boomeranged!
(When rain writhes and brawls through air,
flood be the outcome, *not* balm.)

2. An inundation ambushed Unbelievers,
drowning em in lascivious *Salivation*.

3. It washed away citizens and idols,
never to be seen again.
(The combers emptied into cemeteries).

4. Next, a rainbow macheted the heavens.

5. Noah's ark? Mere lashed together,
patched together timbers,
but engineered well enough
to float Earth's creatures, plus people.

6. Yet, saved from the Flood, folks turned quick
to sexualizing lasses,
to dirtying up *Coitus* as *Fornication*....

7. But God's stalwarts resemble sailors trusting
wood, canvas, knots, and nails,
even amid maelstroms and whirlpools.

8. When water dissatisfies Thee, God,
Thou unleasheth fire—
flames that survive even rain
and brush off blizzards.

9. Stubborn fire that repulses water?
That's what scalds and sears devils!

10. The conditions are *baskweather*—
dry, parching, inflammable.

[Buffalo (New York) 19 *mars* mmxvii
& YUL—Dorval (Québec) 27 *mars* mmxvii]-

XII.

1. Initial punishments for *Sin* are minor—
so as to correct deviations
surgically, almost painlessly.

2. One exception? Those monsters—
who butcher their own offspring,
sacrificing em to dreamt-up demons
of rocks and logs—
are themselves slain by their own parents,
thus x-ing diabolical lineages.

3. God loathes to see tragic steel divvying up babies,
to watch dreadful parents diddle their infants
stabbing down with their knives.

4. Thus, God looses jackals to tear out their throats!

5. (Who dast advocate the survival
of toddlers' assassins?)

6. God upbraids and downgrades mortals:
Their own cancerous abominations cancel idolaters!

7. (They skedaddle, but holes suddenly perforate
their anatomies:
They incarnate *Ebola*.)

8. At *Destruction*, God is cautious in the handling,
so as to destroy everything, perfectly.

[YLW / Kelowna (British Columbia) 17 *mars* mmxvii
& YYC / Calgary (Alberta) 17 *mars* mmxvii]

XIII.

1. A carpenter strips bark from wood;
a blacksmith assembles cast-off pieces of iron.
An idol is cobbled together.

2. But all such *Art* is *Vanity*—
no matter how much rainbow paint
is dashed upon the metal or wood,
nor how loftily each piece is stationed
or nailed into place.

3. Sculptures of dead stone, dead wood,
dead gold, manifest dead gods,
all eunuchs, all quadriplegics.

4. To hunks of metal or wood,
only prays the *con*.

5. How silly to beg for gold coins
from a gilt homunculus!
Better that the idol be smelted
and its gold melted.

6. Idols must be *unbolished* (abolished)!

7. Tricked by *Art*, chumps nominate sculptures
as divinity.

8. (I cannot ratify such asinine assertions!)

9. Better to patrizate—
to take after one's father—

that old bugger!

[Buffalo (New York) 18 *mars* mmxvii]

XIV.

1. *Idolatry* is the capital *Error*!
For all fabricated gods are dead matter—
gimcrackery—
wings chopped off, haloes rusted,
graves developed as landfills.

2. And do not worship the dead as gods!

3. Scold or cajole the dead? Ha! They are dead
to every blandishment, every entreaty.
They are stinking things,
powerless to bellow *Praise* or ululate *Pain*.
Death shushes em.

4. The dead are nothing sacred. They are worms.
Mortal is the religion constructed off their bones.

5. Their only history is in their dental records.

6. Nor can monarchs play gods.
They are perfumed dung, gilded grave dirt.
No matter how attractive a monarch be,
his or her image is only a profile, a *bas-relief*,
that merely brands a coin as true,
but never his nor her soul.

7. (*War* happens because different nations
hosanna different idols, but all of em are false,
just an eerie mash of char and wood.)

8. Idolaters will stab their own babes
and spread the blood over witless elements.

9. Idolaters are bottom-feeders,
plague-spreaders,
dead-enders.

10. To pray to idols is *Poetastry*—
a condign lyre—
the professional riffs of liars.

[Buffalo (New York) 19 *mars* mmxvii
& Edmonton (Alberta) 23 *mars* mmxvii]

XV.

1. Even kings, tyrants, poets, philosophers,
tumble into graves—
as soon as God wills.

2. Sanguinary *Folderol* composes
their comfy *Scripture.*

3. God worries, troubles; *Mortality*:
So stars deteriorate, then are snuffed.

4. Artist! You crave to paint God?
Vain and vicious thou art—
unless thy canvas is shadow
and thy palette is light.

5. God is not a trophy, but shackles.

[Edmonton (Alberta) 23 *mars* mmxvii;
& YUL—Dorval (Québec) 27 *mars* mmxvii]

XVII.*

1. Hell's captives?
Joy's exiles, *los jodidos.***

2. They cringe at their mirrors;
their own shadows appal em.

3. Their urchin mouths bristle thorny curses.
Their jaws leak blood as they speak.

4. Snakes hiss at—and gouge—em;
lions growl at—and shred—em;
vultures javelin their beaks into the rancid flesh.

5. Hyenas rape em, thus whelping *crototes*—
man-mimicking monsters,
strutting on their hind legs,
and whose anuses double as eyes,
so that they're only able to see—briefly—
as they void their bowels.

6. Boulders tumbling down
from crumbling mountains
kill off these infidels,
but never enough—
fast enough.

7. Spears lunge, plunge smartingly;
Horses start, careen
like cannonballs opposing.
Broken shields lie all about.

[YUL—Dorval (Québec) 27 *mars* mmxvii]

* "What is Hell? Your definitions."—LeRoi Jones, *The System of Dante's Hell.*
** Mexican Spanish: The fucked.

XVIII.

1. Pitying his nation, God showered down quail—
winged manna—
to grant skin-n-bones
this skinny, bony delicacy.

2. But God hurled down on Israel's persecutors
odious rodents and vermin—
snaggle fangs and wolfing claws—
starving to rip chunks off oppressors.

3. When cretins watch their spawn expire,
then those bitches and sons o bitches know
whose God is tops!

4. Their land dries up to desert, is bask,*
and when blood clinks out their corpses,
slinks out, in sobbing gobs,
the sand gulps it up, slurping.

5. Our attackers waver like candle flames in gusts.

6. Masters groan as equally as slaves, dying;
and the present dies as fast as a king.

7. Eventually, whole nations disappear,
becoming as disappeared—
as are coffins.

8. Thus, their every trace vanishes—
like a conquering army's million footsteps
displacing desert sand
(for an instant).

---

* Very dry.

9. So deep sunken down are
the doubled-up dead,
our foes seem never
to have ever existed.

[YUL—Dorval (Québec) 27 *mars* mmxvii
& YAM—Sault Ste. Marie (Ontario) 30 *mars* mmxvii]

XIX.

1. Post-Flood, the world was scoured clean—
sanitized, baptized spic-and-span.
Gone was overhangin clouds;
up leapt grass outta thrown back waves.

2. But malefactors spawned new malignancies;
so that serfs again swung low into cotton;
or cotton-pickin machete swingers next waded
into sugar-cane jungles;
harvests became boodle in treasuries;
warhorses got harnessed to chariots;
chariots got outfitted with scythes;
the plutocrats took command
and beseeched preachers to indoctrinate the destitute
that their hungers and pains are inborn,
i.e., *Sin*-borne.

3. Commenced afresh *Filth*.
Virgins' ankles embraced centaurs' hooves;
axe-murderers swung at turbans;
scabrous kings gibbeted seraphic nymphs.

4. Spurning bumbling hubby
and/or fumbling groom,
mamas sold pussy for bread.

5. *Anger* tripped up their heels; *Lust* dizzied em.
Down deep, deep down, they plummeted,
while angels cheered on high,
jeering at these flaming, crisping falling.

6. Degenerates screamed, *Basta*! *Basta*! *Basta*!*
Friday-faced, gloomy, the scarlet ladies charred.

7. Globally, frogs and locusts burst outta cold mists,
and wracked green crops brown and black.

8. Lions turned sharks, killin for sport, not nutrition.

9. Animals and elements mixed up—as if trumpets
could be beaten like drums.
Likewise, crows became blizzards
and coal became wolves.

10. Fire now ate up water.

11. The iniquitous toppled into
the dark liquidity
of crypts.

12. God concocted such ruckus,
even warrior rulers crumbled like sand.

[YAM—Sault Ste. Marie (Ontario) 30 *mars* mmxvii
& Ottawa (Ontario) 10 *avril* mmxvii]

---

* Italian: Enough. The epithet equals a barley-fumble, i.e., a call for a truce by the losing side.

ADDENDUM TO SOLOMON

I.

1. What's dumber than a head-bashed-in cadaver?
A bachelor.

2. Empty tequila, rum, scotch, and vodka!
Yet, no bottle's as empty as bachelorhood.

3. The solitary man has solace?
He quarrels only with his mirror;
he yells only at his own ears.
Nice, eh?

4. The single person is sovereign, aye!
Still, the joyously wedded are imperial.

5. Yep: A wife can be brassy as a cop,
sassy as a barker.
Annoying!

6. But a wife eases cold and softens pains;
she erases hunger and terminates thirst.
Only a jerk complains!

7. Guess what? A wife's treasurebox
unlocks for hubby's key,
and keeps it oiled, sturdy,
and slicks it with grease.

8. Spread the table with brown bread,
red wine, and white Macedonian feta cheese:
Next, thy spouse spreads herself upon thy sheets.

9. Man is knife; woman, butter;
the bed, bread.

10. To sport among pillows, that is rejuvenating.

11. Couple lavishly—and tipple wine leisurely.
(How mellifluous be wine-slicked throats!)

12. *Love* is sunlight, vanquishing shadows,
terrorizing the dark.

13. To decide for *Chastity*? Pitiful!

14. *Chastity* is gobbledygook, gibberish.
Love is rhyming couplets.

15. The undisturbed bridal chamber
is a mausoleum.

16. The true man rests his lovers' legs
upon his shoulders,
while he raises and jabs
his concatenating baton
to orchestrate
his wife's epical, lyrical *Delight*.

17. The best wife squats at her husband's chest,
plants her sodden muff on his leg,
while she lets his insurgent shaft
pole and prod her urgent mouth.

[Panamá City (Panamá) 23 *septembre* mmxvii
& Winnipeg (Manitoba) 1 *octobre* mmxvii]

II.

1. Misogynists,
preferring gin to vaginas,
die extinct.

2. Don't wanna be crotchety?
Quit crochet!
Conjoin crotches!

3. The needle-eye-thin slit of the beloved
is always a grin,
never a grimace.

4. A bachelor—that botch, blotch—
vegetates in his dingy hovel—
as much a booby
as are priests,
tinkering with their fuck-up *Theology*
(if perfectly bad-ass at *Buggery*).

5. Rather perish of *Satisfaction*
than cherish *Pity*

(or nourish *Piety*
the abstraction of *Charity*).

[Panamá City (Panamá) 23 *septembre* mmxvii
& Winnipeg (Manitoba) 1 *octobre* mmxvii]

III.

The soft night's moon glows fair;
Refreshing is her love.
Our tequila pours clear—
Pale as the light above.

Godiva-white, but gold
As the Gioconda—
Da Vinci's auburn mould,
Terracotta Rwanda—

She's open as the wind!
Her words—white as her teeth—
Or grapes got cotton-ginned,
Are the airs my lungs breathe.

[Panamá City (Panamá) 24 *septembre* mmxvii]

Apéndice de Salomón III.

La luna brilla diáfana en la noche suave;
Refrescante es su amor.
Se vierte claro nuestro tequila,
Pálido como la luz de la noche sobre nosotros.

Blanca Godiva, pero dorada
Como la Gioconda,
El molde castaño de Da Vinci,
Ruanda terracota,

¡Libre como el viento, es ella!
Sus palabras, tan blancas como sus dientes,
O cual uvas desgranadas como algodón,
Pensamientos primorosos respiran mis pulmones.

(Ciudad de Panamá, Panamá, 24 *septembre* mmxvii)
Mexican Spanish translation by Ana Paula Austin Ferreira.

IV.

1. Her *Beauty*'s finest—if she's thy wife.
Her spry frame is *Light* itself,
outdazzling the auburn tint
the fired-up oil-lamp casts gainst the bedroom wall.

2. Her moans, growls, groans, and sighs
utter the most devout, resolute *Poesy*—
one-part Sappho and one-part Sade.

3. (The true poet earns such unassailable *Revenue*!)

4. Come nightfall, undress.
Come dawn, delay in dressing.

5. As quenchless as hellfire is *Lust*;
but endless lovemaking is heavenly.

6. If *Love* be absent, a vineyard's a graveyard.

7. Kindle many sparks—fierce batches—
shower from the flame-sundered log.
Die, likewise, by living flamboyantly!

8. *Orgasm*'s presumptuously ungodly cry
is the mortal body demanding *Immortality*....

9. (Note: The enemies of *l'Amour*
are skeletons, boasting bits of gore
where their hearts pretend to throb.)

10. Intimations of saintly yielding, of Caesarian falling,
of blood pinking a white dress and bed,
such scenes commence the virtuous *Marriage*.

[Winnipeg (Manitoba) 30 *septembre* mmxvii
& 1 *octobre* mmxvii
& Kapolei (Hawaii) 17/10/17]

VIII.

1. A poet who dares question *Love*?
That poetaster is a squashed skull,
a squished out heart,
has bile for blood,
and holes for eyes.

2. (English is a sorry language for *Love*!
French tongue be better.)

3. Disagreeable and inconsequential are poets
who do not vilify the stingy clerics
and mangy intellectuals
who tut-tut *contra Love*!

4. (Inadequate emotional *Complexity*
bedevils Ivory Tower poets' verses.
Such inklings look tar—or tarnish.)

5. To mount one's bawd, O bard,
is to climb, panting happily,
to Heaven!

6. It is to evolve!

[London (Ontario) 4–5 *octobre* mmxvii]

IX.

1. Love is never *Dishonour*,
save where it is unwelcome.

2. When night falls chill, don't we wanna bundle up?

3. Priceless gabbing is pillow talk:
Gold coins split in half.

4. No true lover is ever bamboozled
by dandelions ballyhooed as sunflowers:
Craving sees through the *Counterfeit*.

5. Better to go grassin greasily in *plein-air*,
gross-out, *alfresco* couplin,
than plunk in a pub
and wrangle with one's shadow.

6. (An honest bitch moans for her lover—
while sweating under her husband.

7. Hard to tie down that slippery fish
as she gasps, wiggles, thrashes!
Best let her go.

8. Like black bats slicing the moon's white,
thy Moorish fingers knead her vanilla, Venetian breast,
Othello!)

9. Be thou sated in belly—and in bed,
and swallow, swill, voluptuous kisses—
those jiggly oysters—
glorying in orgies.

10. Pitiful, unmindful, it is,
to grind the wind.*)

[London (Ontario) 4–5 *octobre* mmxvii
& YHZ—Enfield (Nova Scotia) 13 *octobre* mmxvii
& Kapolei (Hawaii) 16 *octobre* mmxvii]

*** To act in vain.**

X.

1. Winter's dark, Gothic, miserable cold—
this niggardly, black-ice season—
tires out even *Light*.

2. But dead-centre in Summer,
on those dog days when canine tongues loll out
like flaccid cocks,
drag your lips, sizzling, over hers—
that sweetie who's "too hot to handle,"
and suck down kisses by the litre and the gallon,
until her brimming pussy drizzles,
bullish for your fussily swizzling tusk.

3. Rollick and roll in April muck;
or spring into Spring
by seesawing on bedsprings;
get all muddy and grimy with night and sweat:
Ha! That's the living *Resurrection*!

4. (Withering is old age; is Fall.
Then, every summer feels like a steady winter—
with flowers of frost.)

5. Lookit! A lover must expend largesse—
to the nth degree—
on the daintiest detail.

6. Or pray for a strong spouse—
whose thighs pincer you so tightly,
you'll never want to part. Rightly.

7. (But if thou must slough off
a wife's characterless soul—
her disconsolate face—
that's no sacrifice.)

[Kapolei (Hawaii) 15–16 *octobre* mmxvii]

XI.

1. A man's a horseman; his bride's his filly:
To mount and ride, to spur and graze;
such urges *Chivalry.*

2. To whicker, whinny, dicker, and gambol—
in lovesport;
to crack the hymen and heave aside sheets,
that's what defines the poet, the *picador.*

3. To be gay; to horse about; to tilt to kisses;
to revel in open purse, open bar, open legs;
to chow down on wet, pink salmon
tart with strawberry juice:
That's the proper lover!

4. God hears no complaint from the married
who are fertile in their juices
and religious in vouchsafed *Venery.*

5. God credits no guff re: *Displeasure*—
no bitching or backbiting—
if two lovers are a-bed.

6. Let saints—puritans—gripe:
Even nuns worship makeup.

7. (Ain't prudes cranky hypocrites?
They condemn belles for their cosmetics,
but lick the powder off putains' faces.)

8. But beware the wife who dishes bad meat,
or whose *belle-chose* is tough to hack.
(She's a black widow?)

9. Beware the wife whose kisses
are just farts in your face.

10. (What woman is not a hellish *Woe*
boasting a heavenly face?)*

11. Beware the lover whose kisses are stingy
and whose bed is more mattress than blanket—
or more blanket than mattress….

12. What harries the heart?
A hussy who peppers her port,
or who slings more salt than meat,
more sugar than pie.

13. What havocs the bowels?
A lover whose kin overindulge,
who love to tap out your fridge,
empty out your cupboard,
throw up in your sink,
toilet in your yard,
who expect royal permit,
but return *Ingratitude* and *Insolence*,
and who only share their plagues, contagions,
diseases, disputes, and tumults.
Their every visit is a preview of Hell.

14. (Note: The dead don't ride horses
nor bulls.
Moral? The dead can't foop!**)

15. The blood-flooded fosse,
the bone-brimming fosse,
always more ditch than garden bed,
is murderous of *Love*,
is more tyrannical than *Chastity*.

---

* Editor: Strike this verse!
** Cf. Austin C. Clarke.

16. *War* is not only hacking off heads
and lopping off limbs,
it is also *Castration*—
enforced *Chastity*
and *Rape*.

17. (Despite his face as familiar as weeds—
that visage flattered by warmongers' applause—

Mars

ain't

Venus.)

[Kapolei (Hawaii) 16 *octobre* mmxvii]

XIII.

1. *Love* hates the rich;
ejects Midas from Venus's bed.

2. *Love* isn't frivolous, isn't tame (or tamed);
isn't fickle; isn't faint-hearted; isn't "easy-going"
(especially abed).

3. *Love* is *Treason* whenever *Law* is prudish,
peevish, petulant, or petty.

4. *Love* is *Crime* wherever police attack *Poetry*.

5. *Love* urges naked truth; bare facts;
rewards nakedness;
embellishes nudity.

6. *Love* isn't whim; isn't fanciful; chimerical.
It is untempered *Verity*, faultless *Veracity*.

7. *Love* is candid and voids any discrepancy
between *Desire* and *Satisfaction*.

8. *Love* urges the virgin to disloyalty to *Chastity*;
to repent from it;
and thus increase in *Beauty*.

9. *Love* seeks to please, never to appease.

10. *Love* resents dawn and welcomes dusk.

11. The prisoner of *Love*
occupies Utopia, embraces Nirvana.

[Kapolei (Hawaii) 17/10/17]

XIV.

1. Love, a raptor, swoops down and clutches kings,
mere pigeons in comparison.

2. *Love* busts trophies;
it strips monarchs to their marrow;
it paralyzes heroes.

3. Insidious and seditious is *Love*!
It seeks out chinks in armour;
defects in weapons;
it hobbles athletes
and addles geniuses.

4. To love too much is to approach *Perfection*—
if *via* a quagmire.
But *Beauty* urges the lover
to thrash through quicksand.

5. *Love* is *ad hominem*, delinquent, sassy in invective,
whenever prudes attempt to argue it's defective.

6. (Tediously malicious, impudently inclement,
each prude's just a limp, shrimp-dick,
and/or a ham-fisted boar.)

7. Usually haughty, decked in *haute couture*,
and a gourmet, dishing up *haute cuisine*,
a narcissist, loving, grovels in dirt,
shovels down crap.

8. The empty bed winks at lovers
as each passes by.

9. The *salope*'s slot's a sieve,
and drains a sot's seed and his coins.

10. To be as scraggly as a tattered tartan;
is to be unlovely, eh?

11. But to be a loose lass with a tight quim,
is to be pretty lovely.

[Kapolei (Hawaii) 17/10/17]

XV.

1. To shimmy into—then make shambles of—
sheets: That's *Love*.

2. That husband who'll not breed his wife?
Makes her another man's whore.

3. Who won't dance—hath no *Appetite*;
hates April; is troubled by dew;
is as sterile and as prickly as a grove of cacti.

4. Be neither clerk nor clergy if thou desirest *Fucking*.

5. No one loves a prude: Too overcast.
Yuck!

6. It's "psychophants" (bureaucrats), psychopaths (cops),
poetasters (priests), who prefer
Prudery to *Love*.

7. Cowardly is the castrato; effete's the eunuch!

8. A true valentine don't vacillate!

9. *Love* requires ballyhooed gusto!
The lover must bellow like a bull—
be as upstart and roaring as an elephant.

10. Handsomely generous, the true lover
stuffs his beloved as if feeding sausage
to a pig.

11. A woman's knees serve best as elbows
to arm-like legs,
pincering her eager lover's back.

12. She poises his lump-based shaft twixt her thighs;
next, agile and curvy, her sultry churning skins
his manhood dexterously,
while her tits lunge and lurch.

13. And no intolerable blushing!

14. *Love* befits the mad, the obsessed: True!
But the false lover ends up in Bedlam;
he or she goes to Hell.

15. Better to nosh mackerel (quim)
and suck down brine (*cum*)
than it is to tumble into the fosse*—
butt-up, face-down—
like a trench-sprawled corpse....

[Kapolei (Hawaii) 17–18 *octobre* mmxvii]

* Cf. £, Canto I.

ECCLESIASTICUS

Allí en tu boca escribiré mis versos!
—José Martí, "Bosque de rosas"

I.

1. To simpletons, *Wisdom* is mumbled ciphers,
such as,
"A bloodied horsehead sports a headless king's crown."
Yet, here's the deciphering:
When pacing the *State*, guard thy head.

2. *Wisdom* stimulates mutinous brawls,
colossal brawls,
for it klaxons *Disapproval* of governments.

3. To obey God is *Wisdom*'s root;
Its flower? *Longevity.*
Its harvest? *Eternity.*

4. (God presides over humans stuffed
in cartons—
gone to humus.)

5. Fermented, distilled, and distributed
in drafts (paper),
Wisdom intoxicates, inebriates.

6. *Wisdom* urges drastic proficiency in *Protest.*

7. Where *Idealism* ends, *Corruption* begins.

8. Then, golden sighs go fluttering
across rippling blackness.

[YUL—Dorval (Québec) 18 *avril* mmxvii]

III.

1. Mothers' curses haul down homes
and turf out brats;
but a father's blessings fare no better—
if one's unwise.

2. *Sin*—forgiven—melts like frost in sunlight.*

3. Intellectuals are shifty, shiftless, seditious:
They think *Opinion*—lamentable booty—is *Sobriety.*

4. (Their palates are rusty;
they're half-asleep due to anemia
and/or booze.)

5. Eyes without light are stab wounds;
Knowledge without *Wisdom* is *Anarchy.*

6. Bull-headed scholars treat libraries like china shops;
They act daredevils, and croak,
their jugulars slashed by paper edges
sharp as smashed, jagged ceramics.

7. Because the unsaved commit such gaffes,
they don't get to become gaffers (old men)
or GILFs.

8. Do I damage my reputation with my readers?

[Halifax (Nova Scotia) 20 *avril* mmxvii]

*** Forgiven sins don't *apricate* (bask in sunlight); they disappear.**

IV.

1. If *Wisdom* forsakes thee, thou art ruined.
Why accept *Harm*? Why seek a *Downfall*?

2. (*Life* is a barrel of stones in which infidels—
butter-soft—get battered into monstrosities.)

3. *Wise* are orators: Their tongues teach.

4. (Just as *Fidelity* displaces debates,
so does a king's decision disappear squabbles.)

5. Face shouting cannon: *Truth* urges *Insurrection*.

6. Avoid slothful speech and/or wrathful deeds.
Do not let thy parley be aptotic (uninflected).

7. Be God-like:
Inflexible and zealous.

8. Note: God is neither off-hand in deed
nor second-hand in knowledge.

[Halifax (Nova Scotia) 20 *avril* mmxvii]

V.

1. *Wealth* is not *Power*! But *Wealth* buys *Power*.

2. Even kings are seduced—purchased—poisoned—
by *Wealth*.

3. The problem with billionaires? They're rich:
Their golden shovels can dig a billion graves.

4. Plutocrats get pissed off royally—
if not worshipped as photogenic magnates.*

5. (They are cinematically charismatic,
yet repellent up-close:
The filthy-assed duffers go weeks without bathing!)

6. Envy not triumphs that the worldly trump!
They're gonna plummet deep—
slumping into Hell!

7. Preferring to grapple with swine,
they oust their "dead-end" wives from their beds.

8. (Beware, philandering alcoholic!**
Thy "love-matches" end as dogfight, catfight,
cockfight, fistfight:
Adultery's 100% unpropitious.)

---

* See that vulgarian's Caligulan presidency.

** The loathsome plutocrat's a scabrous gent, mangy at crotch and blistered on pate. His burps—burping, upchucking ("tweeting")—is how the twit capitalizes on *Gluttony, Villainy*.

9. Spurn these varmints!
In the end, their organs, revolting, disobedient,
war against their brains.

[Halifax (Nova Scotia) 20 *avril* mmxvii
& Windsor (Nova Scotia) 21 *avril* mmxvii
& Enfield (Nova Scotia) 21 *avril* mmxvii]

VI.

1. Fire and/or worms corrode the haughty
to ash and/or bones.
Fire and/or worms dismantle em, limb by limb.

2. I sugar-coat nothing!
Sinful skin dons a glaze of maggots.

3. Remember thy *Mortality*!
Thy pillow is your first headstone.
In bed, nightly, is thy corpse splayed-out.

4. The living embody *Music*;
but the dead are lost scores.

5. *Mercy* is God's prerogative;
it's not guaranteed, dumbo!

6. God's *Affection* is never despondent!
Never hath His *Love* any misgivings.

7. That's His *Simplicity*: *Romantic* and *Gothic*.
Never is His *Love*—or *Hatred*—ever suppressed.

8. How gracious that God overlooks
skoppoloit (frolicking)
and *hoyting* (romping),
or we'd all be dead!

9. Only God straightens the circular
and/or cyclical
quandaries.

10. Like God, deathless are ideas.

**[Halifax (Nova Scotia) 20 *avril* mmxvii
& Windsor (Nova Scotia) 21 *avril* mmxvii]**

VIII.

1. Fucking's *Generosity*—equivalent to *Monarchy.*
Fornicating greedily's tantamount to *Charity.*

2. Coital instinct is grimy, but also *Liberty* (gratuitous).

3. Malicious is the celibate.
Insidious is *Celibacy.*

4. A snazzy pussy, snares, throttles, the avid cock.

5. She yet incites the unwary to ride her backside
like a bull.

6. (She's a brawny trollop, this one:
Got a voice of lava, eh?
Right suitable for thou,
her unscrupulous consort!)

7. Diddle old beauties and cuddle young ones:
Cometh unto each as hard as a tower!

8. (In the vinegary brothel,
unpersuasive is the saint's soldiering.)

9. Rapture each unto a froth:
Churn each bowl to get good broth.

10. Women are "weak"? Nay, they're wily:
Their dainty slippers trample bowed necks.

[Halifax (Nova Scotia) 20 *avril* mmxvii
& Windsor (Nova Scotia) 21 *avril* mmxvii
& Enfield (Nova Scotia) 21 *avril* mmxvii]

X.

1. *Sovereignty*'s upheld by God—
and/or by gold
and/or by gunpowder.

2. A reckless king loots the Treasury and paupers his people.

3. Today's pompous king is tomorrow's purple corpse.

4. A dead king gives life to worms. That's nice.

5. (Flesh ain't gold; it gangrenes, it degenerates.
Precarious, the body is dust—in abeyance.)

6. Don't fellow-travel with the rash and/or the vile.
Bloodshed is *Comedy* to them;
Treachery be *Black Comedy* to them.

7. Any secret you pass em will catalyze *Sedition / Treason*.

8. (Presenting saccharine grins,
then blabbing nauseating limericks,
next, sick fucks stab each other.)

9. Avoid the orbits of big-mouth, blasphemous hookers:
They undo saints through rabid *Slander*—
degrading em in the public market
and then in the courthouse,
via miserable Latin
and savages' rationales.

10. (Eyes that sip *Beauty* do often gulp poison.)

11. Pay a wench for a glee spree,
and end up bankrupt,
pimp-jumped, head-bashed-in.

12. Don't oppose judges! Unassailable is their respect.

13. A new friend is as good as new wine;
but an old friend is as excellent as vintage wine.

14. Blessèd is the labourer;
negative is the narcissist who lacks bread.

15. God ain't wishy-washy:
He's blunt at killing, straight-forward at damning.

16. He puffs out sails and smooths seas;
or He topples masts and smashes ships.

17. *Damage* is unfixable if sins are unforgiveable.

18. (Lion-savage locusts attack;
wasps don't fall sluggish.)

19. But obstacles invite miracles;
and *Scripture* mandates the hegemony of ink.

20. (Perhaps a treasury of quotable verses?)

[Halifax (Nova Scotia) 20 *avril* mmxvii
& Enfield (Nova Scotia) 21 *avril* mmxvii
& Plattsburgh (New York) 28 *avril* mmxvii
& Montréal (Québec) 29 *avril* mmxvii]

XI.

1. Small is the bee, but greatly sweet its honey.
The surplus *Capital* of its *Labour* is nectar:
La dolce vita.

2. *Vanity* is *Corruption*:
It is whitewash, prettifying an outhouse.

3. Do not complain unless you have
unignorable slights, slurs:
What good is wasteful grumbling?

4. *Disgust* is a proud, arrogant emotion.

5. Do not attempt multiple tasks,
for, to be found wanting at even one,
diminishes any successes.

6. Old age and accomplishments
best old age and *Admonishment*,
or old age and general *Inadequacy.*

7. The greedy and decadent fleece you by *Stealth*
(*Strategy*);
like rats, they're invisible,
but as eviscerating as black holes.

8. Even kings may face assassins,
who operate vulgarly,
who are quick at chopping (down),
who lurk, eager to cut a regal throat.

9. Even kings may end up dethroned,
sleeping under rain,
while paupers don their crowns.

[**Montréal (Québec) 29 *avril* mmxvii**]

XII.

1. Feed no bread to the debauched,
lest they vomit it upon you
to spit this swill in your children's faces.

2. Fornicators are irrepressible:
Wasps can't sting their shameless genitals
because they clutch too closely,
are just too clotted together.

3. Never gratify *Gluttony* and never ratify *Lust.*

4. Gold and *Fame* magnet parasites.

5. The envious are bright copper in their beaming,
but tarnish green as soon as they weep,
beholding thy triumphs.

6. When a cobra bites his unskilled charmer,
only the *con* is surprised.

7. Likewise, when a backstabber thou hast befriended
redoubles *Aggression* against thee,
grin at thy *Stupidity.*

8. Never be laid-back, easy-going, lenient,
prone to suck back sedatives or to dream,
or you'll bloody your bed, your throat cut.

9. Best be gimlet-eyed, shrewd, never drowsy.

[Montréal (Québec) 30 *avril* mmxvii]

XIII.

1. Lions fang lambs to bones:
Plutocrats crack open scrawny folks' bones
to vacuum their very juices.

2. When a bankable man stumbles, bootlickers
scramble to act as his crutches, even his cushions.
But when a pauper trips, falls, passersby
scoff at his pathetic situation,
and psychos kick his pestilential form.

3. Instantly doth *Wealth* parade a fool as a sage;
instantly doth *Poverty* costume the sage as a fool.

4. *Shaming* is what the moneyed do;
Sharing is what the have-nots do.

5. So what if gold beautifies a corpse?
It's *Waste*.

6. How can rich and poor unite?
Can a rabid wolf and a fat-gut pig
form a commonwealth?

7. Anyway, them that hath no coins,
them don't get no feast!

[YUL—Dorval (Québec) 30 *avril* mmxvii]

XIV.

1. The miser demands burial in a gold casket.
But, quick, his heirs dump him in a garbage pit,
melt the casket into coins and gewgaws,
and feast and play until the *Wealth* is zero.

2. The skinflint is a white shirt, black tie,
and a maw seething with maggots.

3. As narrow as a needle's eye,
as surgical as a needle's point,
is the penny-pincher,
who thus rebukes the fraudulent.

4. (But the scrooge who swallows his gold,
taking his scrounged coins to the grave,
must know his corpse will be cut open,
that hands will swim in his gore
to rescue the gilt.)

5. *Joy*? Satiation of desires.

[YUL—(Dorval (Québec) 30 *avril* mmxvii]

XV.

1. God disembowels the insolent
and trepans tyrants' diamond-wreathed skulls.

2. He swats czars from thir thrones;
He bats—clubs—their crowns.
Their blood whips out—
like a flood bursting a dam.

3. Lances fang forth, stab oppressors to the dirt.
White metal pours ruddy into fatted bellies.
Spilled guts bleed all over underpants.

4. Scythes slice through prongs; kings stoop down,
their manhoods dripping gore.
The mess glows as dark as coals.

5. Huns get bashed up; their armour skewered;
chain-mail becomes scarlet sewers.

6. God dashes down a hundred heads in helmets,
all decapitated.

7. Arrows burst barricades and ribcages.
Flames growl, crimson-jawed.

8. Recall that Pharaoh's army got liquidated
in the Red—blood-tinted—Sea.
That gang of warmongers got incinerated—
in water.

9. The clashing heaps of em
became definite jumbles
of indefinite junk.

[Venezia (Italia) 12 *mai* mmxvii]

XVI.

1. God designed *Eternity*; it obeys His formulae.
(It is based off of Heaven.)

2. The Lord populated the world with excellent creatures,
but all, even the saints,
must go into the earth.

3. Living is aging—waxing, waning;
and dying is the end of the body:
This is the jinx that Adam and Eve brought home to us.

4. The generations are buds, extended leaves,
and then dead, shed leaves.

5. It's not an excessive *Inventory*,
but graveyards reallocate the living.

6. *Truth*: A mother can die
even as her newborn exits
her birth canal, itself dead.

7. *Truth*: Dark dust drifts into place.
Everywhere.

[YUL—Dorval (Québec) 30 *avril* mmxvii]

XVII.

1. The *Respect* that God shows mortals is
upside-down, for we don't merit it.

2. We are gawky, brazen, glitch-prone freaks!
We's all ready candidates for *Castration*,
for genital *Mutilation*.

3. Don't we constitute a Rogues' Gallery,
quite rightly disenfranchised?

4. Cankerous and cantankerous because lecherous;
sickly, treacly, and cranky, because greedy;
Self-Sabotage unto *Suicide*, that's us.

5. Lookit! God's engraved His *Constitution*
with a stone signature.

6. His *Constitution* is tough *Thought,*
and distressing *Reflection*.
In its light, only saps can cavort and snicker.

7. A superior Cyclops, God's oracular eye sees all,
and He commands *Death* to execute all evildoers.

8. (Thus, opiates are appropriate—
to tamp down our *Sorrow* and *Pain*.)

9. Sunlight out dazzles all on Earth;
yet, other stars prove our sun puny.

[YUL—Dorval (Québec) 30 *avril* mmxvii
& Nackawic (New Brunswick) 1 *mai* mmxvii]

XVIII.

1. Mortals always protest, when dying,
"Jeepers, too quick thou cometh, *Death*!"

2. They're resentful and perplexed
that they gotta plunge
back into the dust from which they arise.

3. Thus, they mount urgent, last-ditch orgies,
praying that emergency sweating, the faultless penis
vaulting the vagina's oozing moistures,
plus the eventual, muddled blizzard of the man's roe
(that vague, slushy mess marbling cunny hair),
may flout *Death*'s writ.

4. Ha!

5. Scraping the bottoms of damsels' butts
don't rebut dying.
Anyway, no ginny dons a grimacing mask.

6. *Death*—that doleful *Sleep*—
be our miserable *Destiny*.

7. (*Laughter* is the first medicine,
but *Death* is the final palliative.)

8. And *Poetry* offers temporary balm—only.

9. (Inks wrinkle and warp our reflections
til they are as withered and wretched
as our hearts.)

10. *Charity*, when grudging, slits donors' eyes
and recipients' throats.
Such *Benevolence* is as frivolous as a placebo.

11. *Luxury* begats pig-sty revellers.
(What can assuage their jaws, their secateurs?)

[Nackawic (New Brunswick) 1 *mai* mmxvii
& Grand Falls / Grand-Sault (Nouveau-Brunswick) 1 *mai* mmxvii]

XIX.

1. The doge's *dumpennente* (johnson) besieges silk,
parting the skinny-thighed mama's ribald foliage.

2. His pupils take in—
fall into—
her pupils.

3. He is like a pony—pancaked down—
dizzied by peonies's opium.

4. (Her words? Cream of marzipan—
and sweet as coconut oil.)

5. But reckless is he who, lapping fish broth—
briny female chowder—
goes whole hog, and scarfs the tart.

6. Are her nether parts dirty?

7. The piggish ain't half-hearted,
but fully wolfish in their *Lust*.
(Coarse and brutal is their *Etiquette*.)

8. Spear unsparingly—unerringly—
into gashed meat.
If so, so what?
To not be exiled from *Love*!

9. (The liquor bottle chuckles at first,
and then it hisses.)

[Grand Falls / Grand-Sault (New Brunswick / Nouveau-Brunswick)
1 *mai* mmxvii]

XX.

1. Better to take *Umbrage* than take refuge!
Hoist fists, never white flags!

2. Bid galoots adieu! Rip up fake *Peace*!
Set crossbows, catapults, quarrelling.

3. Keep silent generally,
but *always* brazenly foghorn *Truth*.

4. (Blunder with the tongue, stab the heart!)

5. The garrulous upset *Gaiety*.
They are wasps, roaring, stinging.

6. A dagger windfall: That's *War*.

7. By slaying poets, the conqueror commits suicide.
(O! But who will do vengeance for poets?)

8. The marketplace imperils scruples.
You may haggle, bag a better price,
and still purchase crap,
at dastardly cost.

9. Parasites and swindlers adore suckers.

10. Deviants turn spirituals into limericks.

11. Value *Sanctity*. The sanctimonious? Never!

[Grand-Sault / Grand Falls (Nouveau-Brunswick
/ New Brunswick) 1 *mai* mmxvii]

XXI.

1. Sin has lion's fangs, is ravenous,
and will devour your lineage
right down to the 7th generation.

2. *Sin* is as biting as pincers, scissors, and axes.
Beware.

3. *Insolence* delves into bowels
to divvy out blood and bile.

4. *Insolence* wastes thy substance
in lawsuits, surgery, and/or repairs.

5. Smoke issues from fire; bloodshed follows *Insult*.

6. Those who defy *Correction* stumble into Hell.
Burdensome, thoughtless, is their suffering.

7. Poets become laughing-stocks
when their prophecies—jinxed—fail.

8. Feeble poets pose as philosophers,
and get exposed as charlatans.

9. Take a loan to erect thy roof?
Thou art no better than the beggar
who gathers stones to mark his grave.

10. Take a loan?
Misfortune will be gruesome in thy belly.
Grapes shall shatter thy teeth.

11. Bloodless is a sap's cock-loft:
His skull's a sieve;
nay, it's a wind-tunnel.
Nope, it's gristle-and-grey-matter
sloshing bout in a tumbled helmet.

12. Only dolts resent schooling!
They think a school is *Enslavement*:
Letters are manacles; numerals are fetters.

13. *Disgrace* is eavesdropping, snooping.
It is to act, not like *beaux-clercs*,
but like rats—
torn apart—finally—by hounding dogs.

14. Throttle gossips, whisperers, slanderers!
Don't let em circulate their *Propaganda* shenanigans.

15. Wise, you'll arouse so much hatred,
stone after stone will be thrown,
wherever your face appears.

16. Ain't you me?

[Grand Falls (New Brunswick) 2 *mai* mmxvii
& Perth-Andover (New Brunswick) 2 *mai* mmxvii
& Woodstock (New Brunswick) 2 *mai* mmxvii]

XXII.

1. *Lassitude* = wallowing, hog-like, in *merde*.
You stink, and all flee your disgusting estate—
just as finches flee falcons.

2. Gossip is as uncouth as a wedding march
at a funeral.

3. As quickly as they are overheard,
backbiters' butts gotta be whipped raw.

4. Why not?
They are cancerous kooks, hazardous cranks;
a rictus—a frozen grin—severs each face.

5. Mourn the dead, but not fools:
Everyone must die, but retards choose *Idiocy*.

6. Mourn the dead for seven days: Yes.
But fuck-ups should mourn their birthdays—
everyday that they breathe.

7. Picket fences can't hold back a flood;
nor can a bungler stand against *Trouble*.

8. Nitwits are like turrets torn down,
towers tumbled after.

9. Pillows can't stand in for pillars, eh?

10. Earthquakes don't crumble well-built homes;
Crises don't unbalance the wise.

11. The tongues of the wise are glittering swords
emerging from gold-studded sheathes.

12. Spurn a friend?
That's as nasty as throwing stones at birds.

13. To critique a friend is *Etiquette*;
to slander a friend is *Treachery.*

[Woodstock (New Brunswick) 2 *mai* mmxvii]

XXIII.

1. *Passion*, that excoriating fire,
even drives fathers to fuck their own flesh!
Their dongs plunger their own daughters' dowries.

2. They are sullying bullies,
raping even their own mamas.

3. Fornicators deem all *Congress* syrup,
to be drooled upon, or sapped from,
their own children.

4. They are unnaturally hungry
for their own broods' hymens, or anuses,
and/or *Innocence*.

5. (Such yahoos are as nasty as G.I.'s
who perch their asses,
dripping diarrhea,
on the edge of wells,
to foul enemy water supplies.)

6. They bend to pump at a rump
or ratchet up a snatch.

7. Adulterers thrive in—live in, live upon—night.

8. Each iambic, maniacal heart
bleats with intractable *Lust*.

9. Sly wives mask their bastoods
with their husbands' surnames.

10. Some mad, bad, glad, bigged-up wives
sortie to exotic cities,
where they expel their puppy,
then roast on coals the cherub,
and fork the sizzling flesh,
feasting on chubby limbs
and organs of gourmet spice.

11. Then, returned to hubby and home,
they weep that the child was stillborn
and had to be buried abroad.

12. These skunking, slinking punks stink up
cradles, cribs, Kindergartens.

13. They are bothersome sows.
Their snouts sink into each others' sodden slit-holes.

14. (Whenever one's crotch sops,
her lover's face slops.)

15. Smear and shellack their shameless selves with honey,
so insects lacerate em, sting, bite, scrape, gouge,
and flood each gash with lethal pains.

16. *Tragedy* often only subsides in *Death*.*

17. Servants—forced to improve—don't lack bruises.

18. Hard-pressed, they face blustery whips, bursts of slaps.
That's why they're productive, not impoverishing.

*** If only I could draft tragedies**
that sound tragic—
even in dialect.

19. Dust-ups, hither and thither—
produce gristle and slabs,
so each body seems to've received
a scarlet, slimy kiss.

20. Anyway, all unsaved are suicidal.
They weep so they can sup on their snot.

[Woodstock (New Brunswick) 2 & 3 *mai* mmxvii
& Fredericton (New Brunswick) 4 *mai* mmxvii]

XXVI.

1. A jealous wife, imagining rivals,
is as excruciating as thorns
thrust under fingernails.

2. Like quicksand to a traveller is
the stentorian wife to a sottish husband.

3. (He is better unhoused,
if she'll not renounce brawls and spats.)

4. A squawking wife's a war bugle,
so Post-Traumatic-Stress-Disorder
afflicts her hubby.

5. Her bawling tirades bruise his intellect.
She's as alarming as swarming hornets!

6. (A harridan is a boil;
a termagant is a tarantula;
and a scold is a needle.)

7. A minx squirts her muff at strangers:
Tears never wet her face, only jizz.

8. The adulteress flutters eyelashes:
Her *Sluttery* butters up backsliders,
easing—greasing—their slalom to Hell.

9. A slattern's like spit on a sidewalk.
With each and every illicit orgasm,
she adds dirt to her father's grave.

10. Slime-buffed are her teeth;
sans-culottes be her duff.

11. But a chaste wife is a diamond—no less.
Her orderly home's akin to sunrise.

[YFC—Fredericton (New Brunswick) 4 *mai* mmxvii
& Marcon (Italia) 6 *mai* mmxvii
& Mestre & Vicenza (Italia) 7 *mai* mmxvii]

XXVIII.

1. Lies ramp like lions, mangle victims.
Lies sow roses with worms.
Lies turf kings out their gold caskets.

2. When lies are gilt, *Truth* is ash.

3. Stones that, customarily, batter bankers,
must strike down liars.

4. Behind striding stallions, drag liars, naked,
and leave their bloodied, blotchy fragments
for rats and buzzards to claw and gullet.

5. *Slander* drives the righteous into exile.
Vineyards vanish under brambles.

6. *Slander* downgrades palaces into sewers.

7. *Fraud* crumbles marble-columned banks to dust.

8. Thy breath can fan a flame;
thy spit can snuff it out:
Thy mouth allows both possibilities.
Choose the mode that models *Truth*.

[Vicenza (Italia) 7 & 8 *mai* mmxvii]

XXIX.

1. Why aren't the wise scolded for their *Charity*?
Because they have roofs, and their cupboards are full.

2. *Life* requires wool or silk,
meat or bread,
wine or milk,
plus a roof and a fire:
Own all in surplus
before sparing any portion.

3. Appreciate that *Hunger* gnaws one's mind;
thus, gold is valued less than grain.

4. Note: Renting is fake *Ownership*.

5. Silver in thy purse?
Thou shalt not need spurs.

6. Gold renders fire hotter, brighter.

7. Always bank on a pound of coins:
Never let *Disaster* dissolve *Income*.

8. To borrow and not repay?
That's *Fraud*; that's *Impoverishment*.

9. (Let bankrupts cover their faces!
Their butts show....)

10. To vouch for—or insure—strangers
is to be kayo'd by *Debt*.

11. *Insurance* is gambling, plus *Greed*:
To heap up lucre, and dole but little out,
save to dissuade lawsuits.

12. Tis better to stoop, ragged in a cave,
than be a guest, dependent on *Charity*.

13. If and/or when thou art a guest,
ask nothing.

14. *Misery*? To coast from couch to couch,
and munch water if that's what's tabled.

15. To host another is also *Vexation*:
Be charitable, lest thou be slagged as a skinflint.

16. Still, ingrates sneer,
"Grant us the finest wine,
the best oysters, and your bed—
with your wife and/or your daughter(s) in it—
and stint on nothing!"

17. Beastly figures are such country Fascists,
with their night-black culottes,
their sulphuric tongues!

18. They'll deem your groceries theirs,
squander thy provisions,
spoil thy preserves,
boot you out your own house and bed,
and requisition all thy females
to squirt out usurpers.

19. Dust'll swirl thick as smog
as looters' pick-axes poke holes
in thy walls—
so they can ransack all thy stores.

20. If thou fall prey to such robbers,
choose *Exile* or *Suicide*:
Remember: Kings stab themselves,
they don't let serfs do it!

[Bologna (Italia) 9–10 *mai* mmxvii]

XXXI.

1. When dining with plutocrats and/or governors,
repress *Hunger* lest it segue into *Gluttony.*

2. If heading a banquet, stuff others first.
Rank thy stomach secondary.

3. Do not accept every plate tendered;
do not hog the buffet.

4. Would you nibble on boots
even if dished up on a silver platter?

5. (Is Venus lovely when she bites
on a lamb shoulder
and blood spurts from her mouth?)

6. Meditate as you dine,
and you'll need not medicate while you digest.

7. Chew neither strenuously nor loudly.
Eat like a desert prophet: Fastidious.

8. Be the first to announce *Satisfaction*;
and do not grouse for seconds.

9. Gluttons and/or drunkards prove sick:
Shit burps from the mouth; piss leaks out the eyes.

10. The light diner does not sweat and fart all night.
He rises while dawn streaks the heavens,
and his stomach is muscle.

11. Better is diet discipline
than hospital doctoring.

12. The millionare fattens on pastries;
the toiler diets on dew.

13. A little bread, a little wine—
draughts of *grappa Prosecco*—
some olives, a few sardines,
then milk, cheese, maple syrup:
Thus, thou dine better than princes.

14. Imprudent *Consumption* be impudent *Citizenship.*

15. Be merry at table and cheery in bed.
Who orgies in a cemetery?

16. Wine is *Life* if sipped, but *Death* if gulped.

17. A drunk swordsman is apt to slice up shadows
or dice up spouse and spawn:
Blood washes down his walls
and washes away his home.

18. Worse, a sot will ram any muff—
his mother's, or his daughter's.
(Witness Lot.)
His slushy chitchat echoes bordello inmates' moans.

19. When wine jollies a neighbour,
do not reproach his *Gaiety*
lest he turn surly;
better that he feel sleepy, not sorry,
once *Sobriety* returns.

20. A charitable biliionaire is as good as a saint.
His prosperity feeds, clothes, houses, the needy:
Parliamentarians shout his praises.

21. Private *Clarity* weakens public *Welfare.**
Public *Clarity* = *Charity.*

22. But never parade stolen goods
as charitable donations!

23. And don't blithely give away *Property*!
It's collateral for thy old age.
(Remember Lear, eh?)

[Mogliano Veneto (Italia) 10–11 *mai* mmxvii]

*** Rather, "Make shame more shameful by making it public." Paris graffiti, *mai* 1968.**

XXXII.

1. Lightning outpaces thunder;
likewise, applause pursues *Modesty*.

2. Imitate the *Serenity* (*Sovereignty*)
of an unread book.

3. The just neither stumble nor mumble:
Their step is light; their speech is right.

4. Their government, because beautiful,
is never at all sorrowful.

5. *Nobility*: The poet, the musician, the singer....
Ignoble: The priest, the professor.
The Elect? Lovers.

6. Profs' twisted words snake from their twisted guts.
Their brainfolds—snarled—snuggle vipers.

7. (Like a hammered iron wedge splitting stone,
such is *Corruption*, splintering *Exchange*.)

8. When one builds and another demolishes;
when one speaks and another is silent;
who is doing God's work?

[Mogliano Veneto (Italia) 11 *mai* mmxvii]

XXXIV.

1. *Hunger* is plebeian as saliva
and as biting, forceful, as crab lice.

2. The famished hunch over their luncheons
and/or chow down in troughs of *Sleaze*,
seamy, but seemingly tasty.

3. The trenched cream is extra sugary,
side-to-side sugary, and feels fatty in the mouth.
But it is *Poison*.

4. The famished pray for the rumbling business
of bowels, prosecuting *Waste*.

5. They eat until each gnashes dust,
deeming it delightful.
They exult in—and exalt—excrement.

6. Teeth gnaw carrion;
tongues lap bloody turds,
mistaking em for dew-steeped strawberries.

7. Unimportant are *Death* and *Birth*:
The sun annexes all shadows—
even ourselves—
we disintegrating petals.

8. Some become kings; all become corpses.

9. (To die in a castle,
with clattering notables fawning,
seeking a place in one's *Will*—
or a prestigious accolade or post—
is exactly like expiring in a pig sty,
with stinking swine rushing to eat thy flesh.

10. So, do not worship monarchs!
Even though their mugs authenticate coins,
they're only dressed up maggots.)

[Tropea (Italia) 4 & 5 *juin* mmxvii
& Mogliano Veneto (Italia) *mai* 11 mmxvii]

XXXV.

1. Should they deliver the altar only perfume,
the righteous yet offer up gold.
Redoubtable—indubitable—are their gifts.

2. God's bias is not wholly for the poor,
but only for saints.

3. Yet, to purloin bread from the hungry
withers the babe in the belly;
dries up the mother's milk;
shrivels her breasts;
starves every newborn to bones.

4. The murderer of infants is less repugnant
than those who deprive the labourer of their bread.

5. Pitch, when touched, besmirches, befouls.
League with the rich? Bathe in pitch.

6. (They prefer Medusa to Venus;
Midas to Moses.)

7. But the righteous carve beef for the homeless,
pour wine for shut-ins.

8. God preserves the just from storms;
He reveals shelter;
He guards against faltering and against halting.

9. Champagne poured while blues singers moan,
mumbling through blue smoke?
Diamonds in blue velvet.*

[Venezia (Italia) 12 *mai* mmxvii]

*** Cf. Fred Ward, *Riverlisp*.**

XXXVI.

1. The Lord's fist destroys dexterously:
His arm delivers staggering sockdolagers.

2. His *Art* is *Genocide*; His *métier* is *Massacre.*

3. He anatomizes every unbeliever—
atomizing em—
down to each, last, solitary, mortal atom.

4. Rouse God's *Wrath* so that He cripples
thy persecutors
while He's yawning,
strips em briskly down to bones.

5. Heathens' helmets will heap up, but won't roll,
due to the arrows studding—daggering—
felled faces and necks,
so that they mimic lopped burrs.

6. The God-directed thrusting of Hebrew blades
gusts out—blazes—opponents' innards.
Conquistadors, blood flushing out, blush at their dying.

7. Survivors of God's "First Strike" tee-hee their luck.
But soon the lacerated adversary feels lashing flame:
Smoking pitch leaves their corpses black
and hairless as babes.
They mirror tooth-marked jujubes.

8. Such twits are garrulous;
their verses are cursings;
their writing is graffiti.
Naturally, brimstone will skewer their skulls.

[Macdonald-Cartier International Airport (YOW)
19 *mai* mmxvii]

XXXVII.

1. A woman sprawls before any man
who pleads marriage?
Maybe.
But a proper love summons *Bliss.*

2. Her beauty and her steely legs
are like lamps set aloft
streaming light down gold pillars.

3. A husband becomes a father,
and finds *Longevity via* his giving wife,
and *Eternity via* their offspring.

4. The wise husband breeds his wife:
He capitalizes upon her *Beauty.*

5. Likewise, butterflies and bees collaborate
with the garden,
corroborating *Beauty.*

6. (Non-stop, marital, madcap *Fucking,*
neutering *Chastity,* that's *Love.*)

7. A fenceless property invites trespassers, plunderers.
Likewise, a bachelor got no home, but only hotels,
motels, flophouses, pubs, bus shelters...

8. A bandit who skips from town to town,
skulking along roadways;
and the bachelor who lacks a fixed address;
well, both are drifters, refused *Respect.*

9. They end up in disfiguring wisps and shreds;
they model rag-ends.

10. Heartless, brainless, bloodless, and soulless
are those ghouls who oppose *Love.*

[Macdonald-Cartier International Airport (YOW)
19 *mai* mmxvii]

XXXVIII.

1. *Death*? The birth canal readies an abyss.

2. The dead are arid shoots.
The dead are *Beauty* destroyed.

3. When the beloved die, temper thy tears,
lest *Grief* distemper thy heart.

4. Grief diseases *Virtue.*

5. Your parents died yesterday; you die today;
your children die tomorrow. Face facts.

6. *Mortality = Anxiety.*

7. Gold-throned kings and rock-pillow peasants:
All dread dying.

8. Gold-crowned queens and blue-jeaned proles:
All worry for their graves.

9. Accursed by ill-bred bastards,
you'll be glad to die,
and they'll be glad to gulp thy wine
and piss it on thy grave.

10. Thy surname will know infamy
and thy progeny will go extinct.

11. *Survival?*
One-foot-in-the-grave, yessum,
but one-foot-squishing-wine-grapes.

12. (Even when a road is cleared of obstacles,
one may stumble, *allowably*, exactly twice.)

13. Flesh is so frail, it vanishes at thy perishing.
But a virtuous name survives *Eternity*.

14. Better is inconsolable *Destitution*
than carrying a leprous name.

15. He levels all pests into graves:
God tramples on, stomps down, bugs.

16. Reeds—not weeds—are harvested.
Valued are the saints; the malefactors be chaff.

17. (God-granted *Prudence* offers better *Security*
than 700 sentinels girding a city's walls.)

18. Suitors push away a jilted woman;
War-vet comrades stone a coward;
bankers sic cops on debtors;
hunters' arrows pierce farmers' heels
(so they keel face-down, hard);
toilers jab pitchforks through the lazy:
So, don't the wise shackle the imprudent?

19. A woman despises her rival;
cowards pooh-pooh heroes;
merchants castigate lenders;
farmers curse pasture-marauding hunters;
and the lazy hate toilers:
So, *Envy* poisons their provisos, eh?

20. No worse *Envy* exists
than that of the infirm for the healthy.

[Tropea (Italia) 1 & 2 & 4 & 5 *juin* mmxvii]

XXXIX.

1. God's earthly ambassadors? Doctors!
Even kings kowtow to em.

2. (During famines, poets may be carved up,
wolfed down, but never doctors.)

3. A physician is first a gardener.
The pharmacist pounds greens to juice,
adds water—or wine—or milk,
to brew—or distill—medicines.

4. The physician domesticates God's genius.
Thus, doctors dictate *Perfection*.
(How else will thou survive?
How else can thy body profit?)

5. Might other occupations conjure moral precepts?

6. Busy with harnessing a plough,
tending the shaft of a goad,
flicking rhythmically a whip,
and seeking always a fresh, stud bull,
how can an ox-driver acquire *Wisdom*?

7. (An ox-driver's verses are furrows
in the field, the content is fodder—
paper best off as grain.)

8. Diligent with brush, vigilant with eye,
how can the portrait painter,
fixated on fixing images,
scruple to glean *Wisdom*?

9. Ditto for the blacksmith!
Blast-furnace heat yields *Inspiration*;
a hammer incises stylus-like;
the deafening metre beaten out
casts simultaneously *Song* and *Sculpture*:
In those hands, copper tenses for a pounding;
or one hears the sizzling plop
of wet, liquid lead,
or the din of sledgehammers blitzing iron.
But where's the *Leisure* to fashion *Philosophy*?

10. First setting hand to clay and foot to wheel,
ensconced in muddy *Chemistry*,
the potter soon fires concrete-hard
what is originally as pliable as water,
crafting ceramics from this white heat,
soon pimped out with glaze and dyes.
Where's the time for *Philosophy*?

11. The ox-driver, the painter, the blacksmith, the potter,
though skilled at their works,
are never asked to govern.

12. Though their trades build up civilizations,
not one gets appointed a judge,
nor are their opinions sought out
(nor respected, if overheard).

13. (*Faith* assembles a village; *Credit* crafts a city.)

14. Note a harlot's professional, compliant quality.
Awesomely dramatic is her "curtain-opening"
neath a dude!

15. But how is either wise?
They are as unlike as egg whites
mixed with coal.

16. Decidedly ain't a trollop
exuberant as a hunter,
spry as a hunter,
tireless as a hunter,
yet never ever wise?

17. Pillars prop up governments.
Pillows topple governments.

18. Progeny and prizes secure one's name,
but *Wisdom*'s better than honours or children.

[Tropea (Italia) 3 *juin* mmxvii]

XL.

1. Only clarkes—clerics—clergy—
draw nigh the Most High—
principality of *Pleasure*
plus *Power.*

2. They scope out a diamond-bright,
marble-white *Paradise*—
where rippling *Luminosity* shivers all the air,
that atmosphere as bracing as gales,
but smelling of lilies, a distillation.

3. Poring over mottled scrolls,
clerks imbibe *Wisdom*;
and thereby affirm antique prophecies—
or scuttle em, rebut em.

4. (Hell is also churchy:
A sun-burned, sun-scorched Bible Belt.)

5. Clarkes who jot parables, proverbs,
never fall into *Obscurity*;
their signatures—and poems—
are never blotted out.

6. Nations congregate before clerics
to hear sermons that yield slogans,
mantras,
or allegories as sly and biting as alligators.

7. (*Permission* is *Poetry*; *Prohibition* is *Prose*.)

8. Scribes' deaths are never foppish.
Hygienic—immaculate—are their graves.

9. Scribes must hate every place that isn't Heaven,
that lacks a library.

10. (Every Believer heeds the command,
"*Tolle legge*":
Take up the book and read!*)

11. Clerks remind us how God's *Injunction*
halved the Red Sea, split it into two reservoirs,
to let Hebrews scape cross sudden sodden desert,
then let the divided, mountainous waves,
slap, clap, together,
flushing down the pursuing Gypsies.

12. The jumpy waters, the obscene foam,
composed an instant array of historic, dissolving acids—
a mass, briny grave—
the convulsive seething of visceral waves.

13. Also, Egyptian lances snapped, shields shattered;
spears gored the pagan priests;
blood sprayed over hieroglyphics
suddenly as unfathomable as Greek.

14. Plus, weird engines slew thousands:
Catapult stones boomeranged back at the Gyps.

15. Twitchy blades twisted in Gyp generals' fists
and stabbed suicidally their shocked chests.**

16. Spy, even now, Cairo's cataclysmic rubble:
Vitriolic smoke, crumpled temples.

---

* Cf. St. Augustine, *puis* George Grant.
** Imagine Genghis Khan as Yukio Mishima.

17. Clerics annotate God's expeditious *Wrath*:
He purges babes, dames, sires, thrones,
blowing all away like dust.
His *Anger* is as relentless as the tide.

18. He swamps proud mountains under lousy marsh;
turns watermelon into cacti.

19. God's *Rage* is unabashedly barbaric.
He dices *Eternity*
into personalized, corpse-sized portions.

20. God's *Wrath* is plain:
Hail flogs and flattens crops;
lightning ignites grass huts.

21. Clarkes instruct us that the Most High
provides all that mortals need:
the liquor of the grape, mud for bricks,
marble for floors, wood for roofs,
the taste of sleep in wine.

22. Also *Coitus*. (Earthy *Grace*, worldly *Menace*.)

23. (Irrevocable? The kiss, the caress, and *Coitus*:
Ensure any or all are welcome.)

24. Clergy warn we mortals that God harasses,
wounds, all miscreants,
loosing upon em sabre-toothed wolves,
serrated-jawed vipers,
and/or adversaries' gnashing swords.

25. What is worse than poison or prison?
Misprision.

26. As for clarkes who are poets,
a bard must live long to be wise.
But how else can a scribe's verses become proverbs,
or whole poems rival sermons?

27. One must compose
Ivory Tower poetry, Skid Row poetry,
and *Scripture* (Adept poesy, Devout poesy).
One must be a total poet, a totalitarian for *Poetry*....
Then, *Poetry* can be as profitable as beekeeping.*

28. Understand that the mind is a compass:
Its four stops are *Sex*, *Health*, *Capital*, and *Death*.

29. In response,
wield a vinegar pen and/or a honey stylus.

30. (Poetasters simply dump dirt on the page.

31. Their speeches become
slushy laments or puked up elegies
or coughed up hymns.)

32. Being a Poet, I've pondered *Scripture*,
and am tasked to thunder out its ideals—
ideas—
in ink.
Who else has this *Responsibility*?

33. Never must *Poetry* seem a pedantic belch—
or clamouring, yammering stammers.

34. Never may a poet sound
as throaty as a goat—
nor as languidly moaning.

35. (And never gossip;
then, you never eat crow.)

36. I have an undamaged voice?
Hope so: If it's insolent.

---

* Cf. S. Plath, T. Hughes, V. Mortensen.

37. The sycophants reject *Restraint*,
and, therefore, *Safety*.
Their minds are as dark as their assholes.

38. Shameless, they die, screeching,
as their bowels, spear-snagged,
get torn—tugged—out their bodies.

39. Never do I emit contraband songs.
No dull elegies; no pissy, death-bed wheezing.
No pre-fab rhymes.

40. I have a clucking *Conscience*.
How else can a herald arouse and fret
the *Unconscious*, chronically?

41. Prose goes extinct, so boast a name
poets will favour.

42. *Defeat* is an alienating *Emotion*.

**[Tropea (Italia) 3 & 4 *juin* mmxvii
& Mogliano Veneto (Italia) 11 *mai* mmxvii]**

XLI.

1. Breath = *Toil:*
A diabolical equation....

2. Fishers must squabble with seas and nets
before wine can squall into their cups.

3. Hunters must traverse lead-tint moonlight stealthily
before they may gulp glacier-tapped vodka.

4. Lumberjacks hear the chipping thuds of their axes
before they can chug-chug jugs of ale.

5. Poltroons—perpetual schoolgirls—scuttle,
skedaddle from saddle to saddle,
rut from bed to bed,
clucking and cooing in their labours,
until their faces, in Kabuki rictus,
cry out onerous* *Exultation.*

6. (Escorts sound like laundry women—
sucking, squirting, squishing, swishing, sloshing—
but this *Labour* prefaces *Liquidity,*
cash-flow, and flowing liquor.)

7. A phallus adores every ounce of a moll—
her gushing, luscious orifices—
so that the ram of *Lust* tups the hog of *Gluttony*—
and their conjoined throats hurl purling groans
in the pitchy moment—
the jolly *Melancholy* that's *Climax,*
avid howls subsiding into shuddering moans.

* Oneiric.

8. *Anger, Envy, Lust, Greed, Illness, Debt, Scheming*:
All nag and upset *Sleep*.

9. Wrestling with bedsheets, struggling for breath,
tussling with pillows, and sweating, and snoring,
such are those possessing a harried *Conscience*.

10. And if sleep comes, it summons horrors
as bad as those that disturb old soldiers
reliving nightmarish, lethal battles.

11. Awake? Fears become phantasms.

12. But no dissident may relax or feel *Equanimity*.
Uh-uh!

13. God jitters the unjust with unrest;
thus, He rousts em out their beds.

14. *Beauty* is as *Beauty* does.

15. Come *Victory*, *Triumph*,
dispense winnings as spoils;
turn trophies into *Largesse*;
pay off loyalists.

16. Boot-lickers screech *Praise* to your face,
dribble saliva and tears as they bow, prostrate,
but as soon as your back is turned,
they league—shameless in shadows—
with your assassins.

17. There's no *Love* in their hearts, only blood.
In sordid processions, giggling,
they revile you *even* to your mother.

18. Likewise, a stallion jounces a knight, prancing,
then tramples him, soon as he pitches off.

19. Anyone who eyes you suspiciously
got no gusto in his/her lungs
to hullabaloo thy deeds.

20. Remember: Villains sob,
then ready their secret knives.

[Tropea (Italia) 4 & 5 *juin* mmxvii]

XLII.

1. To fuck errantly is to pimp your father
and whore your mother.

2. It is a pristine *Degeneration*;
disorderly whelping—
sculpting a derelict congregation.

3. (Namely, orangutangs ear-marked—fingered—
for the circus.

4. The guys are *Evolution* that's slumped, sagged.)

5. The slut's bubbling slit sucks up,
glugs down, a shaft,
as she squats, and daddy-o doth dicker.

6. Next, the loud, big-head contralto yodels
while his hairy hand tugs her hair
or half-strangles her throat.

7. She's unexpectedly manipulated.
He screws fur, fangs, and claws.

8. The blatant pro squeezes out recessive beasts—
slimy brats and bloody twats....

9. So's birthed a menagerie of cocksuckers—
a consortium of mongrels...

10. (Their stink, once unstuck, stains all.)

11. Best not play the formalistic libertine!
Scruples must not be random.

12. The *Comeuppance* is, to go downhill.

13. (No unanswered questions in the cemetery!
Our very being entails our ending.)

[Tropea (Italia) 5–7 *juin* mmxviii]

XLIII.

1. Be scrupulous about accounts,
and divvy inheritances equally.
Elsewise, suffer courthouse repercussions!

2. Balance precisely weights and scales,
whether much or little is being valued.

3. Merchants should profit, but never thieve.

4. Avoid mercenary marketing:
Usury is *CONTRA NATURAM.**

5. Treat every purchase, every trade,
as not only final,
but as your very last.
Barter and/or buy as if staring into thy grave.

6. When banking, register every transaction in ink.
Whether giving or receiving, ink is your witness.

7. Conduct business before rigorous mirrors
and under scrutinizing magnifying glasses.

8. In *Business*, the pen is pedantic;
the eraser, scholarly.

9. Gold finances *Will.*

10. Be punctilious bout your cupboards
and vigilant in your sheets.
How else will ye guard *Rapture*?

[Tropea (Italia) 6 & 7 *juin* mmxvii]

* Cf. Pound, Canto XLV.

XLIV: Ancestor Hymn.

1. Let us now laud famous men:
Applaud unprecedented antecedents!

2. Dead are their deeds, but dynamic
they're still; still historically heroic they be.

3. They are living proverbs. Spotless:
The monumental instrumentation of poems!

4. Oracular, oneiric verses are their words.

5. None were unclean rumps—
a clump of poetasters.

6. With gusto, their names were sung in their times.

7. Say their names are gone? So what?
Their rhymes and melodies persist.

8. Noah earned epic poems, for he kept *Humanity*
afloat when God drowned hatefully
the privately sinful *Silent Majority*.

9. Abraham be sung, for he fathered nations—
just like Atilla the Hun,
who clogged morgues with obligatory homicides—
and jammed women with genealogies
spewed off his loins

10. (The meritorious half-light of *Anthropology*
salutes weeping nudes,
whose breasts jump as armies sweep em off,
jigging.)

11. And Abraham was loyal to the Lord—
nearly slaying his own son to bless God's name.
So, God gifted Abe with nation-spouting sons.

12. *Fucking* is counterpart to eating.

[Tropea (Italia) 9 *juin* mmxvii]

XLV.

1. Daughters worry every father:
They fear that she won't marry;
they fear that she'll go gaga for a bum;
they fear that she'll whelp bastards;
they fear that she—or hubby—will test sterile;
they fear her husband will be a lech.

2. Guard a strong-willed daughter,
lest *Shame* be ushered to thy door.

3. Don't let her flounce about,
flaunting her gleaming hair, bouncing her bubbies,
twerking her butt!

4. Don't let older women instruct her in *Love*!
They'll teach tricks, not *Trepidation*.

5. (Women urge on *Wickedness* in women!
Beware.)

6. Treat your daughter like a jewel,
distanced from greedy eyes, lustful hands.

7. A bastood's *Gestation* disrupts accounts,
interrupts harvests, proves the virgin a tramp.

8. Just as winds accost and sow foam all about
open water,
so is the daughter-turned-doxy—open to all
masculine, propulsive impaling....
Plus, her brood may be your enemy's.

9. If she's raped, she'll feel rivets of *Agony*;
but you will know rivulets of tears.

[Tropea (Italia) 6 & 7 *juin* mmxvii]

XLVI.

1. Encircled, Joshua beseeched God's *Aid*:
His reply?
To thunder boulder-huge hailstones on conquistadors;
pulp em to shivering, scarlet blobs.

2. It was kinda hard for Vandals, anyhow,
to make a run for mountain tops
after leapin from pitchin ships.

3. The cretins sprawled—as slime and jelly—
all the way down the bouldered slopes—
millimetre by inch—
a red-and-white, Caucasoid meringue.

4. Faces got splintered into pieces;
teeth bit through cheekbones.
Blood blubbered bitter,
pelted pebbly soil.

5. Joshua wielded the *shillelagh*—
that Irish stick that demolishes skulls
(when polished to a sheen, its oak lets
ya wipe off dead blokes' grey-matter.)

6. *Lobotomy*-triggered, sprang forked-out eyes:
Sanguinary liquid—black—was a mud-mask.

7. Joshua's luscious muscles,
licorice-pungent in tint,
assigned the combatants atrocious blows,
as he helped out at *Genocide*,
wasting 600,000 wankers….

8. Caleb maintained legendary *Vigour*
right up to his centenarian demise:
Plus que 100 years old, and still whelping.

9. Libelled despite his *Virtue*, Samuel yelled,
"I've stolen zero, zip:
Neither pastures—herds—nor a pair of shoes."

[Tropea (Italia) 11 *juin* mmxvii]

XLVII.

1. At God's clap, clouds hunker and hover,
shake down snow or pour out rain.
Thus are wells replenished,
and wheat puff up stores.

2. Snowflakes resemble molecular feathers:
Their white rollicking unfurlings
plume pines and spruce.
Every barren tree hints at a pearly crucifix.

3. Snow accosts the foamed sea.
The flakes resemble bone bits a cyclone scatters.

4. Frost salts fields;
pools don icy breastplates.

5. Snow at night? A kaleidoscope of salt
and basalt.

6. Fragrant is the southerly wind, as God wills.
Due to its dew,
ligaments align anew; nerves croon each-to-each.

7. Gusts hunch among cordial woods.
Intensified comes *Bliss*.

8. Lavish is the gusty breathing—
the ravishing breezes—of immodest April
as is the unfolding of fruit-spiced blossoms.

9. May arrives, pistachio-green;
infinite dew studs grass.

10. Eye the lightning-scratched,
lightning-scrawled sky.
Ogle nasty, pasty lightning
that chars eyes as they blink!

11. Yet, superior to lightning is God—
that dazzle, disorienting and enlightening.

12. God sparks fires that liquidate forests:
God decides on fire-garbled ruins.

13. Punishing be his *Inferno*,
broiling trespassers ceaselessly.

14. Last-minute *Murk* or irresistible *Radiance*?
God chooses.

15. Anapestic rain or a cloud's thundering yawp?
God judges.

16. The sea inhales, exhales, pebbles, shells.
Note the trembling, white-lace fringe of froth.

17. At times, the ocean is dainty gurgles;
at other times, it's dastardly throbs....

18. Skimming white froth off black broth is the ship,
in dizzying nights of pure tar—no stars.

19. Sailors squint at the dawn to suss out—
within the pale cavern of the light—
whether *Gloom* or *Glitter* broaches the sea.

20. Sailors face Gothic waves that smithereen
wood and shamble canvas.
Such saltwater *Disquiet* can overwhelm lungs....

21. (If only sailors could rest easy where eels
love their anchors.)

22. Sailors carouse among isinglass-tipped waves,
but end as worms among seaweed,
on darkling shingles—
on distant and *War*-distraught,
War-fraught shores.

[Tropea (Italia) 7 & 9 *juin* mmxvii]

XLVIII.

1. Because Moses approximates *Divinity*,
devastated be his challengers.

2. Only Moses was elevated—to bear God's *Law*,
seared into stone tablets—
to Israeli-tutored *Humanity*.

3. God's *State* is founded on Moses and Aaron:
Marble pillars, a gold throne,
the stone-carved *Law*.

4. In the Palace of the *State*—Government House—
Aaron wears white silk instrumentalized with gold chimes,
so that each step and gesture communicates *Music*.

5. Before Aaron's Ministry came in,
Public Administration disfigured *Beauty*.

6. Then, incense—that politic perfume—
got intertwisted with all pronouncements.

7. To Aaron, Government's task is to model *Splendour*.

8. Even peaches seem now the work
of unimpeachable jewellers.

9. No wonder that Aaron's nemesis, Korah—
that beauty profiled in Egyptian hieroglyphics
(buttery leather corseting her lemony waist,
crowning her *belle-chose*)—
sustained God's *Enmity*.

10. That *Coitus fortissimo, zaftig* drab,
plotted, alongside understated, devious henchmen,
to launch a first-rate, last-ditch *Putsch*.
To repeal *The Decalogue*!

11. Jeering at Aaron, Korah *et* her scofflaws—
Rather and Aberrant—
fought to camp out in Government House.

12. Unamused was God. *Revenge* came extra painful.

13. A boulder struck Korah's pregnancy so hard,
her kiddo shot out her maw
and, bawling, struck sharp stones.

14. But what slew her newborn was Korah herself,
plopping dead—a sheer dead-weight—
upon her mewling chick.

15. Next, a thorn thrusting through his boot
finished off Rather rather quick!
The spiky plant-part bit into his foot bone,
squirted venom through his heart.

16. Aberrant saw blood lunge from his side
where Aaron's spear had dug in.
His chunky corpse clunked so hard to the floor
that plaster plunked down off the ceiling below.

17. Haughty, outlaw troops suffered
panoramic *Rot*,
broke down into clumps of trash—
bone, teeth, hair—
exuding a dirty stench.

18. Disembodied garbage strewn among cacti:
Assassins become intinsic bacteria.

19. Korah and her band now nurse on epitaphs.

20. And Aaron is no slouching pasha.
He's an indignant saint.

21. His sons' voices boom through trumpets
of hammered gold.
Full-throttle, full-throated: Their melodies.

22. Established unquestionably now is
Imperial *Decency*—
i.e., measured and meted out *Gravitas*.

23. What was ancient is now unique, that's all.

[Tropea (Italia) 10 & 12 *juin* mmxvii]

XLIX.

1. Wherever he'd turn, in his wake,
Josiah generated bergamot—
that lemon-*louche* and bracing bergamot,
of San Nicola da Crissa and/or Tropea.

2. Whenever others quoted Josiah,
his words became liquor in their mouths;
whoever absorbed Josiah's words,
heard lyres as lyrical and fluid as flutes.

3. Correct info merits *Fame*;
bad teachings summon *Infamy*.

Josiah's lectures were wine-tastings;
his symposia oozed ouzo and *vino locale*.

4. His derogatory murmurs,
though muted,
still sand-blasted errant ears.

5. (To hide *Folly* is wise; to hide *Wisdom* is suicidal.)

6. Never did Jeremiah need to struggle
into his armour,
which was *l'Amour*.

7. An architectural resuscitator, Nehemiah
engineered the rebirth of rubbled walls.
All his structures were as smooth as breath.

8. His cordial blueprints arranged maximum sunlight,
succulent breezes, the gusty bacchanalia of fountains.

9. His buildings, decked out with ivy-latticed walls,
soon boasted sparrows' wings—
chrome-brilliant—darting, flashing.

10. (His firm—Varcon—laid out streets
where sunflowers showcased glitzy burning—
those gold-leaf incendiaries—
wherever they trespassed.)

11. Nehemiah paved over—with bricks—
the pits holding the bones and ashes
of the calamitous kings of Judea—
who'd presided over an Eliotic Waste Land,
whose governments were hapless chapters
of *Kleptocracy*, *Hypocrisy*, and *Blasphemy*.

12. (Bankrolled by *Big Money*,
their *Plutocracy* pursued bankrupting,
unproductive *Luxury*.

13. These ugly Israeli kings turned their bung-holes up
to the knifing, sordid sticks of foreigners!

14. Wanton as always were peasants' deaths,
lacking even the shabby glory that mercenaries win.

15. These lousy monarchs got repealed:
Like consumptive, *Death*-sentenced lawyers,
neckties manacled their hands;
next, circumcised were their necks.)

16. Nehemiah's city soon steeple-stabbed the sky:
No *Lego*-block Pisa was his creation.
Brutalism was eschewed.

17. From birth was Joseph an unparalleled governor:
From sweet *Infancy*, he was as wise as a prophet.

18. At death, his body was steeped in bergamot
(exuding nuances of tea roses),
then sheathed in gold leaf
(as crisp as pie-crust,
each tissue was applied slowly,
under the eagle-eye of that art critic, Berger);
and then he was ushered into a marble tomb,
pick-axed out a mountainside,
at that Doukhobor redoubt,
Brilliant.

[Tropea (Italia) 15 *juin* mmxvii]

L.

1. Knowing that a cistern waters *Faith*,
Simon commanded the trenching of a reservoir
able to hold—unreservedly—a sea.

2. To police the city, Simon girdled it
with a palisade and a walkway,
staffed with a hundred bow-and-arrow snipers.

3. Whenever he broached his curtains to walkabout,
reconnoitering the city, folks beamed—
just as cavemen do when the sun shatters clouds,
or when the sun silvers the sea;
or when the detergent moon scours turgid night....

4. Whenever Simon stood among his brethren,
he seemed a palm tree garlanded by fallen coconuts.

5. His government profited even the senses.

6. Thus, I, Jesus, son of Eleazar, son of Sirach,
loathe all apostates, all savages.

7. I denounce, thus, Assyria, Babylon,
and all those shit-holes that populate Washington.

8. Their strategy is *Greed, Gluttony, Lust, Wrath,*
Treachery, Blasphemy, Treason.

9. Due to their garish, unpolished whiteness,
they resemble untamed ghosts.

10. Breed em stinging wounds
that'll feed maggots in broad daylight!

11. Tear off their human masks!
Sight their wolf-skulls and blood-spewing jaws!

[Trenitalia Train 22674, Tropea-Lamezia Terme (Italia)
& Trenitalia Train 3684, Lamezia Terme-Cosenza (Italia)
15 *juin* mmxvii]

LII.

1. Elijah? Pure, deathless fire!

2. As appalling as Apollo
and his incinerating self,
his eyes spark ignition;
his touch is a torch.

3. Didn't Elijah cause a corpse to leap up—
though half-decayed, stinking—
and stand again, hearty and cheery?

4. That cadaver'd been rancid snow.
Elijah'd had to judge whether *Resurrection*
was generally in the dead's best interest....

5. Soon, folks carted a freight of corpses—
to Elijah for his "healing."
But he quick declared, "The dead should stay dead!"

6. (Anyway, the sickly be all rustic decadents,
pitiful in their palsies and groans.
Were they not better off
lying under the soil
than stumbling or staggering over it?)

7. Frog-marched monarchs to guillotines,
did Elijah;
he had courtiers shackled down
even in their sick-beds.

8. Naturally, *Death* couldn't touch Elijah!
In a whirlwind of blazing horses, in his fiery chariot—
a cloak of flame—
he got borne up to Heaven.

9. The next-best prophet, Elisha,
with marvels and omens, regaled all.

10. Hezekiah had the foresight to demand
that his city be battle-ready,
that water be winched up from wells.

11. Aroused stupidly by the warm damp
of his own guts bleeding out,
Slacker saw his prong jerk up
as his belly drained flat.

12. His Assyrians got air-conditioned,
reamed out like *culeros*,
thanks to spears—
diabolical icicles—
analyzing em.

13. Those who survived that tsunami of spears—
a blizzard as black as rotten bananas—
soon faced hollow bellies.

14. The Assyrians voted to eat their young,
their wounded, their elderly, their diseased,
and everybody morbidly obese!

15. Died off now, ashes are their echo.

16. Isaiah witnessed the sun spin backward.
Thus, he could render a compass pointless!

[Tropea (Italia) 13 & 15 *juin* mmxvii]

SINGULAR CIRCULARS

I. — *The Letter of Jeremiah.*

1. Yo! Babylon's grotesque gods
are arty, exotic, but inviting,
thanks to gold or ebony,
studded with lurid garnets
or syphilis-jaundiced-tint jade,
or glaucous, tubercular pearls.

2. Naturally, the Babylonians credit
these gargoyles—
these jacked-up gutter spouts,
with cartoonish superpowers.
But, Israel, *nota bene*:
All these gods are frauds.

3. Gleaming with gold-leaf,
or patina'd with copper,
the sawn or carved
or baked or hammered visages
leer—repulsive and/or beckoning.
Yet, Israel, these so-called gods
cannot utter even a grunt.

4. Idiots will dig up, smelt, and work gold
to fine-tool this gimcrackery,
or crown these preposterous derelicts!
(These putatively omnipotent dolls
really model pubescent fashionistas,
craving ornaments to dress up
their spineless and male-gaze-sexualized
self-images!)

5. Unscrupulous theologians will, at night,
sneak into temples and strip these fetishes
of every valued accoutrement—
and then hand the denuded and eyeless
statuary or busts
to superstitious prostitutes
in trade for *fellatio*.

6. The credulous robe these dead objects in silk
and shod em in leather,
these fancy clods (not beings)
can't walk, talk, or fuck;
can't keep emselves from being denuded,
scraped bare,
rusting (if iron or tin);
burning and splintering (if wood);
or shattering (if ceramic);
can't heal anyone,
can't enrich anyone,
can't dissuade or even delay *Death*....

7. Of course, the dust and dirt of the feet,
sandalled or not, of unwashed idolaters,
begrimes the faces of their gargoyles,
these asinine fetishes.

8. Say that one idol brandishes a sword,
or another waves an axe?
Robbers hee-haw at both these charlatans!

9. A vase or a bowl is useless once busted.
Ditto for the Babylonian statuary—
this tarted up rubble, gussied up trash!

10. Priests like to illuminate these dirt-slimed jobs.
But no matter how many candles are lit,
not one chases away shadows.

11. These dreaded Babylonian entities—
are rat-bit (because rodents,
having eaten the idols' stingy food offerings,
remain famished);
and worms and beetles burrow and nestle
in the cavities and folds,
becoming the only *Life*
that these dead deities boast.

12. On their heads and faces,
spot gull guano, sparrow splatter,
pigeon poop.
Cats doze at their feet, or piss there.

13. Israel, ya call these nincompoop,
junk piles, "gods"?

14. Aye, Israel, the gold leaf of these "Lumpen" lumps—
mere wood, clay, stone, or metal—doth glitter.
Uh-huh!
But only because beggars clear off the grime
smeared thereupon
by worshippers' soiled feet and fingers.

15. These thingies are *Vanity*,
for they are insensate.
Just dead weight. Period.

16. But, if metal, they're easy to melt down
and repurpose as *pissoirs*, urinals, chamber pots.

17. (If one of these decorative mannequins falls—
clunk—over,
a living dolt has to stand the flimflam upright.)

18. Just as they do for the dead,
folks leave these inventions gifts.
But thieves are the sole beneficiaries.

19. *Cordon-Bleu* chefs prepare *Michelin Guide* meals
for these stultified statues.
But as soon as the temple gates close,
the priests feast on these gourmet dishes,
and joke and hurl back wine,
while kicking away the rats.

20. Let plutocrats toss coins at the feet of idols!
The priests collect and count em at dusk,
and use these moneys to pay off trulls
and bankroll their kennel.

21. Women burning bran for incense,
to salute statues,
would be better off smoking it!

22. When one of Bawl's believing bitches tumbles
before a priest's prick,
and she derides her bran-burning sister
for not having been selected for this ceremony
(a Sodomite spectacle),
she ought to desist!
All it is, is just bumf!
Bawl can't care what a woman does,
for Bawl is just a soulless gewgaw!

23. All idols are the monstrous toys
of carpenters, blacksmiths,
goldsmiths, jewellers, painters, potters....

24. Worthless! Helpless! Powerless!
These vain idols—regardless
of all their gold, silver, ivory, diamonds,
gems, jewels, iron, and incense—
can't back kings,
can't guillotine traitors,
can't rescue martyrs,
can't distinguish the valuable from the extinguishable,

can't scare off thieves,
can't house, feed, clothe, heal, teach, anyone,
can't keep emselves from being rebranded
(so Thor can become Medusa,
or Venus can become Priapus).

25. Babylon's pathetic gods, O Israel,
are easily melted down for scrap.
quick burnt up or broken into smithereens,
soon carted off as boodle,
fast chopped up or defaced,
swiftly tagged or grafitti'd over,
et cetera.

26. And how can anyone complain—*sincerely*?
The *Vanity* of these inanimate things is exposed
as they moulder or are mangled
or are manhandled.

27. A padlock on a Treasury is useful;
as is a pillar supporting a floor.
But idols are functionless—
except as dildos.

28. A Babylonian godlet is no better than
a reeking corpse flung into an ash heap.

29. All idols are corrupt creations.
They are only suitable as
anthropological oddities,
as archaeological specimens,
as theological failures—
dead letters.

[Tropea (Italia) 19 *juin* mmxvii]

II. — *The Prayer of Azariah & The 3 Jews.*

1. Hank (a.k.a. Shadrack), Meshell (a.k.a. Meshack),
and Azariah (a.k.a. Abednego), strolled and pirouetted
amid waltzing, promenading flames—
as if their furnace were the likeness
of a Bermudian beach—
balmy, sultry, and moist.

2. All prayed now to God:
"Thou regardest our tears
as if they were burnt sacrifices
of thousands of bulls or rams
or 10,000 newborn lambs.

3. "O do not tally our sins.
Do not pass us by."

4. The theologians of the Babylonian Court,
overhearing Azariah's prayer,
and confounded by the failure
of this miniature, privatized *Holocaust*,
demanded that pitch, coal, naphtha,
brushwood, tallow, fat, and napalm,
plus gasoline and other fossil fuels,
be adduced as accelerants to the blaze,
intended to incinerate and silence
the exasperating, Hebrew trio.

5. Well, the intensified inferno lobbed fireballs
61 feet up, above the furnace.
But, queerly, a few went astray
and burnt to crisps
all mocking theologians.

6. Hank, Meshell, and Azariah
now saluted God
in unison.

7. "All praise to the God
that dwarfs all other gods."

[Tropea (Italia) 20 *juin* mmxvii]

III. — *O Susannah!**

1. Though only a Babylonian exile,
Jenson was bankable, and so manned
this beaut of a bride.

2. *Bellissima*, gammy, and *guapísima*,
Susannah had sex appeal to damn a saint.

3. Elders—Judges—voted by the Hebrews
to try criminal and/or civil cases,
conclaved to decide verdicts
usually at Jenson's manse—
a virtual palace—
and his clerks assured that the judiciary
utilized first-class offices and furnishings—
airy with sunlight and aired-out by breezes—
and lunched on lamb and refreshed with wine.

4. Habitually, at noon, Susannah would stroll
a leafy, thus shadowy, grassy path
on her estate,
to her bath, *au naturel*.

5. Two Judges—Elders—
chose to spy on Madama Susannah Jenson,
having reconnoitred a view-plane—
through olive topiary and emerald leaves and brush—
to scrutinize, inscrutably, the pedestrian Godiva,
while she passed by
(as liltingly as that *Gal from Ipanema*)—
traipsing unawares to her bath.

6. That marrony, cinnamon bride,
wading into lapis lazuli.

---

* Cf. *Oh! Calcutta!*

7. Daily, the twinned lechers savoured
the sunbathing and/or skinnydipping drama,
the *plein-air* peep-show.

8. Well, both Judges craved to take Susannah
judiciously—and injudiciously—
without prejudice to any orifice—
and so found frustrated *Fulfillment*
(wanking, frigging, each other),
shameless in their voyeurs' lair.

9. Both gave off the musty smell of years.
They were *Lust*'s withered antiques.

10. Conspiring, perspiring, at their clandestine eye-hole,
they machinated to prosecute, to persecute,
each of Susannah's inlets....

11. A day later, the Judges secreted themselves
on the primrose path, near the marble bath,
and awaited the gleaming glory
of Susannah's *Nudity*.

12. She dropped her "bralette":
Each breast was a sun;
each nipple a moon:
A gold-bronze sun with a beauty-spot moon.

13. Sun-shades, sun-tan oils, sunburn ointments,
all lay in the accommodating grass,
a tantalizing array.

14. So, once her maids had retired and closed gates—
sealed off the garden enclosed—
the two Elders confronted the scared, stripped *femme*,
and declared their *Decision*.

15. "Either we use you any way we like,
or we'll testify that we've caught you
committing *Adultery* with a deaf-mute lad,
and you'll be stoned to death
and he banished."

16. While the Elders / Judges stood
erect
(as usual at high-noon),
Susannah, no longer at ease—
but also no longer afraid—
screamed, "Help! *Rape*! Help!"

17. But the Judges screeched, "*Treason*! *Adultery*!"

18. The shuttered garden was unlocked,
and Jenson's household eyed the two Judges,
skull-faced,
each holding one arm
of the naked, squirming, jiggling
(evidently D-cup-supreme) Susannah.

19. They swore they'd observed Susannah
twerk her "bare-ass" rump
at her paramour's groin.

20. Immediately, two misogynist misters
bent to dredge up stones
to hurl at Susannah's clear and obvious *Femininity*.

21. But the Judges intoned, "Nay:
No *Judgment* can be exercised
until the missus is tried
before Master Jenson tomorrow—
once back from his business junket."

22. Now was Susannah padlocked in a room
in the mansion basement, guarded,
until she could be let out to testify.

23. The next day, ushered before the kangaroo court,
Susannah was veiled sumptuously.

24. The scoundrel Judges ordered her unveiled
so they could lust after her afresh,
before she'd be drubbed and bedraggled,
ripped apart,
under a steady fusillade of stones.

25. The *Lust*-cankered Elders testified
they'd caught Susannah—
in flagrante delecto—
"servicing" a "dummy,"
but he'd dodged their clutches,
being sweaty, youthful, lithe, and muscled.

26. Believing the scoundrels' witnessing,
onlookers screamed,
"Gotta stone her to death!"

27. Traumatized, Jenson sat stone-faced in an armchair.

28. Susannah cried out,
"O God, Thou knowest my *Chastity*'s honest!"

29. No matter: *The Silent Majority** crowded about
as Susannah was led to the nearest stone pile—
to be bathed by stones;
to be pummelled and battered into a pit.

30. But one youth, who'd lagged back
from the homicidal horde,
felt God-prodded to butt in:
"I, Daniel, refuse to accept executing
this innocent woman,
who's been slandered by geriatric eunuchs—
due to their unsanctified, unnatural,
and unreciprocated *Lust*!"

* Nixonian.

31. The guilty Elders called for Daniel's seizure,
and now tagged him as Susannah's covert lover.

32. "We thought her date was a retard,
but now that we spy the boy up close,
we state that Daniel was the culprit
diddling Susannah while her mouth
slurped up his drool."

33. Guards scrambled to grapple Daniel.
He yelled, "Prove that I'm lying!
Prove that Susannah's lying!"

34. Some who already held rocks
had to let em fall, relunctantly.
There'd be time for a double-stoning—
undoubtedly—later.

35. Shortly, two pale Judges quailed
as they were separated from each other,
so that Daniel could evaluate their *Veracity*.

36. Daniel asked Judge I, "Tell us,
by what tree did you see Susannah
offer her 'bumper' to my 'swipe'?"

37. Sweating ferociously, Judge I answered,
"An orange tree."

38. Similarly questioned, Judge II asserted,
"A fig tree."

39. Thus exposed as prevaricators, neither Elder
could explain away their discrepancies.

40. Each fell to accusing the other
of having concocted the game plan
to entrap Susannah and coerce her
into *Adultery*.

41. Daniel lectured th'Assembly,
"Y'all almost—due to *Misogyny*—almost
slew horribly a pure woman and wife,
almost slandered her family and husband,
based on the base allegations of two Judges,
hiding their foul *Lust* behind judicial garb.

42. "And keep in mind that these two hoods
have likely trapped other wives (privily)
into behaving as a tantrum of slags.

43. "(Maybe some of you wives present
got blackmailed into satisfying
these two-faced, fork-tongued vipers?)

44. "Jenson, trust me with your sword!"

45. Daniel now tasked the cowering Judges
to expose and tug each other's phalloi.

46. As soon as, despite mutual *Terror*,
each Judge's rod stretched upright,
Daniel swung down his sword,
slashing free twice half an arm
and its fist-clutched penis.

47. Then, the loathsome pair were jerked
to the quarry,
to be bashed and crushed by flung stones,
while they flailed,
blood puking from their halved arms
and now-unmembered groins.

[Tropea (Italia) 20 *juin* mmxvii]

Baruch IV.

1. W*isdom*? It's *The Decalogue,* moron!
Those 10 Commandments fire up the sun
and spark the stars.

2. God's People, never prioritize Fascist laws!
Such "Best Practices" urge on curses:
Treasuries of fool's gold,
anthologies of massacres,
orgies of mamas plucking suckling babes
off their own teats
to ground em underfoot.

3. O Israel, God is ever *Just.*
Obey His Constitution,
and enemies' citadels dissolve to rubble.

4. To spurn God's statutes, *Governance,*
is to empty the *Treasury,*
round-up the pregnant for summary abortion.

5. Our daughters get tarted up,
pimped,
colluded lewdly with lice.

6. Our sons, if not slain outright,
will be shackled at the neck
and dragged over stones and thorns.

7. We learn the *Tyranny* that's *Love* outlived.

8. When will our mirrors see heroes again?
When we are *Just.*

[Tropea (Italia) 19 *juin* mmxvii]

TABLE OF VERSES

(of published–or accepted—works, in order of appearance herein)

"Beloved Reader": *Share & Care: The Story of the Nova Scotia Home for Coloured Children*. By Charles R. Saunders. Halifax: Nimbus Publishing, 1994. X.

AAR Centennial Roundtable: "Furthermore": *The Journal of the American Academy of Religion*. 82.3 (September 2014): 593–594.

"Genesis I": Trans. Galia Vurgan.

"Joseph Repulses": *Vallum*. 11.1 (2014): 10.

"Moses (Memoirs)": *Braided Way Magazine*. February 5, 2019.
http://braidedway.org/moses/

"Exodus XX (Gloss)": *ottawater*. 15 (January 2019): 17.
http://www.ottawater.com/ottawater15.pdf

"Samson II": *Canadian Literature*. 237 (2019): 83–84.

"Samson III": *Poem*. 6. 3–4 (September-December 2018): 297–299.

"Samson IV": *Maple Tree Literary Supplement*. 23 (April-July 2018). ISSN 1916-341X.
http://www.mtls.ca/issue23/poetry-george-elliott-clarke/

"Ruth I": *Maple Tree Literary Supplement*. 24. 2019.
http://www.mtls.ca/issue24/poetry-george-elliott-clarke/

"Ruth II": *ottawater*. 15 (January 2019): 18–19.
http://www.ottawater.com/ottawater15.pdf

"Ruth III": *ottawater.* 15 (January 2019): 19–20.
http://www.ottawater.com/ottawater15.pdf

"Ruth IV": *Maple Tree Literary Supplement.* 24. 2019.
http://www.mtls.ca/issue24/poetry-george-elliott-clarke/

"Ezra III": *Maple Tree Literary Supplement.* 24. 2019.
http://www.mtls.ca/issue24/poetry-george-elliott-clarke/

"Ezra VI": *ottawater.* 15 (January 2019): 20.
http://www.ottawater.com/ottawater15.pdf

"Ezra VIII": *Maple Tree Literary Supplement.* 24. 2019.
http://www.mtls.ca/issue24/poetry-george-elliott-clarke/

"Job (Addendum)": *The Nashwaak Review.* 40/41.1 (Fall/Winter 2018/19): 8–10.

"Screed 1": *Grain*. 41.2 (Winter 2014): 62.

"David (Marginal Notes)": Trans. Yin Xiaoyuan.

"David (Excerpt from II Samuel 11)": *Maple Tree Literary Supplement.* 23 (April-July 2018). ISSN 1916-341X.
http://www.mtls.ca/issue23/poetry-george-elliott-clarke/

"Ecclesiastes III": *The Trinity Review.* 131 (Spring 2019): 8–10.

"Ecclesiastes XI": *The Trinity Review.* 131 (Spring 2019): 11–12.

"Solomon 1: 1–10" ["The Lecture of Solomon: I"]: *ottawater9.* [www.ottawater.com] (January 2013): 23.

"Solomon 2: 1–7" ["The Lecture of Solomon: II"]: *Toronto Review of Books*. October 15, 2013.
http://www.torontoreviewofbooks.com/2013/10/two-new-poems-george-elliott-clarke/

"Song of Solomon III": *Grain*. 46.2 (Winter 2019): 100.

"Song of Solomon VII": *Braided Way Magazine*. June 4, 2019. https://wp.me/p4R8ZR-OD

"Experience 1: 1–9": *Toronto Review of Books*. October 15, 2013. http://www.torontoreviewofbooks.com/2013/10/two-new-poems-george-elliott-clarke/

"Enoch 1: 1–19": *Vallum*. 10.1 (2013): 43–45.

"Enoch 2: 1–19": Trans. Anna Yin.

"Enoch 3: 1–18"; "Enoch 5: 1–29"; and "Enoch 6: 1–20": *Descant*. 163. 44.4 (Winter 2014): 33–39.

"Enoch 4: 1–18" and "Enoch 7: 1–34": *Maple Tree Literary Supplement*. 23 (April–July 2018). ISSN 1916-341X. http://www.mtls.ca/issue23/poetry-george-elliott-clarke/

"Wisdom of Solomon II": *African American Review*. 51.3 (Fall 2018): 234–236.

"Wisdom of Solomon IV": *The Trinity Review*. Spring Journal (2018): 14–16.

"Wisdom of Solomon VI": *The Pangolin Review*. 8 (January 8, 2019). https://thepangolinreview.wixsite.com/mypoetrysite/issue-8-jan-8-2019

"Wisdom of Solomon VII": Trans. Raed Al-Jishi. *Sobra News*. February 8, 2019. Saudi Arabia. https://www.sobranews.com/sobra/30115

"Wisdom of Solomon VIII": *The Pangolin Review*. 8 (January 8, 2019). https://thepangolinreview.wixsite.com/mypoetrysite/issue-8-jan-8-2019

"Wisdom of Solomon IX": *The Pangolin Review*. 8 (January 8, 2019). https://thepangolinreview.wixsite.com/mypoetrysite/issue-8-jan-8-2019

"Wisdom of Solomon XIX": *African American Review*. 51.3 (Fall 2018): 233–234.

"Addendum to Solomon III": Trans. Ana Paula Austin Ferreira.

"Addendum to Solomon XIV": *The Nashwaak Review*. 40/41.1 (Fall/Winter 2018/19): 17–18.

"Ecclesiasticus III": *Vallum*. 15.2 (2018): 24.

"Ecclesiasticus V": *African American Review*. 51.3 (Fall 2018): 233.

"Ecclesiasticus VI": *Vallum*. 15.2 (2018): 23.

"Ecclesiasticus XI": *The Malahat Review*. 204 (Fall 2018): 84–85.

"Ecclesiasticus XXII": *LRC: Literary Review of Canada*. 26.5 (June 2018): 6.

"Ecclesiasticus XLVI": *The Malahat Review*. 204 (Fall 2018): 86–87.

"Ecclesiasticus XLIX": *Kola*. 32.1. 2020. [Forthcoming]

"Ecclesiasticus L": *The Malahat Review*. 204 (Fall 2018): 88–89.

"The Letter of Jeremiah": *Kola*. 31.1. 2019. [Forthcoming]

BIBLIOGRAPHICAL REFERENCES

From: *The* KJV*

Genesis (Selected)
Samson (Repressed)
The Saga of Jezebel
The Book of Ruth
The Book of Ezra
Job (Conclusions)
Ecclesiastes
The Song of Solomon
The Book of Amos
The Book of Nahum
Plus Miscellaneous Scriptural Fragments

The Book of Enoch**

From: *The Apocryphal / Deuterocanonical Books*****

Wisdom of Solomon
Ecclesiasticus, or the Wisdom of Jesus, Son of Sirach
Singular Circulars

* Inspired by the Scofield Reference Bible, ed. Cyrus I Scofield (Oxford: University Press, 1909).
** Inspired by *The Book of Enoch, the Prophet*, trans. Richard Laurence (Chicago: Lushena Books, [n.d.]).
*** Inspired by *The New Oxford Annotated Apocrypha, 3rd Edition*, ed. Michael D. Coogan; assoc. eds., Marc Z. Brettler, Carol A. Newsom, Pheme Perkins (Oxford, 2001).

ACKNOWLEDGEMENTS

In February 2011, Aqua Books of Winnipeg (MB), organized a "Mondo Clarke" that saw me sip *Punt e Mes* in that most unlikely space. The Library of Parliament's Parliamentary Poet Laureateship of Canada (2016–17) sustained me in Halifax (NS), Montréal (QC), Ottawa (ON), Iqaluit (NU), Yellowknife (NT), Vancouver (BC), Kapolei (HI), and other sites. After readings at the Vicenza Poetry Festival *and* the Vicenza Jazz Festival, I enjoyed a three-city tour of Italy (Venezia, Pisa, and Cosenza), organized by Profs. Marco Fazzini, *et al.*, in May 2016. (A further tour, in May 2017, took me to Bologna as well as to Vicenza and Venezia.) The Hackmatack Children's Choice Book Award programme saw me jog about New Brunswick (Fredericton, Nackawic, Grand Falls / Grand-Sault, Woodstock, and Perth-Andover) in early May 2017. Dr. Sonia Labatt, Ph.D., and Victoria University (*via* The E.J. Pratt Professorship at the University of Toronto), sent me packing everywhere else, from Halifax (NS) to Havana (Cuba); from Vicenza (IT) to Venezia (IT); from Marcon (IT) to Mogliano Veneto (IT); from Nice (FR) to Niagara Falls (NY); from Nantes (FR) to New York City (NY); from Puumala (Finland) to Panamá City (Panamá); from Berlin (Germany) to Buffalo (NY); from Cuidad de México (MX) to Valle de Bravo (MX); and from Cable Beach (Bahamas) to Cosenza (IT), *et cetera*. This same treasure permitted month-long residencies in Tropea (IT) and jaunts to Roma (IT) in 2017 and 2018, with essential stops in San Nicola da Crissa (IT), 2016–2018. University invitations—Acadia, Alberta, Algoma, Bahamas (Nassau), British Columbia (Kelowna & Nanaimo & Vancouver campuses), Cape Breton, Dalhousie, King's College, Memorial, Ontario Institute of Technology, Salamanca, Western Ontario—brought me to their host cities. Reading Series—Blue Metropolis, The Fourth Annual Erotic Poetry Salon, Saskatchewan Writers' Guild, and Thin Air—transported me to their domains (Montréal [QC], Durham [ON], Regina [SK], and Winnipeg [MB]). The 2019 Sage Hill Writing Spring

Poetry Colloquium posted me to St. Peter's Abbey (Muenster [SK]). If my verses deserve curses, I am to blame. If my pressings seem blessings, my benefactors own your applause.

The usual suspects—*The* John Fraser, Riitta Tuohiniemi—encouraged. Michael Mirolla, Giovanna Riccio, and Paul Zemokhol edited, here and there. M. NourbeSe Philip urged thoughtful correctives. I alone am responsible for every flaw and/or folly.

The translators herein are Raed Anis Al-Jishi (Arabic), Ana Paula Austin Ferreira (Mexican Spanish), Galia Vurgan (Hebrew), Anna Yin (Chinese), and Yin Xiaoyuan (Chinese). (I thank Fawn White and Evan Fallenberg for directing me to Ms. Vurgan. El Jones connected me—nicely—to Raed Anis Al-Jishi. Stephen Brown was the poet-bridge to Ms. Ferreira.)

Michael Mirolla said yes immediately to this project when I proposed it to him, way back in 2011. I'm proud to be associated with Guernica Editions, and I anticipate, with relish, the conclusion of this epic poem in *Canticles III*.

David Moratto executed the design of this book. The titular font and section titles reflect the artistry of William Clarke (1935–2005). Digitized in 2011 by Andrew Steeves of Gaspereau Press, *Bill Clarke Caps* is a font my late father drafted—with yardstick, pencil, and ink—in 1969. The body text is *Dante MT Std*, however.

George Elliott Clarke
Carmel-by-the-Sea (California)
31 *août* mmxix

ABOUT THE AUTHOR

The 4th Poet Laureate of Toronto (2012–15) and the 7th Parliamentary/Canadian Poet Laureate (2016 & 17), George Elliott Clarke is a revered artist in song, drama, fiction, screenplay, essays, and poetry. Born in Windsor, Nova Scotia, in 1960, Clarke was educated at the University of Waterloo, Dalhousie University, and Queen's University. Clarke is also a pioneering scholar of African-Canadian literature. A professor of English at the University of Toronto, Clarke has taught at Duke, McGill, the University of British Columbia, and Harvard. He holds eight honorary doctorates, plus appointments to the Order of Nova Scotia and the Order of Canada at the rank of Officer. He is also a Fellow of the Royal Canadian Geographical Society. His recognitions include the Pierre Elliott Trudeau Fellows Prize, the Governor-General's Award for Poetry, the National Magazine Gold Award for Poetry, the Premiul Poesis (Romania), the Dartmouth Book Award for Fiction, the Eric Hoffer Book Award for Poetry (US), and the Dr. Martin Luther King Jr. Achievement Award. Clarke's work is the subject of *Africadian Atlantic: Essays on George Elliott Clarke* (2012), edited by Joseph Pivato.

END OF THESE CANTICLES,
but CANTICLES II WILL RESUME.